Progress
Toward Development
in Latin America

Progress Toward Development in Latin America

From Prebisch to Technological Autonomy

edited by
James L. Dietz
and
Dilmus D. James

Lynne Rienner Publishers • Boulder & London

338.98
P964

Published in the United States of America in 1990 by
Lynne Rienner Publishers, Inc.
1800 30th Street, Boulder, Colorado 80301

and in the United Kingdom by
Lynne Rienner Publishers, Inc.
3 Henrietta Street, Covent Garden, London WC2E 8LU

Library of Congress Cataloging-in-Publication Data
Progress toward development in Latin America : from Prebisch to
  technological autonomy / edited by James L. Dietz & Dilmus D. James.
  Includes bibliographical references.
  ISBN 1-55587-179-8 (alk. paper)
  1. Latin America—Economic policy. 2. Technology transfer—
Economic aspects—Latin America. 3. Debts, External—Latin
America. 4. Capitalism—Latin America. I. Dietz, James L., 1947–
II. James, Dilmus D.
HC125.P775 1990
338.98—dc20   89-77636
                                                          CIP

British Cataloguing in Publication Data
A Cataloguing in Publication record for this book
is available from the British Library.

Printed and bound in the United States of America

The paper used in this publication meets the requirements
of the American National Standard for Permanence of
paper for Printed Library Materials Z39.48-1984.

Contents

Part 3   Strategies for Development:
         Toward Renewed Growth and Equity in Latin America

Preface

This book is dedicated to the memory of James H. Street (1915–1988), whose professional career was spent primarily in the Department of Economics, Rutgers University. Jim Street was one of the first economists to intensively study Latin America from the institutionalist perspective.[1] From the first article he published on the similarities between Latin American structuralism and institutionalism (1967) to one of his last works on economic development (1987a), Jim was an untiring advocate of a closer collaboration between structuralist and institutionalist economists.

Both editors worked closely with Jim for much too short a time, but he was an important influence on our work and thinking. We hope this book will help to bring structuralist, institutionalist, and other like-minded economists and policymakers a greater shared understanding of where Latin American development and development policy has been and where it is—and where it ought to be—heading. To the extent that we and our *compañeros* who have contributed to this book are at all successful in furthering this goal—and the joining of structuralist and institutionalist writers here is but one modest step in that direction—we like to think that Jim would have been pleased.

The title of the book owes a debt, in an all too obvious way, to the influence of Albert O. Hirschman, a most insightful observer of Latin America.

All of the contributions, with the exception of Chapter 3, were prepared especially for this book and are published here for the first time. All of the contributors have worked hard to meet their deadlines and to think about their subject matter in new ways. Both editors are extremely grateful to them all.

A special note of thanks to Lynne Rienner, who has been particularly supportive of critical research that attempts to extend the boundaries of traditional knowledge. Her encouragement of, and suggestions for, this project at an early stage of its development were most valuable. *Un abrazo.*

Thanks, too, to Pam Ferdinand whose intelligent editing of the manuscript has improved its presentation significantly.

Note

1. For a short introduction to Street's work and life, see Dietz and James (1988) and James (1989). Also see Street (1988) for a modest autoevaluation of his work.

1

Trends in Development Theory in Latin America: From Prebisch to the Present

Dilmus D. James
James L. Dietz

Four recent historical events will profoundly influence the shape of Latin America's future in the 1990s and into the next century, events that can contribute to the forging of a new theoretical paradigm. First, since 1960, there has been a growing and increasingly profound recognition within the region that science and technology are forces to be reckoned with. The other three events are inextricably intertwined: the debt crisis; the resurgence of neoliberalism both in theory and practice; and the economic slump during the mid-1980s.

Science and Technology

In the 1960s, Latin American nations began to express their dissatisfaction with the North-South process of technology transfer. Empirical studies revealed restrictions in contractual agreements covering technology transfer from abroad that were deleterious to the host country. Purveyors of technology, particularly multinational corporations (MNCs), were accused of garnering monopoly rent through transfer-pricing mechanisms, market discrimination, and the exercise of superior bargaining power. Complaints were aired repeatedly regarding how poorly the technology being imported meshed with the character of local factor endowments, available skills and inputs, and market size. It was firmly believed that modern technology weakened the rate of labor absorption and contributed to the highly skewed pattern of income distribution characteristic of most Latin American nations.

One reaction to these concerns in the late 1960s and early 1970s was to establish regulations on imports of technology in Argentina, Brazil, Mexico, and the Andean Pact countries. A second, and more positive, reaction was to establish national councils expressly charged with overseeing science and

1

technology (S&T) issues. Argentina and Brazil initiated national research councils in the 1950s, but in the 1960s these began to take on increasing importance. As Amadeo (1979: 154) put it, "the decade of the 1960s is the landmark in the formal evolution of the S&T institutions of Latin America. Uruguay (1961), Chile (1967), Venezuela (1967), Argentina (1969), Peru (1968), Colombia (1968), [and] Mexico (1970) established new institutions aimed at the planning, coordination, and promotion of scientific and technological activities."

Interest in augmenting Latin America's internal technological capacity received a further boost in the late 1970s, much to the surprise of many development economists within and outside the region, when it was found that some technical learning and innovation were already taking place. Jorge Katz and associates (see Katz 1984a, 1984b, 1987), in a revealing series of case studies of Latin American manufacturing enterprises, found that intraplant innovations actually were quite common, and that through time their cumulative impact on productivity probably rivaled or surpassed the productivity effects of introducing updated equipment. Other research indicated that some of the "top tier" economies in Latin America also were making substantial strides in two areas that typically demonstrate a domestic technological capacity; namely, exports of products and services with a high technological component ("technology exports") and the production of capital goods.[1]

Despite the fact that S&T has emerged as an acknowledged ingredient in any path to socioeconomic development, there is yet a long distance to traverse. Various chapters in this book show that there remain serious problems with the types of technology imported and the conditions under which these are obtained; that fully effective programs of internal research and development (R&D) have yet to be realized in most countries; and that the necessary socialization of science and technology within the Latin American culture is incomplete. Further, there has been inadequate internalization of technological dynamics into prominent theoretical and influential thinking on Latin American development, within both the structuralist and neoliberal schools. Significant alterations in cultural values, social modalities, allocation of resources, and power structures are prerequisites to more rapid technological progress and social development in the region. Accommodating these alterations will not be easy, but, since 1960, at least S&T policy is firmly ensconced on the agenda, although there remains much to be done before science and technology will be able to make the contribution they are capable of making, as Chapters 9 and 10 more fully suggest. But it cannot be doubted, as Adler's (1987, 1988) and Solingen's (1989) work on Brazil and Argentina demonstrate, that effective S&T policies are both feasible and indispensable if Latin America is to enter First World status.

The Debt Crisis

Even considering the eroding effects of inflation on the value of the dollar, it is astonishing that the outstanding external public debt of Latin America could go from slightly over $7 billion in 1960 to an estimated $426 billion in 1989, an annual increase of 22.8 percent. The tale of the initial impetus for the debt crisis, its evolution, and the proliferation of suggestions for dealing with it has been spun many times over (for one of our views, see Dietz 1986). Our intention here is merely to recapture the flavor of how events unfolded and earmark debt as an unavoidable policy consideration that must be linked to any future development strategy.

Anxiety about seeking returns on surplus petrodollars garnered by the petroleum-exporting countries generated a lending frenzy among commercial banks, matched by borrowing binges of various intensities by Latin American governments. Growth of debt was explosive in percentage terms during the 1970s, and an enormous hike in absolute terms followed during the 1980s. Rising incremental capital-output ratios (that is, a declining "bang in income per buck" of investment) hinted at, or should have raised concerns about, serious difficulties in converting these massive financial inflows into productive investment projects that could cover the costs of borrowing. Some countries, unfortunately, bypassed productive outlets as they used loans to expand spending on the military; swelling negative totals in the "errors and omissions" entry of the balance of payments accounts made it clear that huge transfers of flight capital were leaving the region as loans flowed in the other direction, loans that were financing this hemorrhage of funds.

During the 1970s, there was an increasing reliance on private institutions, mainly commercial banks in developed countries, as a source of borrowed funds, the reverse side of the coin being a decline in multilateral and bilateral official lending. This meant that: (1) a smaller proportion of loans were on concessionary terms; (2) there was a huge increase in short-term debt; and (3) much more of the debt was subject to market fluctuations in rates of interest as bankers attempted to protect themselves from high and rising world inflation with variable interest rate contracts.

The stage was set for disaster, which came in the early 1980s as a precipitous drop in petroleum prices hurt the credit standing of petroleum exporters in Latin America; as a determined effort to drive down inflation in the United States sent interest rates through the roof; as a global recession set off by the inflation squeezes eroded Latin America's ability to export; and, as a natural result, as rising deficits on the current account of virtually all countries in the region led commercial bankers to be very reluctant to continue lending to the region. All of these factors contributed to the nearly decade-long debt and growth crisis of the 1980s.

This is more or less where the situation has stagnated. Monetarist experiments (Foxley 1983) and the International Monetary Fund's (IMF) imposition of conditionality on loans have led to a tremendous compression of the Latin American economies, an even greater compression of imports, and a still greater compression in the importation of fixed investment goods necessary to fuel industrial expansion. Latin American debtors face the wriggling, higgling, and maneuvering over actual and threatened dispensation of payment, while the menu of temporary expedients to avert disaster, including debt-equity swaps, the unloading of debt at deep discounts in secondary financial markets, debt rescheduling, negotiations around the Baker Plan, and the stalled Brady Plan gloss over the full importance of the debt overhang that continues to threaten the region's future development possibilities.

Our reason for recounting the general schema of the debt crisis is to stress that whatever development paradigm emerges from the ruins of the 1980s, be it neostructuralist (as suggested in Chapters 4, 9, and 11) or otherwise, the disposition of the debt problem must be addressed within the new strategy, and functional policy implications concerning future behavior of all major actors must be clearly delineated so that the crisis not only can be overcome but cannot recur.

Most Latin Americanists would agree that the ability to borrow facilely during the 1970s postponed the day when Latin American countries had to face painful internal readjustments in their economic, social, and political structures. The irony is that, currently, there is such an overwhelming preoccupation with the external debt crisis among policymakers that long-lived and intractable internal problems have been suffering from relative neglect or have been assumed not to exist; this gives a whole new meaning to the term *crowding out*. Some managerial effort obviously must be expended in negotiation with one's banker, but someone has got to mind the store, too.

Neoliberalism

During the 1960s and 1970s, development economics, as a subdiscipline, experienced a marked shift toward employing the analytical tools and policy prescriptions of orthodox neoclassical economics. We can think of no better way to symbolize the rise of mainstream economics within development theory than by examining the two *Pioneers in Development* volumes produced under the auspices of the World Bank. The first volume (Meier and Seers 1984), designed to include the major contributors to development theory during the 1940s and 1950s, is dominated by heterodox economists such as Albert O. Hirschman, W. Arthur Lewis, Gunnar Myrdal, Raúl Prebisch, Paul N. Rosenstein-Rodan, and Hans Singer—the inclusion of conservative writer P. T. Bauer seems tantamount to tokenism. The companion volume (Meier 1987), intended to cover major contributors to development theory during the 1960s and 1970s, focuses on five economists, including Theodore W. Schultz, Arnold Harberger, and Gottfried Haberler; the first two are members of the neoliberal Chicago School, and the last is certainly allied with economic orthodoxy. Orthodoxy, then, had triumphed to an extraordinary degree over a relatively short period.

The influence of the new orthodoxy was, of course, felt in Latin America. Sporadically, countries in the region had implemented orthodox, monetarist stabilization programs during economic crises (resulting in stop-go cycles), and, occasionally, experimentation with mainstream policies would be tried for longer periods. But it was in the span from the early 1970s to the early 1980s that neoliberalism (sometimes referred to as neoconservatism) really came into its own. Tried partially and episodically in Brazil and Peru, neoliberalism came to hold almost total sway in the Southern Cone countries, perhaps showing its most pristine form in Chile after the 1973 coup. And it is neoliberalism, with variations, that still dominates policymaking in the Latin American nations attempting to live up to IMF conditionality (see Chapters 4 and 5).

The policy arsenal of neoliberalism has included cutting back government spending, slowing the rate of monetary expansion, imposing wage controls, deregulating prices and financial markets, closing some state enterprises and selling others to the private sector ("privatization"), rapidly opening the economy to merchandise and financial flows ("liberalization"), and devaluating/depreciating the local currency.

To use Chile as an example of the impact of neoliberal policies, as they took effect: there were two very poor years in 1975 and 1976, but then the economy apparently began to improve. From 1977 to 1981, gross domestic product (GDP) grew between 7.3 and 9.9 percent. Inflation, which had been running at more than 600 percent in 1973, receded to under 10 percent by 1981. A $3.3 billion fiscal deficit in 1973 was transformed into a $0.5 billion surplus in 1981. And labor productivity rose, ostensibly because of the greater efficiencies resulting from international competition following the opening of the economy.[2]

Then, however, the situation turned sour, with a decline of over 14 percent in GDP in 1982 and a slight decline in the following year. Government deficits returned, and inflation rates could not be held at the lower rates achieved in the early 1980s. During 1982/83, real wages fell by 18 percent from their 1979–1981 levels, which put them on a par with wages in 1969. It is difficult to determine what proportion of blame for this downturn to assign to neoliberal domestic policies vis-à-vis adverse external shocks in the early part of the decade, making it easy for neoliberal policy supporters to point their finger at an adverse external environment. The same, though, could be said for Chile's good growth record over the last three years; the commodity terms of trade improved from an index of 73.0 in 1985 (1980 = 100) to a preliminary estimate of 101.0 in 1988, so that neoliberal economics equally cannot be credited as the cause of the upturn. Suffice it to say, however, that most Latin American economists do not look on the record of neoliberal accomplishments with much favor. The stop-go syndrome appears to be alive and well in Latin America, reflecting underlying structural rigidities that monetarism cannot abolish by fiat.

The Mid-1980s Slump

Judging from the latest data available, many Latin American countries have income distributions that are among the most highly skewed in the world, and there is little or no convincing evidence that the lower-income strata improved its relative position during the buoyant growth characteristic of the 1970s (Tokman 1982). Still, it was some consolation that, from 1960 to 1980, the absolute conditions of the populace in general seemed to improve. William J. Dixon (1987) calculated the Physical Quality of Life Index for twenty-two countries in the region and found that all showed varying degrees of improvement.[3]

The 1980s, however, was a period of absolute deterioration in income. From 1980 to 1988, real GDP per capita fell by a disturbing 7 percent. There still are no definitive answers to the question of what happened to equity and welfare in Latin America during this decade, but there are some persuasive indications. Miguel D. Ramírez (1989: 159) cites a study by Mexico's Instituto Nacional del Consumidor, conducted in 1984, that showed that a number of low-income families had given up meat products (11.4 percent), milk (7.5 percent), fish (6.7 percent), and fruits and vegetables (3.3 percent). He also reports (156), citing World Bank sources, that real wages fell in Mexico substantially during 1981–1983, the decline being greatest in the agricultural sector (31.3 percent).

Frederick Ungeheuer (1989: 64) gives a journalistic account of continued poverty in the region and speaks of "an enormous group, 60 percent to 80 percent of the population, whose situation is approaching the despair of sub-Saharan Africa or Bangladesh." He goes on to claim that close to 10 million in Argentina have a family income of less than $100 per month, and 15 million more are barely above that level (in 1985, Argentina's population was about 31 million). The World Bank (1987) reported that large increases in food prices accompanied the declines in real wages, the adverse impact of which has been particularly acute for rural labor and the urban poor. Real wages in Mexico, for example, fell by an average 28 percent between 1981 and 1983 and fell slightly in 1984. At its peak, open unemployment in some cities of Mexico stood well above 1981 levels (Gregory 1987: 67). Further, an increase in infant deaths caused by diarrhea, and a slowdown in the decrease of infant mortality rates in Latin America can, according to the Inter-American Development Bank, "justifiably be attributed to the crisis" (IDB 1989: 67).

As the data continue to be evaluated over the next several years, the spotlight will be trained, justifiably, on the plight of lower-income groups. Equally important from the standpoint of policy formulation, however, is the wrenching experience of the middle class. As an unscientific example of a single individual in Mexico, but one we do not think is atypical, a close friend of one of us was earning the equivalent of between $35,000 and $40,000 in the early 1980s as a professor in Mexico City. His current salary is worth approximately $5,000. One cannot help be reminded of Crane Brinton's *Anatomy of Revolution* in which he found that a serious deterioration of the position of the middle class seemed to be a recurring theme in the English (Cromwellian), American, French, and Russian revolutions.

Shortcomings and *Fracasomanía*: The Need to Go Forward

Forced import substitution industrialization (ISI) began during stabilization crises, both world wars, and the Great Depression in Latin America, but it was only after World War II, under structuralist inspiration, that ISI was advanced as a long-term strategy of development. Orthodox economists criticized ISI from the beginning, and as the strategy took shape a variety of shortcomings became evident. The twin socioeconomic problems of skewed income distribution and redundant labor remained stubborn under ISI. As the protective ISI tariff umbrella spread, and as economies began to initiate the production of goods requiring more sophisticated technology, skills, and material inputs, cost differentials between domestic and world production widened, and, irony of ironies, ISI became more import-intensive, although producer goods replaced consumer goods as key imports. Agriculture and mining were clobbered by overvaluations of domestic currencies that discouraged exports, and, as the internal terms of trade between agriculture and industry increasingly favored the latter, the agricultural sector took on an added burden. Skewed factor prices, combined with other policies, favored the most capital-intensive sectors and the more capital-intensive industries within them, encouraging firms to adopt capital-intensive production techniques (although the availability of alternative technologies, regardless of factor prices, was probably quite narrow). The labor-saving bias of ISI production, however, undeniably aggravated the problems of inequity and unemployment and contributed to a large ratio of underutilized capacity in the manufacturing sector. In general, the hothouse atmosphere of protection tended to reduce the incentives for pursuing cost-cutting innovations or improvements in product quality, and the highly differentiated degrees of protection within the industrial sector channeled entrepreneurial talent into lobbying for extended preferential treatment that would favor its interests, rather than into more productive directions that would have represented a better allocation of its skills.

Two observations on Latin America's historical development path seem warranted: First, generally speaking, the difficulties of ISI were recognized by many Latin American economists who are outside the neoliberal tradition (see Bitar 1988; Ffrench-Davis 1988; Rosales 1988; and Chapter 2, below); second, we must carefully distinguish ISI in practice from structuralist thought. Osvaldo Rosales (1988) points out that many of the excesses and misdirected policies of ISI were inconsistent with the recommendations and cautionary remarks coming from the Economic Commission for Latin America and the Caribbean (ECLAC), very often from Raúl Prebisch himself, a point that Alexander also makes in Chapter 2 of this book.

Undeniably, there have been periods when state-initiated economic measures got completely out of hand in Latin America, and while these policies could only be seen as constituting a caricature of ISI, much of the blame was assigned to it, and to structuralist thinking, because of ISI's interventionist stance. Alejandro Foxley (1983) describes the plight of many economies in the early 1970s before military juntas took over and implemented the neoliberal economic experiments. There can be no denying that the economies were pretty much in shambles in Brazil and Southern Cone countries (although outside interference in Chile cannot be ignored, either). Mexico, during 1978–1982, was a case of interventionism gone wild with expansionary policies. But, simply because particular interventionist states exceeded the limits of good policy does not imply that state intervention in the Latin American economies is, per se, unjustified.

Neoliberal doctrine suffers from an inability to perceive that market failures are common, even pervasive, in the context of a developing economy. There are real and constraining structural bottlenecks in human capacities, transportation systems, communications infrastructure, agricultural production, and fiscal systems, among others. There seems to be a failure in neoliberalism to accept the possibility that public expenditure can complement ("crowd in") private economic activity (Bitar 1988: 54), although one would think that the large orthodox literature on public goods and externalities would have put this issue to rest. Building a national highway system in the United States hardly "crowded out" private expenditure on means of transportation; apparently, neoliberalism in the developed world operates on somewhat different, although unexplained, premises.

The existence of beneficial externalities resulting from state intervention thus are usually downgraded or ignored. That the capital goods sector generates national technical learning, or that achieving dynamic comparative advantage in selected industries might require deviation from unfettered market forces, seems not to have found a place in the neoliberal basket of theories, despite compelling contemporary evidence from South Korea and Taiwan, just to mention two of the most often cited successes in recent development history (see Chapter 10).

Part of the explanation for this theoretical gap might be an underdeveloped ability in orthodox, neoclassical economics to handle dynamic changes, especially the dynamics of technological change. As Pan A. Yotopoulos and Jeffrey B. Nugent (1976: 183) observe, comparative statics, or whatever else neoclassical economics has to offer, cannot provide a full explanation of historical change. We know of no serious treatment in neoliberal theory that addresses the problem of introducing technological progress into the development equation on a sufficiently dynamic and sustaining basis. Evidently, "getting prices right," letting markets "do their stuff," and relying on private initiative are sufficient for development to "take off"; for neoliberals, this proposition is considered so transparent that no lengthy elaboration is necessary to support its veracity.

Neoliberals can also be faulted for introducing their policies far too rapidly to enable the realization of those structural adjustments in the economy that they claim to desire. As Alexander's chapter indicates, there are powerful ideological overtones at play here. Neoliberal comparative statics rarely take real-world asymmetries into account; the relative ease with which firm-specific technical expertise is lost to deindustrialization following rapid liberalization and the opening of an economy to intense and immediate international competition, and the painful, time-consuming process necessary to regain such experience, is ignored. In combating inflation and balance of payments problems by reducing internal demand and "getting prices right," insufficient consideration has been given in the neoliberal agenda to rigidities in debt-servicing obligations and price inflexibilities of imported goods and services as a whole, rigidities that make the neoliberal policies counterproductive over the longer term.

Finally, economic orthodoxy pays far too little attention to how powerful social and political forces can encapsulate and steer market forces. While it is a truism that the market influences the allocation of resources, when we peer behind buying and selling activities, vested interests are inevitably found to be shaping the rules of the game under which these activities operate; in Latin America, where these vested interests have highly concentrated access to the reaches of power, this tendency is even more deeply entrenched.

Where, then, is Latin American development and development theory heading? Perhaps as a start, we should guard against tossing either the

ECLAC structuralist or neoliberal models out the window completely. In short, we must avoid what Albert Hirschman (1981: 140) has termed fracasomanía—"the habit of interpreting as utter failure experiences that actually contain elements of both failure and success."[4]

After all, the ISI recommended by structuralists ushered in over two decades of powerful economic growth in Latin America. Felipe Pazos (1987) pointed out that fiscal deficits and current account deficits for most Latin American countries were not unreasonable until the lending/borrowing rage in the mid-1970s, by which time ISI opportunities had been pretty well exhausted within the existing institutional milieu. Pazos also cites research in Brazil that demonstrates that protectionist ISI policies did not preclude competition, efficiency, and learning—costs of many manufacturing goods did become internationally competitive. Giving orthodoxy its due, financial variables are real and important; some state enterprises are horrendously inefficient; and a multiplicity of market interventions, sometimes working at cross purposes, often gives confusing signals to the productive sectors (see Chapter 6). No responsible observer of Latin America denies that there have been failures of state intervention. Even less is it our intention to suggest such a simplistic view, particularly given the nature of the ruling and state elites in Latin America, elites whose interests and agendas have been all too often opposed to meaningful change and development of their own social and economic structures (see Chapter 10 for an elaboration).

Unless one chooses to produce an entirely new deck of cards for guiding Latin American development into the first part of the next century—and we do not propose that this be done—some sort of intelligent amalgamation of strategies is needed that integrates the best elements from ECLAC structuralism, neoclassical orthodoxy, and entirely novel elements, to arrive at, for lack of a better term, a neostructuralist approach. This is a challenging, if not a daunting task, especially if one considers regional diversities with respect to historical experiences, cultural values, levels of income, and technological sophistication, among other factors.

The contributors to this book consider where Latin American development has been, in theory and practice, and where it might best aim in the future. In the last chapter, we attempt to pull some of the threads of their thinking together. Our intent, there, is modest but sincere: to suggest what seem to be solid building blocks for a neostructuralist paradigm that can provide a more solid future for Latin American development.

Notes

1. For technology exports, see the articles on individual Latin American countries in Lall (1984). For data on the impressive expansion of capital

goods production from 1975 to 1982 in Brazil and Mexico, and from 1975 to 1980 in Argentina, see Chudnovsky (1985).

2. Unless otherwise specified, data in this section come from various issues of the IDB's (1984–1989) annual *Economic and Social Progress in Latin America*.

3. The Physical Quality of Life Index is a weighted average based on infant mortality, life expectancy, and literacy rates.

4. Emanuel Adler (1988) reminds us that Hirschman used the term *fracasomanía* in a somewhat different way elsewhere in his work; i.e., to "shut oneself off from newly emerging cues and insights as well as from the increased confidence in one's capabilities which should otherwise arise" (see Hirschman 1973: 245).

Part 1

Structuralism as a Theory of Economic Development

2

Import Substitution in Latin America in Retrospect

Robert J. Alexander

Throughout most of the twentieth century, Latin America has gone through its own industrial revolution, and almost everywhere in the region the strategy used to bring this about has been import substitution. Although industrialization and overall economic development have been suspended by the debt crisis for almost a decade, one can nevertheless conclude that, whatever limitations that strategy may have and may previously have had, it was largely successful.

ECLA Advocacy of ISI

In the decades following World War II, the most vocal advocates of import substitution were the economists gathered in the Economic Commission for Latin America (ECLA),[1] led for a decade and half by the Argentine economist Raúl Prebisch, who with his colleagues developed a theory and rationale for the economic development of Latin America.

According to the Prebisch-ECLA analysis, it was a mistake to regard the (non-Communist) world as a single economy. Rather, the argument ran, there are two economies, that of the "center" and that of the "periphery" of the world economy. The former consists of the major industrial countries, those in Western Europe, North America, and Japan. The latter is made up of the so-called Third World countries, which have been exporters, in each individual case, of a very limited number of raw materials or foodstuffs, and importers of most of the manufactured goods they consumed.

According to the ECLA theory, it is the center rather than the periphery that determines what happens in the world economy. The industrial countries' willingness to purchase the exports of the peripheral countries determines the prosperity, or lack of it, of peripheral economies. However, the willingness or ability of an individual peripheral country to buy the exports of an industrial nation has relatively little influence on that center country, affecting only a relatively small segment of its diversified economy. (The "oil crisis" of the 1970s—which occurred long after the ECLA economists had developed their theory—was a major exception to this pattern.)

Although they did not cite Alexander Hamilton's precedent so far as I know, the ECLA economists in effect agreed with his analysis of the U.S. economy in the 1790s when it was "underdeveloped." Hamilton argued that the U.S. economy at that time was like a three-legged stool with only two legs: It had agriculture and commerce but did not have manufacturing. Therefore, he argued, the government should encourage the country's industrialization, making it able to produce domestically many of the products it was then importing. The ECLA economists made a similar argument with regard to Latin American countries in the post–World War II period and urged them to establish industries to produce goods that, until then, were available only from the center.

In any case, the Latin American countries were forced into import substitution by world economic circumstances. Either because of wartime interference with their trade or because of lack of sufficient foreign exchange caused by depression-induced decreases in demand for their exports, the Latin American nations had little choice but to try to produce for themselves. By the end of the Great Depression, the governments of most Latin American countries had become committed to a deepening of the process of import substitution through a deliberate ISI strategy. (The major exception among the larger countries was Argentina, which did not adopt this strategy until the Perón regime in the middle 1940s.)

By the end of World War II, industrialization had gone far enough in the major Latin American countries to provide for domestic production of most basic consumer goods—processed foodstuffs, textiles, shoes, pharmaceuticals—and key construction materials—cement, paints, and other such things. Subsequently, the larger economies also import substituted in heavy industry—steel production and basic chemicals—while the smaller countries undertook import substitution in the consumer goods sector. In a few cases, the larger economies' development went even further, to the mounting of machine and machine tool industries.

The Reaction Against Import Substitution

Import substitution industrialization went on successfully in most Latin American countries through the 1960s, when it began to run out of steam, in the sense that most substitutions that might be economically undertaken already had been accomplished in many nations. Criticism of import substitution began to grow.

The most notable cases of reaction against import substitution, in terms of public policy, were Chile, Argentina, and Uruguay, under the military regimes that governed those countries during the 1970s and early 1980s. In all three cases, the economic policymakers contended that their countries had been mistaken to undertake ISI, which had generated only "artificial" and inefficient industries. Rather, they argued, their nations should open their economies to imports of manufactured goods from the rest of the world rather than try to produce them behind any kind of protective wall. In turn, they should pay for those imports by relying on the few primary products in which they had traditionally had comparative advantage, and on whatever additional primary products for which they might be able to develop comparative advantage.

The most extreme case of reaction against import substitution came in Chile during the first decade of the Pinochet regime, when the so-called Chicago Boys were in control of economic policy. These were economists who had either been trained at the University of Chicago under Milton Friedman and his colleagues, or were students of students of the Friedmanites. Milton Friedman visited Chile to give advice to his acolytes. The man who was charged during most of that time with execution of economic policy was frank with me, before taking office, about his willingness to sacrifice Chilean manufacturing industry on the altar of free trade "rationality." He said that, as a professor at the Catholic University in Santiago, he had participated in a survey of the potential effects of free trade on the Chilean manufacturing sector that had shown that without effective protection, one-third of the country's industrial firms would disappear; another third would be as well off, or better off, than they were with protection (because of the removal of tariffs on essential inputs that they had to acquire abroad); with regard to the other third the results were inconclusive. He was quite willing to sacrifice a third to a half of the country's industrial sector in the name of "economic orthodoxy" and to accept the unemployment of a quarter of the labor force rather than have those people employed in producing goods that could not compete with imports. This was his definition of "economic rationality."

In practice, the Chicago Boys were as good as their word. In a very short time, they cut tariffs, which had in some cases ranged as high as 200 percent and in many sectors were 25 percent and upward, to a common rate for almost all imports of 10 percent, and virtually all types of nontariff protectionism were eliminated. The result was what might have been expected—the decimation of the home products, textile, and a wide range of other industries, and massive long-term unemployment. In addition, deprived of opportunities for profitable investment in industry, those with available funds turned to an orgy of speculation, which culminated in a deep recession in the early 1980s; this recession, ironically, forced the "free enterprise" government of Pinochet to take control of most of the nation's banking system. Depression also convinced the general of the need for jettisoning the Chicago Boys and returning to at least a limited policy of import substitution (see Gatica Barros 1989 for a discussion of the Pinochet government's economic policies).

Criticism of the import substitution strategy was not confined to the traditional adherents of "free enterprise" and free trade; many of the former advocates of import substitution came to the conclusion that they had erred. It is my contention that the ECLA and others had not been wrong in advocating import substitution as the proper industrialization and development policy in the period in which they endorsed it. Their error lay in their exaggerated expectations from the strategy: They believed that the Latin American countries could reach the level of industrialization and general economic diversification achieved by the United States and Europe while relying only on import substitution.

Thus, many of the ECLA economists failed in the 1950s and afterward to see that import substitution was only a phase in the development process. With ISI's exhaustion as the main motor force for development in Brazil by the beginning of the 1960s, nearly half of the population was still more or less out of the market, and similar situations existed in many other countries. A good number of ISI's former advocates became disillusioned.

However, there were leading advocates and practitioners of import substitution who did not have such exaggerated hopes for what ISI could accomplish. Raúl Prebisch was one of these. When he became head of the United Nations Conference for Trade and Development (UNCTAD) early in the 1960s, he urged Latin American and other Third World countries at a similar level of development to alter their development strategy and build on what had been achieved through import substitution. He recognized that further growth and development depended on adoption of a post–import substitution policy. This alteration of strategy involved, among other things, recognizing the fact that many of the manufacturing industries developed as import substitutes already had acquired comparative advantage and were quite capable of competing on an international level. Therefore, one could judiciously remove protection from these industries, and government encouragement should be given to the development of "nontraditional" exports of their products.

At the same time, of course, Prebisch urged the countries of the center to open their markets and even give preference to manufactured goods from the newly industrializing countries that could compete with goods from the highly industrialized countries, and even with domestic industries in those countries. In effect, Prebisch challenged the countries of the center to practice the free trade ideas they had for so long been preaching to the nations of the periphery.[2]

Another strong advocate—and practitioner—of ISI, Brazilian President Juscelino Kubitschek, also realized that import substitution would not be sufficient to complete the process of economic development. With the virtual exhaustion of import substitution as the main impetus to development by the end of his term in 1961, he realized the need for a post–import substitution strategy. The program that he developed for his second presidency (which, because of the political disasters of the early 1960s, unfortunately never came to pass) called for a major program of agricultural development and stimulation of new industrial exports.[3]

Eduardo Frei of Chile also understood that his country had to move on beyond import substitution. During his term of office in the late 1960s, he pushed programs of heavy investment in agriculture, together with an agrarian reform designed to put into use substantial areas of arable land that large landholders had traditionally kept out of cultivation. Further, he induced the expansion of existing industries, such as steel and paper, originally established for import substitution, for the purpose of having them become exporters. Finally, he took the lead in establishing the Andean bloc, which he hoped would make it possible for the six countries involved to carry out import substitution on a much broader level than was feasible for the individual national economies (see Alexander 1978: Ch. 11, for a discussion of the Frei administration's policies).

Thus, Prebisch, Kubitschek, and Frei all realized that ISI was only a part of an at least three-phase process of economic development. The first part of the sequence was the growth of a major export industry—a mineral or agricultural product—that generated foreign exchange income, thus providing the means for importing larger quantities of manufactured goods.

ISI was the second part of the development process, but, when import substitution was exhausted as the major impetus of economic development, a post–import substitution strategy became necessary, a strategy that concentrated on the development of new exports from industry and on the expansion of agriculture, which had lagged behind during the import substitution phase, so that the rural sector could not only supply the agricultural raw materials and foodstuffs that the national economy needed but could bring agricultural workers into the market, thus providing new customers for the still-expanding industrial sector.

The Failure of Latin American Economic Integration

One aspect of the ECLA-Prebisch program for import substitution development in Latin America did clearly fail. An important part of the message that had been preached during the 1940s and 1950s was the need for economic unification. Integration would make it possible to carry through import substitution on a regional or, at least, a subregional basis, instead of a purely national one. At least four integration efforts were made with the blessing of ECLA. These were the Latin American Free Trade Area (LAFTA), the Central American Common Market (CACM), the Andean Pact, and the Caribbean Common Market. Unfortunately, none of these projects was successful.

After almost a decade of campaigning to establish an overall Latin American common market, the ECLA had to settle, in 1961, for LAFTA. This was a good deal short of a full customs union; while providing for the elimination over a period of fifteen years of all tariffs among its members, it did not provide for a common protective wall around the group as a whole. LAFTA was joined at first by Argentina, Uruguay, Brazil, Colombia, Ecuador, Peru, Paraguay, Chile, and Mexico, and later by Bolivia and Venezuela.

At first, annual multilateral and bilateral negotiations were held, during which member countries agreed to reduce their barriers against one another. However, after some apparent success, these sessions foundered, largely because during the first meetings the negotiators were agreeing not to protect industries that they did not have. When it came time to drop protection for existing industries, the process languished. Although the LAFTA still officially exists, it has been virtually inoperable for the last fifteen years.

The CACM, which also began in the early 1960s and included Costa Rica, Nicaragua, Honduras, El Salvador, and Guatemala, was highly successful for several years. Barriers among the member states were largely eliminated, progress was made on establishing a common protectionist system, and intraregional trade grew spectacularly. However, the CACM fell victim, first, of the "soccer war" between Honduras and El Salvador in 1969 and, subsequently, of the violent political turbulence in several of the member states. It, too, is now virtually inoperative (Weeks 1985a).

The Andean bloc was established in the late 1960s by Chile, Bolivia, Peru, Ecuador, Colombia, and Venezuela, and it also sought to merge these six countries into a single economic whole. Modest progress was made for a few years, but then the Pinochet government withdrew Chile, and, more generally, the bloc was subverted by the oil crises of the 1970s and the subsequent debt crisis.

Finally, the new English-speaking states of the Caribbean formed the Caribbean Free Trade Area in the late 1960s, subsequently broadening it into the Caribbean Common Market. It still exists and is relatively healthy, but has certainly fallen far short of the aspirations of its founders to create a single economic unit in which ISI and general economic development could take place on a subregional level. The traditional patterns of trade of each of these territories, which were directed toward the old "mother country" and, more recently, toward the United States, have been very difficult to break.

Import substitution was thus limited largely to a national rather than a regional or subregional basis as integration schemes failed to develop or collapsed under the weight of political divisions. Obviously, that limited the possibilities of the strategy to much less than the vision of the ECLA planners during the decade and a half after World War II.

Success of the Import Substitution Strategy

ISI in Latin America achieved most of the objectives it was designed to achieve. Obviously, the situation varied from country to country, depending upon the size of the national market and other factors such as natural resources and the educational level of the inhabitants. However, as a result of using ISI, the various countries came to be able, to a greater or lesser degree, to produce within their borders the majority of their basic consumption and construction goods. Several have become self-sufficient in many products of heavy industry. Also, as a consequence of import substitution, the larger economies of the area and some of the intermediate ones were in a position, potentially, to greatly diversify their exports, so that their prosperity no longer needed to depend on the vagaries of one particular product market.

A majority of the countries of the region have industries that supply most of the clothing their people wear; indeed, some of the Latin American nations are among the world's leaders in the textile sector. For instance, in the early 1980s, Brazil rated as the fourth-largest producer of cotton yarn, and the fifth-largest manufacturer of cotton woven fabrics, while Mexico was the eighth-largest supplier of the latter (UN 1985: 227, 236).

Heavier types of consumer goods are also widely produced in the Latin American countries. For instance, by 1985, Brazil was producing more than 2 million television receivers, followed by Argentina and Mexico, each producing nearly 600,000 (UN 1985: 221). Colombia, Cuba, Chile, Ecuador, El Salvador, Peru, Trinidad, and Venezuela also manufactured televisions (ECLAC 1987: 682–683). Other goods of this type turned out in the Latin American countries are washing machines, which by the middle 1980s were being produced in Argentina, Brazil, Colombia, Chile, Ecuador, and Peru; and refrigerators, of which Brazil was manufacturing more than a million and a half (nine other Latin American and Caribbean nations also produce them; ECLAC 1987: 680–681). By the early 1980s, Brazil was turning out more than five and a half million radio receivers, almost as many as the United States was and more than were manufactured in France or West Germany (UN 1985: 221).

The Latin American countries also have become significant—and in some cases quite important—producers in heavy industry. By the mid-1980s, Brazil's crude steel production of 9 million tons was only slightly less than that of India and Belgium; Mexico produced 7 million tons, while half a dozen other Latin American countries also produced steel (UN 1985: 651). By the mid-1980s, Brazil was the largest producer of "passenger vessels, dry cargo vessels, and combined cargo-passenger vessels" (UN 1985: 749) and was the tenth-largest producer of passenger cars. Mexico followed Brazil, turning out more autos than did India, South Korea, or any East European country except the Soviet Union (UN 1985: 761). Latin American industry also turned out in substantial quantities such products as steam turbines, tractors, and lathes. Fertilizers were being produced on a large scale by the early 1980s in Brazil, Mexico, and Venezuela, and were being made in eleven other Latin American and Caribbean countries (ECLAC 1987: 684).

Perhaps another way to indicate what has been achieved in industrial development on the basis of import substitution is to look at two of the "intermediate" countries of the area, Colombia and Venezuela. A recent publication of the Colombian government said that

> Colombia's industrial sector accounts for about 21 percent of the GDP. The main branches are food processing, textiles, chemicals, metals, paper, and pharmaceuticals. In the past two decades, the industrial sector has shifted from production based almost exclusively on consumer goods to the more complex production of intermediate capital goods, which now represent more than 80 percent of the value added. While non-durable consumer goods still have an important role, the manufacture of intermediate products has shown significant development. Included in this category are cement, sawn wood, plywood, iron and steel, print, flooring and roofing materials, bricks, tiles and steel, and plastic piping among others. Capital goods production presently includes a variety of machinery and equipment as well as transport equipment (Colombian Information Service 1986).

The Venezuelan economy, which still remains very heavily weighted toward oil production and processing, has nonetheless seen the manufacturing sector become significant. The 1987 economic report of the Central Bank of Venezuela indicated that, whereas in that year "petroleum activity" accounted for approximately 90.3 billion bolívares of the total GDP of nearly 456.6 billion bolívares, "manufacturing industry" accounted for 68.5 billion and was the second-largest contributor to the national income (Banco Central de Venezuela 1988: 147). In terms of value, more than half of the country's industrial output consisted of products from "industries producing intermediate goods," followed by "industries producing consumer goods" with two-thirds the share of the first category, and "industries producing capital goods" with a bit more than 20 percent of the output of intermediate goods producers (Banco Central de Venezuela 1988: 170). The Central Bank's report also indicates that, in 1987, manufacturing was the third-largest category of the economy in terms of employment (998,691 workers), outdone only by "communal social and personal services" (1,568,083) and "commerce, restaurants and hotels" (1,128,726 people employed). The petroleum industry, mining, and quarrying together employed only 58,376 people (Banco Central de Venezuela 1988: 196).

Thus, it is clear that through the use of import substitution, the countries of Latin America have greatly diversified their economies and have provided important sources of jobs and income.

Further, on the basis of the industries established during the import substitution period, the Latin American countries have developed a major manufacturing export sector. Most spectacular is the case of Brazil, where industrial products make up a majority of exports and include such various products as shoes, airplanes, automobiles, steel, and (regrettably) arms. So successful has the country's drive for industrial exports been that Brazil was one of the three nations denounced by the U.S. trade representative as "unfairly" exporting to the United States (a case of the pot calling the kettle black, one might think).

The Role of MNCs in Latin American Industrialization

In a number of sectors, such as automobile production, shipbuilding, and heavy chemicals, as well as production of heavy consumer goods, the MNCs of the major industrial powers have played a leading role. Indeed, in the case of the auto industry, almost all of the firms are subsidiaries of U.S., European, or Japanese multinationals. Of course, that fact results in a substantial part of the profits of these enterprises being repatriated to the MNCs' home countries, thus limiting the direct contribution of those firms to the Latin American countries' gross national products (GNPs). It also means that the subsidiaries of the MNCs have been subject to their home offices' global plans, which may not always be seen by the Latin American nations as conforming to their national needs. Insofar as the auto industry is concerned, however, the multinational phenomenon is not confined to Latin America. The presence of foreign-owned multinationals in that industry is also a characteristic of the highly industrialized nations, including Great Britain, Canada, West Germany, and the United States.

On the other hand, MNC-owned firms in Latin America have created hundreds of thousands of jobs, a large part of them in skilled employment. They have resulted in the creation of innumerable domestically owned enterprises in the Latin American nations that provide parts and other inputs for the multinational subsidiaries. The operations of the MNCs have also served substantially to expand the markets for all kinds of other industries, both domestic- and foreign-owned.

It is worth noting that while MNCs were participating in establishing manufacturing in the Latin American countries, older investments of the multinationals in public utilities, mining, and petroleum were being nationalized. Also, the Latin American governments have generally kept foreign enterprises out of the steel and other industries that they feel to be "strategic."

What is perhaps the final comment on the MNC question was given to me a quarter of a century ago by President Kubitschek, who, in his drive to industrialize Brazil, enthusiastically invited foreign firms to participate. He commented that it did not make much sense to him to argue about who was to own industries that did not exist. The first priority was to get the industries established, after which there would be plenty of time to discuss the question, to whom should they belong.[4]

The Effect of the Debt Crisis

One thing that has tended to discredit import substitution in the eyes of many has been the almost universal stagnation of economic development during the 1980s. However, the cause of this stagnation has little or nothing to do with import substitution; it is a consequence of the international debt crisis that had been brewing for some years and became glaringly obvious in 1982 when Mexico declared its inability to continue payments on its debt, soon followed by several other Latin American countries.

The debt crisis was due to two things: the drastic increase in petroleum prices during the 1970s and U.S. monetary policy. The crisis thus really began in 1973–1974, with the first increase in the cost of oil from between $2 and $3 a barrel to approximately $15 a barrel, which brought about a dramatic increase in the foreign exchange earnings of the oil-exporting countries. Most OPEC members, especially those of the Middle East, were in no position to use all of that growth in revenues to develop their own economies. As a consequence, they placed a large part of their additional dollars abroad, particularly in deposits in commercial banks in Europe, North America, and Japan.

This presented a serious problem to the banks, which had both to pay interest on their greatly enlarged deposits and to use those funds to earn income from which to pay interest; this led to a sudden willingness on their part to make loans in Latin America that they would never before have contemplated. For their part, the Latin American countries were willing to borrow to finance their development plans, and for other purposes.

Until 1979, this situation did not generate a real crisis in Latin America. With their policies to a large degree oriented toward expanding exports of "nontraditional" products, especially manufacturing goods of those industries that had been created during the import substitution phase, many countries were able to increase foreign exchange income sufficiently to more than meet the requirements for servicing their new, commercial bank loans.

Then, in 1979, oil prices jumped again, from $15 a barrel to close to $40; and Paul Volcker of the U.S. Federal Reserve established a policy of drastically increasing interest rates, which very soon had worldwide repercussions. Latin American countries began borrowing mainly to pay the interest and amortization on the debts they had acquired earlier, rather than to finance development projects or other activities.

Finally, to say that the fact that the debt crisis had nothing to do with the Latin American countries' import substitution during an extended period of time is not to say that the governments of Latin America all spent well the foreign currency they borrowed; that picture is very spotty, varying from one country to another. The point is that the import substitution phase of Latin American development had largely been completed by the time the debt crisis appeared. The fact that the leaders of the various Latin American governments might have used the sudden access to large foreign resources in the 1970s to carry out a post–import substitution strategy, and that many of them, particularly the military regimes so prevalent at the time, did not do so, is no argument against their countries' use of the import substitution strategy in previous decades.

The situation became increasingly untenable for the Latin American debtor countries after 1979. Not only was their debt infinitely greater than it had ever been before, but it was qualitatively different from what it had been in the past. Instead of mainly owing long-term loans at relatively low interest rates to international and foreign government lending agencies, they owed short-term debts at very high—and frequently changing—interest rates. Thus, some countries were faced (considering both interest and amortization payments) with having to pay back in a given year the equivalent of a quarter to a third of their whole debt.

Since the debt crisis formally began in 1982, it has been met, on the one hand, by one stopgap after another—"bridge loans," "emergency loans," and a variety of other such devices—offered by both foreign governments and the creditor commercial banks. Domestically, the crisis has been confronted by a series of "austerity programs," sponsored by the IMF, that have been disastrous, as further economic development has been virtually abandoned, drastic reductions in per capita income have followed, and increasingly grave social crises have emerged.

In the face of this catastrophe, both Latin American economists and political leaders have searched desperately for the answer to the question of how their countries got into such a mess. Not a few of them have accepted the "wisdom" of the IMF and the U.S. government that the original cause of their problems was the proliferation, behind protective walls, of "artificial," "uneconomic," and otherwise nefarious import-substituting manufacturing industries. Acceptance of such irrational "rationality" is truly throwing out the baby with the bathwater.

Possible Alternative Development Strategies

Of course, the import substitution strategy is not the only one that could be used to achieve economic development. At least two others have been touted by elements in the economic and political communities: the Marxist-Leninist-Stalinist strategy; and export-oriented rather than domestic market–oriented industrialization.

Only one Latin American country has resorted to the Marxist-Leninist-Stalinist approach to development for any substantial length of time—that, of course, is Cuba—but the Castro regime's record in terms of economic development is certainly not a brilliant alternative to import substitution. During the 1960s, Cuba's GNP and per capita income both dropped substantially (Roca 1975: 516). Although the 1970s showed a recovery from the situation of the previous decade and the establishment of some new industries and other sectors (such as fishing), the 1980s, particularly since 1985, have seen a marked slowdown in the Cuban economy.

Nor has Stalinism brought an end to the dependence of the Cuban economy on a single export product and a single customer. Sugar is still overwhelmingly important, and all the island has done with regard to depending on a single customer has been to substitute the Soviet Union for the United States. In recent years, the only modification of Cuba's dependence on sugar has been a large increase in its export of (of all things) oil; this oil comes not from Cuban wells but from the Soviet Union, which has purposefully sold (at relatively low prices) more oil to Cuba than its economy needs, with the agreement that the Cubans can sell the excess in the international market at a considerable profit in convertible currency. However, this has only made Cuba even more dependent on the USSR, which can at any time turn off this spigot of *divisas-valuta*, and there are indications that to some degree the Gorbachev regime has been doing exactly that since 1986.

Needless to say, the Stalinist method of development has involved a very high political cost for Cuba. Freedom of the press, speech, political activity, and any kind of opposition, even from within Castro's own camp, has been weak or nonexistent for almost three decades.

The other alternative development strategy, which has won favor among economists in recent years, is the export-oriented one that has been apparently so successful in South Korea, Taiwan, Hong Kong, and Singapore in the last two decades. Those advocating it have argued that building industries basically to supply the export market not only makes possible economies of scale that the domestic market could not possibly provide, but it also forces those industries, which have to buck very stiff competition in the world market, to be more efficient and cost-conscious than is the case with industries established for import substitution purposes.

There is, of course, some truth in these arguments, but they have very little relevance to Latin America. As I have indicated, Latin America was forced into import substitution by the two world wars and the Great Depression, and the ECLA-Prebisch rationalization was developed only after the process had been long under way. Import substitution was not so much chosen as inevitable, given the nature of the world economy at the time.

Furthermore, the use of the import substitution strategy in the first instance by no means rules out industries that are, at least in part, designed to serve the overseas market. Indeed, I have argued that once the process of import substitution has been largely exhausted as the principal motor force for development, one of the elements that is required in a post–import substitution strategy is the expansion for export by those manufacturing sectors that, as a result of the import substitution learning process, have achieved a position of comparative advantage.

In addition, even when import substitution is proceeding, the supplemental fostering of largely export-oriented industries may in some cases be appropriate. Thus, in the case of Mexico, the encouragement of industries along the U.S. border (*maquiladoras*) to manufacture or assemble parts for goods to be sold in the United States was a useful supplement to the general import substitution thrust of Mexican development, although those border industries alone would hardly have constituted an alternative development strategy. In a somewhat different context, the development of tourism mainly for clients from the United States and Europe in both Mexico and the Caribbean islands was also a useful, although not in itself an adequate, form of export-oriented industry.

The one case in the Americas in which the export-oriented industrial strategy of development seems to make most sense is that of the very small states of the Caribbean. Individually, they have such small populations that they provide almost no basis for import substitution development, and they have so far failed to unite their economies sufficiently to provide a basis for import substitution on a regional basis. So, perhaps the only kinds of manufacturing industries they can hope to have are those that provide inputs for firms in the United States.

Conclusion

In retrospect, then, ISI was a development strategy that was forced upon Latin America by the global circumstances of the first decades of the twentieth century. It found its most eloquent advocates among Latin American economists and its most effective practitioners among Latin American political leaders, and, on balance, was a very effective prescription for one phase of the economic development of Latin America. It is necessary now to build further on these successes, when the resolution of the debt problem makes that possible.

Notes

1. The ECLA became the ECLAC with the addition of the Caribbean region in 1984.
2. Interview with Raúl Prebisch, New York City, February 25, 1964. Prebisch expounded on these views at length in his first report as head of UNCTAD.
3. Interview with Juscelino Kubitschek, New York City, February 25, 1964.
4. Interview with Kubitschek, New York City, November 28, 1966.

3

Structuralism, Dependency, and Institutionalism: An Exploration of Common Ground and Disparities

Osvaldo Sunkel

There has been a situation of unequal exchange between institutionalists and structuralists. Institutionalists have read and studied the work of the Latin American structuralists. Several papers by Street (1967, 1987a), C. Richard Bath and Dilmus James (1976), Street and James (1982), James L. Dietz (1980, 1986), and William P. Glade (1987), among others, are proof of their interest and appreciation, although they have also expressed criticisms. Through their publications a wider readership of institutionalists has been made aware of the contributions of Prebisch, Furtado, Pinto, Noyola, Ferrer, Urquidi, and Seers, to mention only some members of the generation of the founding fathers, and of the UN Economic Commission for Latin America and the Caribbean (ECLAC; or CEPAL, the Spanish acronym), the main institution in or around which they worked. Since those institutionalist authors have already presented the basic characteristics of structuralism and dependency, and since there is an excellent recent survey available in English (Blomström and Hettne 1984), I will not insist on those aspects here.

Unfortunately, the Latin American writers in the structuralist and dependency tradition have not done their homework with respect to institutionalism. To the best of my knowledge, there are only three articles on the subject, which were published in an important Latin American journal many years ago by the Argentine economist Santiago Macario (1952a, 1952b). Macario was a student of Clarence Ayres around 1950 who tried to bring the writings of the institutionalists to the attention of Latin American economists. He provides an excellent introduction to institutionalism and suggests there is much to learn from it. Macario informed me that on completion of his studies he joined CEPAL and that he thoroughly discussed the papers he was preparing with Raúl Prebisch, Víctor Urquidi, and José

Reprinted in abridged form from the *Journal of Economic Issues* 23 (June 1989) by special permission of the copyright holder, the Association for Evolutionary Economics.

Antonio Mayobre. They showed great interest, but there was no follow-up. He also informed me that he is not aware of other such initiatives. While the existence of the institutionalist school of thought is of course known and mentioned here and there, institutionalist writings have not been systematically studied and used in Latin America.

In order to appreciate similarities and differences between the respective approaches, I have had to become better acquainted with institutionalist writings. What I have done is to sample several volumes of the *Journal of Economic Issues*, and I have come to five tentative and preliminary conclusions with respect to: (1) some reasons why we have not developed closer collaboration in the past; (2) some areas of coincidence between the two approaches; (3) some fields where it would be particularly fruitful for structuralists to study the work of institutionalists; (4) some areas where, conversely, it might be interesting for institutionalists to look more closely at the work of structuralists; and (5) a conceptual perspective that might be useful for generating certain convergences between the two schools.

Let me then begin with a word about some possible reasons why Latin American economists have ignored the work done by institutionalists despite its obvious usefulness for understanding the economic development problem. One fundamental reason, it seems to me, is the fact that the discipline of economics is, among other things, a system of power organized in such a way that it reproduces itself over time (Earl 1983; Canterbery and Burkhard 1983; Hamilton 1984). But it is not only a national system of power in the United States; it is also an international or transnational system of power (Sunkel and Fuenzalida 1979).

In most Latin American countries, economics did not become a separate discipline and a distinct profession until the 1940s or early 1950s. During the 1950s, schools of economics became separate entities but were frequently combined with the study of accounting and business administration. The next stage in the modernization of the discipline came through three main channels: (1) the use of foreign textbooks, mostly U.S. and British; (2) foreign economists who came to teach, to introduce curricula reform, and to plan and conduct research; and (3) students who went to study abroad, mostly at U.S. universities, and who returned to become the new local faculty. These three channels were greatly enhanced during the decades that followed, as they became conscious and systematic activities of development aid, supported through international agencies, government organizations, and private foundations.

In the process, many of the most prestigious Latin American schools of economics eventually became imitations—almost subsidiaries in certain cases—of their U.S. alma maters. They were thereby incorporated into the international academic system of power devoted to the reproduction of the conventional paradigm of the discipline, through similar orientations in research, teaching, publications, academic exchange, and funding for all these activities. As with institutional thought in the United States, structuralist and dependency work and thought in Latin America has been segregated and marginalized from these institutions. The result is obvious: Latin American students of economics in the better-known universities are not given the chance to seriously study structuralism, either in Latin America or in the United States.

Some perceived the dangers of this process and tried to suggest a more reasonable system of international academic cooperation and exchange that, while helping to improve and modernize the discipline, would keep it relevant and capable of addressing the development problems of Latin American countries in the context of their historical, environmental, cultural, political, and socioeconomic realities (Pinto and Sunkel 1966).

Moreover, in the last decade and a half the study of the problems and crises of the economic development process—which presumably are at the center of Latin American concerns and are where structuralist and dependency approaches have made significant contributions—has been expurgated from the departments of economics of U.S. universities. The same trend has, of course, been replicated in Latin America (Sunkel 1984; Griffith-Jones and Sunkel 1986).

The worst cases have been those in which the conventional academic establishment has become associated with military governments and therefore has become not only an implicit but an explicit part of the system of power, in which everyone who is not a true believer in neoclassical economics of the Chicago School variety has been expelled from academia, and in which all reference to economic thought and literature not sanctified by the system of power has been suppressed. For this reason, in countries that have suffered long periods of military dictatorships and where neoconservative ideology has prevailed, independent academic work could only be carried on, under great difficulty, in independent research centers outside the university (Street 1983a, 1983b).

Structuralism has been engaged in a running battle with neoclassicism from its very inception, in the work of Prebisch, and through its evolution during the last decades, when it has met increasing difficulty in resisting the revival of neoclassical and monetarist orthodoxy. Structuralism also has had to contend with the other main school of thought having a strong presence in Latin America—that is, Marxism. Although in the origins of structuralism, the Marxist perspective was supportive and helpful, and although both approaches developed more or less in parallel without much conflict, this situation changed in the mid 1960s. After the Cuban revolution, Marxists became more militant and revolutionary and began denouncing import substitution industrialization as a bourgeois and pro-imperialist strategy. In this way structuralism and its outgrowth—dependency—came in for a strong attack from the left. This became, in fact, one of the most important aspects of the dependency debate. Over the years, structuralism has therefore had a very difficult time defending itself both from the right and from the left. This is probably another reason why structuralists have not made the effort to become aware of the contributions of institutionalists. The challenges came from neoclassical orthodoxy and Marxism, and for a long time there seemed to be no need for allies. The situation may be changing now and new perspectives may be opening.

Let me now move to some parallels and coincidences between the two approaches. The origins of both perspectives in the work of Thorstein Veblen and Prebisch are apparently related to the overwhelming prevalence at the time of laissez-faire doctrine and policy prescriptions (Mayhew 1987; Prebisch 1984). In both cases this influence came mainly from abroad, particularly from Great Britain. The North and South American reaction was influenced by the German Historical School but was mostly endogenous, reflecting national interests, peculiarities, and concerns. Sharing some of Marx's insights, capitalism—and in particular, industrialism and technological progress—was seen as a tremendously dynamic force of progress and change, but as hampered by institutions and structures. These institutions must be transformed to allow capitalism and industrialism to develop, while also retaining control over the unbound and partially destructive power of capitalism.

Both approaches are, therefore, reformist and not revolutionary in character; capitalism as a system must be tamed, controlled, and guided, rather than abolished. Keynesianism and post-Keynesianism are welcome, and so are government activism, the participation of the public sector in economic and social activities, the promotion of institutional and structural reforms and change, and governmental planning. But also, civil society, at local, regional, or national levels, is encouraged to engage in reformist activities. Advocacy of social and economic change is clearly a characteristic of both approaches.

The economic process is not seen as a static, circular, repetitive, equilibriating mechanism, limited mainly to what happens in various markets, but as an ongoing, sociohistorical, evolutionary process—the cumulative cause and effect of conflicts and changes in economic, social, cultural, and political forces. Individuals are not considered equivalent to computers programmed to maximize a welfare function given certain constraints, nor are firms seen as computers programmed to maximize profits given a production function and certain financial restrictions. They are conceived as social and cultural entities, relatively autonomous but institutionally and structurally shaped and circumscribed as regards values, norms, behavior, forms of association, and organization. As a consequence of this vision, the recent revival of the neoclassical paradigm, carried to extremes of individualism, hedonism, and utilitarianism, and its corresponding neoconservative ideology, represent to both approaches a formidable challenge to the welfare and integration of society and must be exposed and overcome.

Institutionalist and structuralist thought is always centrally concerned with contemporary socioeconomic reality and the corresponding preoccupation with economic policy. As a matter of fact, moral values and pressing problems, rather than deductive reasoning and controversy, are at the origin of most research and thought. Concern about crisis and injustice seems to be a major initiator of research and policy prescriptions. Prebisch's initial contribution is the outgrowth of his experience as head of the Central Bank of Argentina during the Great Depression of the 1930s, of his perception of the profound inability of his country to face the crisis, and of the irrelevance and perverse consequences of the application of received doctrine and the policies derived from it. As in the case of Veblen and the founders of institutionalism, Prebisch's thought was a vernacular reaction to foreign laissez-faire intellectual and practical predominance, which was seen as detrimental to the national interest. The depression seems to have been a great challenge and stimulus to both schools of thought, generating much activity and creativity in both theoretical and policy matters. As reported by K. Parsons, K. Boulding, and J. K. Galbraith, John Commons and his students contributed significantly to Roosevelt's New Deal in the early 1930s (Parsons 1985).

The further development of Prebisch's thought occurred during the decades of the 1930s and 1940s when, having had to leave Argentina as Juan D. Perón took over, he traveled through Latin America advising central banks, particularly in Mexico and Venezuela. He was confronting problems of economic policy resulting from the depression, its aftermath, and World War II. Observing these economies, he realized that there were great differences among them; he was particularly struck by the sociocultural contrast between Argentina, with a rural sector that was sparsely populated with European immigrants, and Mexico, with its massive rural population of ancient culture. But he also saw fundamental similarities: the virtual absence of an industrial sector and the dependence on a few primary exports. Observation, the inductive methods, and comparative historical analysis were central to his approach, as is also the case with institutionalists.

I could go on, but, as can easily be concluded from the above, institutionalists and structuralists indeed share a common ground or—as Schumpeter would put it—a similar vision of the economic process.

Let me then look at a first aspect of some of the disparities between the two approaches. The institutionalist literature, as it is represented in the *Journal of Economic Issues*, presents certain areas of inquiry that appear particularly strong from the perspective of structuralism. I am struck, for instance, at the thoroughness and comprehensiveness of the philosophical, epistemological, methodological, conceptual, theoretical, and analytical critique of the conventional neoclassical and monetarist paradigm. Although structuralism shares many of these critiques, it is much weaker and more superficial in this regard and has much to learn from this aspect of the institutionalist literature.

Institutionalism is also much stronger as regards the theoretical and conceptual grounding of its approach and its theory of socioeconomic change as a distinct and positive alternative to neoclassical orthodoxy. Much of the effort of institutionalists goes into the analysis of the philosophical basis of institutionalism, the theory of human nature, the theory of institutional and technological change, and the criteria of social value. Structuralism is particularly strong in its conceptual approach and historical interpretation of Latin American underdevelopment and dependency (Blomström and Hettne 1984; Gurrieri 1982; Rodríguez 1980). But, as regards its theoretical and philosophical foundations, only a few references come to mind (Cardoso 1977a, 1977b; Sunkel and Paz 1970; Valenzuela and Valenzuela 1979). One main reason for this weakness is the fact that there is not much place for such fundamental inquiry in the academic and research institutions of Latin America. As already mentioned, our universities either exclude us or do not allow us the time, resources, and research environment conducive to the accumulation of fundamental knowledge. This is in part for ideological reasons but also because the universities are geared toward professional training rather than the pursuit of scientific knowledge. Therefore, if one follows the life and work of the main contributors to structuralist thought, they will be seen to have spent little of their time and effort in academia, except for periods in exile outside Latin America. Most of their time has been accounted for by work either in international organizations or in government, where critical thought and economic philosophy and method are not particularly valued. Institutionalists and structuralists have a different institutional base, and it shows in their intellectual output.

One interesting and promising development in the structuralist approach is the attempt in the 1980s to give some of its central propositions a more formal and mathematical expression. This has been called neostructuralism. Although this interesting effort has revitalized structuralism, it has tended to concentrate on short-term equilibrium and adjustment problems rather than on questions of economic development. Nevertheless, more recently, neostructuralists have been making an effort to relate to and rediscover their roots in structuralism, as shown in the review of this literature by Osvaldo Rosales (1989).

Institutionalism is also particularly strong in the area of technology, of course, and devotes a large proportion of its literature to its study. Technology is absolutely central to institutionalist thought, so much so that it is the driving force of evolution and change in this approach. Technology is seen as closely related to cultural change, thereby bringing into the picture a dimension of development that is completely absent from structuralism. Technological change is seen as a dynamic, transformation-inducing aspect of culture, deriving from the accumulation of knowledge and transcultural inducements; but cultural patterns, in turn, define the extent and nature of its incorporation into cultural change. This intimate relationship of technology—seen as the cumulative development of ideas, tools, and skills—to the culture from which it derives and to which it contributes is a fundamental element of institutionalism. It is an aspect of development theory that has been badly neglected by structuralism, which has had a more restricted view of technology.

But this does not mean, as I think some institutionalist critics have suggested, that structuralism does not give sufficient importance to technology (Street 1977). From Prebisch onward, structuralism has placed great importance on industrialization, which is seen as the bearer of technological progress and the key to modernization. Great emphasis was put on this aspect, but some confusion seems to have arisen about the dependency critique. What structuralism and, particularly, dependence thought have argued is that the nature of the process of transfer of technology has inhibited the development of endogenous technical capabilities in Latin America. Building up a national base of technological capability is certainly crucial to development, and Latin American countries have attempted to create it in various forms but have remained great consumers of imported technology, which, as a neoclassical economist would put it, is cheaper and more readily available. Except perhaps in the case of Brazil, Latin America has not yet developed the will and the capacity to produce, adapt, and select technology, but the region is most definitely convinced that this is a central feature of the development process. As a matter of fact, the process of institution-building in this field, aimed at channeling resources into this area and promoting science and technology, was quite significant in the 1960s, before the onslaught of neoliberalism.

Another area in which structuralists have much to learn from institutionalists is their extensive analysis of the institutional characteristics and corporate structure and dynamics of the U.S. economy, both in general and as regards its different sectors and regions and its main markets and institutions, including, particularly, governmental regulations and policies. The U.S. economy is a determining factor in the evolution of Latin American economies and societies through all sorts of channels: monetary and fiscal policy; interest rates; tariff and nontariff barriers; volume and value of imports and exports; transnational corporations; migration policies; technological innovation; and consumption patterns, to name just a few. It is at least as important for Latin American students to become intimately acquainted with the intricacies of those aspects of the U.S. economy that are crucial for their own countries as it is for them to spend time and effort mastering the latest twist in some highly abstract and probably irrelevant theoretical debate or methodological or statistical refinement. This might in fact be a practical and straightforward avenue for starting significant cooperation among institutionalists and structuralists.

My second set of disparities concerns some areas of structuralist and dependency research that institutionalists might find of interest. I have the impression, for instance, that institutionalist thought has given very high priority in understanding the domestic economy of the United States, almost to the exclusion of understanding the structure and evolution of the international economy and the relationships between the two. Take such fundamental recent statements of institutionalist thought as Marc Tool's *The Discretionary Economy* (1985) and the two volumes of the *Journal of Economic Issues* bearing the title *Evolutionary Economics I and II*, which were "intended to provide a comprehensive, contemporary formulation of institutionalist political economy." Tool's book does not list any international aspect in its index and has only passing references in the text. In the two volumes of the *Journal*, only the article by John Adams (out of thirty articles) deal with international trade and payments. In his words: "American institutional economists have devoted very little attention to the international economy" (Adams 1987: 1841).

I would submit that we have here probably the greatest difference between the two approaches: The institutionalist approach is state—or nation—centered; its object of study is the national economy— fundamentally, the national economy of the United States. The structuralist-dependency approach is world-centered. The national economy of the United States, together with other industrial economies, is seen as dominant, and Latin American and other underdeveloped economies are seen as dependent subsystems of the global world economy. All national economies are therefore significantly influenced, although in different ways, by their participation in the system. U.S. MNCs for instance, which from almost any conceivable perspective constitute a critical institutional core of the U.S. economy, derive a very high proportion of their profits from their operations abroad. Therefore, the U.S. economy is structurally and institutionally interrelated in a very profound sense with the world economy, quite apart from the more obvious external economic relations of trade and finance.

I can think of some powerful historical reasons why these different approaches should have developed. The United States is a continental economy and society, with a strong isolationist tradition, and institutionalism was born in Middle America and Texas rather than on the East or West coasts. Structuralism and dependency approaches reflect almost the opposite historical circumstances. But, given the progressive, massive, and pervasive interpenetration of the U.S. and world economies in recent times, there seems little doubt that a purely domestic vision of the U.S. economy will fail to give a reasonable account of its evolution. The work of the structuralist-dependency school—although one may have to turn it on its head—might give some interesting clues to a better understanding of the highly transnationalized U.S. economy of the late twentieth century.

There are other significant areas of structuralist socioeconomic research that might be worth a glance. There is, of course, the structuralist approach to inflation, which has been frequently reviewed and is well known. But there are other important fields: the debt and development crises of the 1980s; planning and regional development; the state and the transition from authoritarian to democratic regimes; the interrelation between the environment and development; and the whole area of poverty, underemployment, the informal economy, marginalization, urbanization, and social change.

It is impossible to do more than mention these subjects here, but anyone interested in familiarizing himself or herself with the corresponding literature has some readily available sources at his or her disposal: *Revista de la CEPAL (CEPAL Review)*, the *Latin American Research Review*, *El Trimestre Económico*, and *Pensamiento Iberoamericano: Revista de Economía Política*.

Finally, I would like to outline a conceptual perspective that I have found useful in differentiating the neoclassical synthesis from the structuralist approach, particularly as regards the understanding of economic development processes. I believe this may also be a convenient way of exploring the differences between conventional economics and dissenting schools of economic thought in general, and of perceiving the similarities among the latter—including, in this particular instance, structuralism and institutionalism.

My proposal consists simply of distinguishing among them according to the emphasis that each one places on stocks vis-à-vis flows in the economic process. By stocks I mean the classical view of the endowments of human, natural, and capital resources that a society has at its disposal at a certain point in time; by flows, the production, income, expenditure, and transfer streams per unit of time obtained from those endowments. Classical political economy placed a great deal of emphasis on resources, without neglecting the flows derived from them. Conventional neoclassical economics, the mainstream paradigm, on the contrary, has managed to expurgate from its theoretical framework, its teaching and research, and its policy recommendations, almost all reference to the productive resources of society and has concentrated almost exclusively on flows, both at micro- and macroeconomic levels.

This difference in preference of focus has profound implications. The exclusive emphasis on annual or semiannual monetary flows brings to the forefront of interest questions related to the short-term adjustments of the economy, particularly in regard to equilibrium, both macroeconomic—the balance of payments, the budget, the monetary accounts—and microeconomic—firms, consumers, markets, and prices. Mainstream economics excludes from the field of economic inquiry and policy almost all that pertains to that other major part of the socioeconomic process that deals with resources, their dynamics, the relations among them, and with the flows that derive from them, with technology, institutions, power, and culture, which are responsible for the way in which those resources are created, owned, combined, used, abused, and reproduced. Neoclassical economics, of course, mentions these matters in introductory chapters of economic textbooks, but strips them of their real significance by transforming them into factors of production that can be manipulated in any way one wishes according to the logic of the corresponding markets.

Apart from a mechanical kind of demography that allows population projections from which to derive the supply of labor, labor becomes a disembodied commodity without relation to the man or woman who performs the labor, to the family to which they belong, to the social class of which they form a part, and, in summary, to the society and culture that determines skills, habits, values, stratification, and aspirations. This exercise in abstracting labor from its sociocultural environment and making it responsive solely to changes in wages, furthermore, prevents any meaningful cooperation between conventional economics and the other social sciences—sociology, psychology, anthropology—which presumably have something to say about performance, creativity, cooperation, motivation, union activism, and so on, and which, in fact, play a major role in the training of managers in schools of business administration—economists notwithstanding.

Moreover, producers and their families are, of course, also consumers, another disembodied category of neoclassical economics. The degree to which the nature of the laborer's place in the process of production determines his pattern of consumption is glaringly obvious to the most superficial of observations: Working-class, middle-class, and upper-class areas in any city display consumption patterns with respect to housing, health, education, entertainment, food, clothing, and transportation that are worlds apart and that have much to do with what one does for a living (not to mention marginal and slum areas where there is little labor to speak of, or conditions prevailing in the rural areas—not the ones used for upper-class recreational purposes, but where actual agricultural production takes place).

Labor is also disembodied from institutions: the state, the firm, the judiciary, the union, the school, the mass media, the party, and the corresponding rules of the game and bureaucracies. Presumably, ownership, control, information, knowledge, power—the stuff of political economy—

also have something to do with labor, work, and consumption, but again neoclassical economics refuses to have anything to do with such disturbing and confusing matters.

If we move from human resources to natural resources, the process of disembodiment takes the form of stripping down the environment to square acres of land. There might be some reference to different qualities and diminishing returns of land to show that David Ricardo has not been totally forgotten, but any notion that natural resources are dynamically imbedded in ecosystems, that soils, flora, fauna, water, weather, forests, topography, and human activity interact in multiple and complex ways, with generally deplorable consequences for land and also people, in the longer run, is certainly not to be found in conventional economics textbooks. The devastation caused in rural (and urban) areas the world over might have been averted to some extent if economics had also opened a door to the hard sciences—physics, chemistry, biology, and hydrology—rather than closing it with the parametric nails of the technical coefficients of the production function and abstracting, furthermore, from the material, spatial, locational, physical, and environmental bases of all social processes.

Last but not least, there is capital. In recent work on environment and development, I have assimilated accumulated capital to the built-up and artificialized environment: the final product, over time, of the progressive transformation of nature through labor, knowledge, technology, and social organization (Sunkel 1980,1987a). The accumulation of capital, in this sense, is therefore at the center of the process of economic development, since it incorporates technological innovation, brings about specialization and productivity increases, and allows for additional investment and further expansion of the capital base of society. An artificial environment is thereby built up, which sustains progressively increasing levels of living and productivity, although at the risk of undermining it through the abuse of its life-supporting ecosystems.

By focusing explicitly in this way on stocks—their dynamics, the relations among them, the ways in which they generate flows, and the feedback of flows on stocks—structuralists and institutionalists have further common ground to support a joint intellectual effort aimed at a better understanding of economic development and of the strategies and policies that might bring it about and contribute, especially, to the improvement of the living conditions of the poor. I sincerely hope that this discussion will help in building bridges between the two schools of thought—structuralist and institutionalist.

4

Latin American Structuralist Economics: An Evaluation, Critique, and Reformulation

James M. Cypher

The situation today is comparable with that which existed in the immediate postwar period because of the questions that we confront and the absence of answers. At that time, we had the contributions of CEPAL—which offered a theoretical interpretation of development problems and some fundamental policies for development. Today, the "CEPAL Manifesto"[1] of the early 1950s is clearly exhausted, yet nothing has taken its place. It is now more difficult because the objective conditions are less favorable and the task is even greater. This time, it is not a case of encouraging processes already under way, as then occurred with policies of import substitution, but rather it is necessary to reorient and reverse tendencies (toward depression, concentration, denationalization, and inequality) that have become deeply entrenched in the current period. Consequently, new policies of development also require more profound economic transformations. It is not surprising, therefore, that the "New Economic Manifesto for Latin America" that would redefine the role of the "agents" of development, as well as the contents and instruments of economic policy, has been slow to arrive.

—Pedro Vuskovic (1986: 66)

Latin America comprises a vast territory with nations of varied history and social composition. The heterogeneity of the Latin American social formations is such that no set of ideas, however general, could be sufficiently encompassing to describe the pitfalls and potentialities of development for this most-complex subcontinent, nor is it my objective here to create such a description. Rather, I attempt to define and describe situations, conditions, tactics, and policies that have the potential of contributing to a popular form of development for the larger nations of Latin America. (Many of the smaller nations seem to face special circumstances stemming from their limited economic resources and the narrow extent of their development. Whether the

41

case of the smaller nations demands special consideration is a matter that lies outside the scope of this chapter.)

I explore an intermediate terrain that lies between the rapid transformation of social formations (with all the attendant difficulties that such transformations entail) and the acceptance of an unacceptable status quo based on a failed model of neoliberal economic policies. Dependency theory posits an all-or-nothing condition—either catastrophe (the status quo) or an overthrow of the existing social formation.[2] This has proved, for the most part, to be a rigid, nonoperational formula that displaces critical analysis from the examination of existing social structures—leaving the field of policy analysis open to the most retrograde of analytical constructs (in particular, neoclassical economic theory).

The alternative to dependency analysis has been Latin American structuralism—an attempted theoretical paradigm that has increasingly suffered from its own structural limitations. Dependency analysis arose from a reaction to both the assumptions of pragmatic development policy advanced by the Latin American structuralists and the presumptions of historical inevitability imbedded in the developmentalist model of W. W. Rostow and others who proposed this paradigm. The weaknesses of all three of these paradigms—dependency, structuralism, developmentalism—opened the way, in part, for the attempt to hegemonize a doctrine that constitutes their collective negation—neoliberalism in the Hayek-Friedman form.[3]

The rise of neoliberalism was only partially due to the exhaustion of the structuralist paradigm; paradoxically, it was also due to the limited success of the structuralists' endeavors (Pazos 1987: 147–155). That is, the ability of the structuralists to define and introduce a model that challenged the presumptions of neoclassical theory—both in the sense of defining a rudimentary industrial policy and in modestly reinterpreting the nature and function of some of the institutional structures of power in the global economic system—occasioned a response in defense of the status quo.

This response came slowly, and only in the face of a situation that illuminated the degree to which the postwar institutional structure—commonly known as the Bretton Woods system—had permitted a redistribution of global economic power within the advanced capitalist nations and between those nations and the nations of the South. While only a few nations of the South enjoyed this new situation, the significance of a modest power shift that favored some of these nations was not lost on the more astute policymakers in the advanced nations. It was the "energy crisis" of the early 1970s that first raised an alarm. In essence, the energy crisis demonstrated that nations of the South could contest the control of global resources that fell within their territories. This was followed by the recognition, later in the decade, that some newly industrializing countries were making advances in manufacturing production—thereby playing a new role as (subordinated) competitors of the advanced nations. A third matter also was to be noted in the 1970s: Many nations had commenced counterbargaining with transnational corporations that operated in the poorer nations. (Recently, this approach has been referred to as one of assertive industrialization.[4]) During the 1970s the structuralist economists of ECLAC were not in the vanguard in interpreting the significance of this modest but notable shift in global economic power toward the South. In the 1980s their work has, for the most part, been limited to short-run analyses that have inordinately concentrated on the problem of debt renegotiation, stabilization, and structural adjustment.

Throughout the 1980s, there was a concerted attempt, spearheaded by multilateral institutions such as the World Bank, to put the genie of the South back into the bottle. In Latin America this initiative took two forms: First, the multilateral institutions used the tremendous leverage afforded to them by the debt crisis to tie new credits to policies that are the antithesis of assertive industrialization; second, an ideological offensive was mounted against the structuralist model of development. We are basically concerned here with this second aspect—the ideological distortions of the structuralist model and a critique of this model. We seek to understand the potential for a policy realignment based in a neostructuralist approach and to envision what this would entail.

A (Limited) Critique of ECLAC's Structuralist Approach[5]

Raúl Prebisch exerted an extraordinary influence over ECLAC in its formative years. To begin a critical interpretation of ECLAC it would seem logical, therefore, to commence from Prebisch's point of departure— neoclassical economics. Prebisch (1984: 175; 1985: 9) was quite frank regarding his admiration of neoclassical economics during his early years. While he maintained that he was subsequently able to reformulate his views, it is debatable how far he was able to distance himself from neoclassical analysis. In the topics he chose to analyze, in the way in which he and many of his ECLAC colleagues carried out their analysis, and in the broad range of issues and elements that ECLAC treated as exogenous from their analysis there is more than a whiff of neoclassicism. Neither he nor most of the ECLAC economists ever engaged in a frontal assault on neoclassical theory. Nor did they seem to be familiar with the broad body of work, particularly deriving from the institutionalist school, which had undertaken precisely such an assault (see Chapter 3 for elaboration).

Structuralism's point of departure was a critique of one of the mainstays of neoclassical theory—the doctrine of comparative advantage (along with the concept of the international division of labor that flowed from this doctrine).

Prebisch's (and ECLAC's) innovation in this area should not be minimized—theirs was an important, even fundamental, achievement. Likewise, this innovation should not be misunderstood—dispensing with the theory of comparative advantage and a few other elements of neoclassical theory does not, in itself, constitute a new paradigm of economic analysis. Rene Villarreal, a widely published Mexican economist, has argued that ECLAC's structuralism fell far short of a new economic paradigm—it was, rather, "an unfulfilled *rebellion*" (1984: 174, 177).

When ECLAC introduced new analytical categories such as the "center" and the "periphery" and maintained that a "diversified" (nonhomogeneous) production base existed in Latin America, resting on the divergence between the advanced agromineral export sector and the local production base of native cultivators and artisan manufacturers, it provided the building blocks for what might have been a promising new interpretation of the origins of economic backwardness. ECLAC argued that the structure of the global economy was not based on essentially homogeneous trading nations. Latin America—as a trader of basic agricultural, tropical, and mineral products— faced a set of structural impediments that did not confront the manufacturing nations. (This became the origin of the much-discussed "Prebisch-Singer" thesis that has been exhaustively scrutinized elsewhere and need not detain us here [Sarkar 1986: 355–372].) What is to be noticed, here and elsewhere in the work of ECLAC, is the abstraction from historical time. In the Prebisch-Singer construct, the terms of trade for primary products (exchanged against manufactures from the center) were assumed to decline; this accorded with certain theories derived primarily from neoclassical economics. The argument was expressed essentially as a timeless construct; it abstracted from long wave phenomena and held other factors constant—in accord with time-honored principles of neoclassical analysis.

Likewise, the concept of the "periphery" abstracted from historical time. There was no conscious and determined effort by ECLAC to understand the evolutionary dynamics of the social formations of Latin America. Such an endeavor would have drawn ECLAC into a determined effort to understand the dynamics of the economic history of Latin America. Neoclassical economics has no interest in such inquiries, because its theory is timeless and essential—all else is exogenous. A similar bias is to be detected in the methodological approach of ECLAC. There was a search for certain constants—theoretical regularities—that would give shape to ECLAC's analysis, but there was rarely a descent into history as a force; it could be treated as exogenous. Timeless analytical constructs are idealist constructs: They exist outside of historical discourse; they are presumed to be true because they have been demonstrated with (presumably) faultless internal logic. At virtually every turn in Prebisch's writing, one finds the abstraction from historical time and the insistence on abstract and idealist constructs.

"Center" and "periphery" can, in certain instances, be helpful analytical constructs, but there are unanswered historical questions. What occurs when the dynamics of the center change; that is, what happens when the postwar hegemon, the United States, enters economic decline? What happens when the periphery fragments? These were not questions that structuralism anticipated because of the abstract and idealist constructs implicit in its methodology.

Prebisch introduced an assumption into his work that has conditioned most of the research of ECLAC, as well as forming the bedrock of dependency analysis: Causality runs from the external to the internal. However, the degree of involvement with the international economy waxes and wanes as we move from one Latin American nation to the next. There are great variations in the degree of involvement and in the type of products produced and sold in international markets. Methods of production vary, as do the markets in which the products are sold (e.g., monopsonistic, cartel-oligopsonistic, competitive). Over time, nations change their degree of involvement, and export markets rise and fall.

How is one to understand the shifting importance of the external market? At the very least it is necessary to make a comprehensive historical study of the experiences with international production and trade. From this might (or might not) come some ideas regarding "regularities" of trade relationships and how—if need be—they might be altered. Does the external determine the internal? This is a question of an empirical nature, not one reducible to a priori deductions. In at least one major Latin American nation, Mexico, the evidence for the dominance of the external over the internal is difficult to document, even while it is commonly asserted (Cypher 1990). John Weeks's important study of Peru (1985b) likewise finds that internal factors are of the utmost importance in understanding the development dynamic of that nation. It is not intuitively obvious that other major nations fit the ECLAC assumption; Brazil, for example, exported only roughly 10 percent of its GDP in 1986. That the 10 percent determines the other 90 is not a very likely hypothesis.

There is no attempt here to invert ECLAC's approach and argue for the insignificance of the foreign sector. Clearly, in many cases the foreign sector plays a role that far overshadows its relative weight in the GDP.[6] Nonetheless, the burden of proof seems to be on the *ECLACistas* to show that their emphasis on the external sector is in fact warranted. What cannot be disputed, it seems, is the assertion that ECLAC's methodology led to the relative neglect of the internal (or domestic) elements of the socioeconomic formations of Latin America. The posited dualism of the social formation (advanced agromineral exporters vs. subsistence cultivators and artisan manufacturers) reduced extremely complex and historically derived production processes to basic categories. Moreover, it should not be forgotten that the backwardness of the internal sector was viewed as a direct function of the transfer of the "surplus" by the Latin American nations to the "center" nations.[7]

Two important matters worthy of prolonged analysis (the transfer of the surplus and the primacy of external factors) were collapsed and then set aside by ECLAC. Let us first consider the question of the surplus: Economists who employ this concept have always had trouble converting it into an operational form—a predicament Prebisch did not succeed in avoiding. (Presumably, the surplus is some considerable portion of nonwage income.) This, however, is not of crucial importance for the point that I raise at this juncture: Should we concentrate on the part of the surplus, however defined, that is gained by the transnational elements (banks and corporations) or that portion accruing to the national economic and political elite? The answer, I argue, is both—and in proportion to how the surplus is divided. More important, as Arturo Bonilla (1980: 28) maintained, is how the surplus is utilized:

> In reality, the terms of the problem are distinct from the form in which they are presented by CEPAL. Economic development is not merely a question of taking advantage of a capacity to export in order to accelerate industrialization. Rather, I would maintain, the problem should be examined in terms of the capacity of the Latin American economies to generate a social surplus and above all to understand the forms in which it is utilized. . . . To the degree that we fail to arrive at a quantification of the surplus, and a critical study of its utilization, we will be unable to understand the causes of underdevelopment.

Bonilla is alluding to the domestic misuse of the surplus by the economic and political elite and the state. Here, rather than in the exportation of a portion of the surplus, we are to locate the key to underdevelopment. Others, in particular Weeks (1985b: 7–23), have argued that the key is not to be found in the native elite's squandering of the surplus so much as it is in its disinclination to produce a surplus. Neither hypothesis, of course, is mutually exclusive. They both, however, take us well beyond the level of discourse adopted by ECLAC.

Let us return to the second point, which was collapsed by ECLAC's insistence on the primacy of the external—the diverse and disarticulated nature of the domestic processes of production. As I have maintained, ECLAC recognized a significant degree of diversity among the national producers. This might have provided an important point of departure had not there been an overriding tendency to collapse the internal into questions that could be subordinated to those linked to external factors of trade, investment, and exchange. The question of the internal market, and internal forms of production, demands and deserves the most careful consideration.

It is necessary to perceive the distinction between the production base of the advanced nations and that of the Latin American countries. In the capitalist mode of production, production processes are relatively homogeneous—large-scale "monopoly capitalist" producers hold the commanding heights of the economy, receive virtually all the profits, and make the investment decisions that matter. There is a strong correspondence between the needs of the supercorporations and the priorities of the state, although state policymaking is not reducible to meeting the needs of the large corporations. Behind these two dominant institutions lies the "competitive sector"—a residual category of small businesses and unorganized workers—where we find the numerical majority of businesses and workers who eke out a modest existence in the interstices of advanced capitalism.

Nothing so simple is to be found in the Latin American social formation. Here we see *latifundio/minifundio* producers; Indian subsistence cultivators; capitalist agribusiness interests; artisan manufacturers and those who utilize backward (but capitalist) methods of production; advanced domestic manufacturers; transnational corporations; moneylenders; cartel-like banking interests; currency speculators; rentiers of every type, size, and description; a military caste; landlord and political oligarchies; village and provincial-level political "headmen" or "chieftains"; commercial cartels in wholesale and retail merchandising; a vast army of small peddlers, repairmen, and food vendors; and, finally, the unemployed. Not only is there a complex, even bewildering array of producers, but the production processes themselves lack unity—they are disarticulated one from the other. Modern and twelfth-century production methods—and virtually everything between—are thrown willy-nilly together. Nor is there any force that somehow harmonizes the production base; social life is "reproduced," but in the most halting and contradictory conditions. Across a wide range of modes of production only one attribute of commonality is to be found—pervasive monopolies. It is fairly clear that such a disarticulated production base must be a major—I would argue the major—contributing factor to economic backwardness.

If the above is an adequate description of the economy, two outcomes are to be expected: low productivity across wide sections of the economy; and severe imbalances between sectors. In Mexico, for example, once the stage of easy import substitution was passed after the 1960s, relatively high industrial productivity growth (approximately 5 percent per year) was replaced by relatively low productivity growth; from 1970 to 1984, it was below 2 percent (INEGI 1985: vol. 1, 335). The disarticulated nature of production was best illustrated by the growing divergence between industrial and agricultural productivity from the 1950s onward: Agricultural productivity steadily lagged behind industrial productivity, sometimes approaching or reaching zero and negative levels (Cypher 1990: Chs. 3, 4). In Mexico, and in several other nations of Latin America, it was not uncommon in the 1980s to find that 40, 50, or even 60 percent of certain basic foodstuffs were being imported—foodstuffs that had been adequately produced and even exported thirty years earlier. The disarticulation in production was readily reflected in the distribution of income. In Chile, for example, 57 percent of the income was taken by the top 20 percent of income recipients in 1978 (Filgueira 1981: 95).

In many ways, ECLAC set the research agenda, the critical tone as it were, for socioeconomic studies in Latin America. Consequently, there is no large body of literature on Latin American modes of production or their interaction within a given social formation. A body of production-based case studies, informed with a theoretical orientation that would devote adequate attention to the causes of underdevelopment to be found in the sphere of production, does not exist.[8] In part this is due to the predilections of the ECLACistas to locate fundamental causality within the sphere of circulation[9]—most particularly in the transfer of a share of the social surplus abroad through foreign trade and the effects of both transnational corporations and banks.

The Absent Theory of the State

ECLAC sought to articulate a policy that would carry the Latin American economies from a stage dominated by primary export forms of production toward one in which capital accumulation arose from the growth of the internal market. Its long-run objective was to transform the Latin American economies into "autonomous" rather than "dependent" entities. The agent that was to achieve this grand transformation was the state, which was to implement a set of import substitution policies that would eliminate the importation, first, of consumer nondurable goods, then consumer durables and intermediate products (steel, cement, petrochemicals), and, finally, capital goods. This was the policy of horizontal-to-vertical ISI. On many occasions, the ECLACistas emphasized that they had no claim to having originated ISI policies, which had developed pragmatically during the course of the 1930s in many Latin American nations. Rather, they sought to give shape and intellectual coherence to a policy that was already well under way.

Reflecting the weight of neoclassical theory in their work, the ECLACistas attempted to articulate the conditions under which it would be permissible to deny the efficacy of the market and erect tariff barriers against foreign manufactures. This orientation led to a body of literature that attempted to specify the terms under which such transgressions of the "logic" of the market would be justified. In other words, there was a notable tendency to emphasize precisely those concerns that any neoclassicist would highlight—the case to be attributed to "market failure." In and of itself, there is nothing particulary objectionable in such an approach—except when it displaces, totally or partially, other considerations of a more fundamental nature.

ECLAC's conceptualization of the state was limited to technocratic concerns. Its concentration on the microeconomics of tariff policies left the question of "the state for whom, and what" unexamined. To be blunt, there was no theory of the state in ECLAC's analysis. The state was assumed to be an exogenous agent that could be brought in to correct economic imbalances, and, by assumption, it had no interests except those that led to the most efficient and rapid form of industrialization.

But, even the most simple policies of ISI can raise fundamental questions: First, if the backward nation is to cut its importation of consumer goods, it immediately confronts the possibility that the advanced nations that face shrinking export markets will have the capacity and desire to retaliate; second, in order to industrialize a nation, the state will have to engage in massive investments in infrastructure. Where will the funds come from to support these new state investments? This question opens a Pandora's box of options: Direct taxes on the economic elite—particularly the nonindustrial oligarchy who hold vast tracts of land or orchestrate the banking and financial "system" of the nation—will be strongly and perhaps effectively resisted; taxes on commodity exports have been often imposed at this juncture, but this reduces the rate of profit in the agromineral export sector and is certain to be resisted as well; taxes on the economic underclasses are not an option given their dire circumstances. This, then, may leave only foreign borrowing—a strategy that Prebisch readily acknowledged would have to be integral to an ISI policy, and, from the perspective of the 1980s, one riddled with pitfalls. Moreover, and this point has been emphasized on many occasions, any attempt to increase the domestic production of manufactures will demand the increased importation of machinery, equipment, and technology to provide the underlying basis (that is, the capital goods) for the increased domestic production of manufactures. This, then, increases the demand for "hard" currencies—which, in turn, increases the need either to export or import borrowed funds.

Furthermore, it is immediately clear to the old agroexport-banking elite that an ISI policy will create a new industrial fraction of the elite that will vie for power within the state apparatus. The special favors and treatment received from the state—which the old elite have come to regard as theirs by right—now are placed at risk. The ECLACistas apparently believed that a populist coalition could overwhelm these interests. Research into the populist coalitions of the Southern Cone during the 1940s suggests, however, that they were effective only when strategies were developed that accommodated or coincided with the interests of the old oligarchy. For example, the depression of the 1930s forced many agroexport interests in Argentina to reorientate their production toward industry. When the Peronist surge began in the 1940s, these interests were positioned to take advantage of the new policies; at the same time, these were years of strong global markets for those whose capital remained in agroexport production. While the populist policy did discriminate against agroexport interests and in favor of domestic industrialists, the old oligarchy had been somewhat split by historical circumstances. In Chile, at roughly the same time, the populist coalition left the old agroexport interests untouched, while extracting the funds needed to promote their new ISI policies from foreign mining interests (Conaghan 1988: 21–30).

The lesson from all of this seems to be that the state can introduce ISI policies only under unique historical conditions that afford almost costless change. ECLAC, drawing their optimism from these cases, did not have an adequate understanding of the political precariousness and uniqueness of the populist policies of ISI that they came to champion: When the losers feel rather deeply their losses, the populist coalition is faced with disintegrating pressures that it cannot withstand.

Implicit in ECLAC's theory of ISI is a conceptualization of the Latin American industrialist as a historical agent analogous to that found earlier in the advanced nations. But, in Latin America, when members of the elite shifted their capital from old-line agroexport pursuits to industry, they took with them the social mores of their former culture. They had become adept at the arts and sciences of sharp trading and at the manipulation of their political environment for their own ends. In short, they were merchant capitalists, not industrial capitalists. While industrial capitalists can be expected to participate in the development of their products—that is, they engage in the more or less intermittent improvement in their productive plant, labor force, and product—merchant capitalists will endeavor to exploit every fissure in the marketing process in order to maximize profits. In Thorstein Veblen's parlance, one can distinguish between the captains of finance (rentiers) and the captains of industry. Latin America has been burdened with an abundance of the former and a paucity of the latter. The reason for this disequilibrium is to be found in the several hundred years of colonial domination that inculcated the rentier ethos into the very marrow of Latin American society.

For ECLAC's version of state-led industrialization to come into existence it is necessary that the state itself create an industrial bourgeoisie. ECLAC has yet to define and analyze how this might come about. (There is, nonetheless, an important body of literature that discusses how this function can be and has been undertaken by the state in Latin America [see Evans 1982: 210–247].) A particular difficulty, in this regard, is the inculcation of a new ideology that embraces and nurtures a dynamic and dominating attitude toward technology. If any one factor can be singled out as the Achilles' heel of the structuralists it has been their tendency to glide over the profound social and cultural changes regarding the use and understanding of technology that must be made if ISI policies are to work.

Not only did the idealist and ahistorical conceptualization of the state propounded by ECLAC soar above the social reality, the state as a new locus of accumulation also escaped the scrutiny of these analysts. ISI policies grant to the state a new and relatively large, if undefined, portion of the economy. The state will now build a vast infrastructure; it will deploy powerful "development banks" and a cadre of technicians to fund, construct, and operate important state-owned industries; it will be involved in an extensive program of public education and labor training; it will operate a qualitatively and quantitatively new state apparatus—complete with a sizable cadre of economists/planners who will out-think the market. All of these new areas of activity open up avenues for primary accumulation by state functionaries who can exploit (in countless unanticipated ways) the decisionmaking power now afforded to them. ECLAC assumed the existence of a selfless corps of highly trained state technocrats who would bring ISI's policies to successful completion. There have been surprisingly large numbers of such individuals who have played major roles in the various ISI programs in Latin America, but they have, of necessity, had to confront or coexist with numerous other state functionaries who have embraced no such altruistic principles. Predatory state functionaries have worked directly with the rentier interests in the private sector to utilize the leverage of the state for their own pecuniary interests. To acknowledge these realities is not to deny the efficacy of any and all forms of ISI policymaking. Rather, it demands that such policymaking be accompanied by a sophisticated and historically derived theory of the state.

The initial intuition of Prebisch and the ECLACistas was accurate enough—the vicious circle of backwardness would have to be broken by state intervention—but their orientation toward the external sector led them away from a systematic study of the state in Latin America: its history; its constraints and limitations; and its potentialities. Moreover, even within the confines of their own analysis, they often were not sufficiently alert regarding the contradictions hidden in their recommendations of state intervention. Their conceptualization of the state—an efficient technocratic entity standing outside of society—offered no role for direct participation by the underlying population. In Mexico (where state policies often approximated those advocated by ECLAC), this situation led, in certain respects, to the creation of a new "political class" that operated the levers of state power. Unconstrained by either organized labor or the peasantry, this "class" proceeded to merge the policies of the state with those sought by the *haute bourgeoisie* (Cypher 1990: chs. 3, 4, 6). The experience of the Mexican state illuminates the dangers implicit in programs that rely upon the introduction of technocratic programs operated by technocrats, without restraints imposed by the middle class, the peasantry, and the working class.

ECLAC as an Institution

As an institution, ECLAC has occupied a distant third place behind the IMF and the World Bank in the United Nations' grouping of "development organizations" (Payer 1982: 16–17). The IMF is well known for its close adherence to neoclassical economic analysis (Brett 1983: 7–86). The Bank's enthusiasm for these formulations has shifted over the decades, but its biases have always been on the side of orthodoxy. ECLAC is a minuscule organization in relation to its "sister" institutions. It has always faced the danger of being too outspoken. While it has had a large impact on policymaking attitudes throughout Latin America, ECLAC has been forced to walk a tightrope where one step too many to the left would bring it into open confrontation with the most economically and politically conservative elements in Latin America and/or the Fund and the Bank.

Any critique of ECLAC must be tempered by an acknowledgment of its institutional setting. Considering this, Prebisch and his colleagues have demonstrated their shrewdness. Even in the dark ages of high neoliberalism, in the 1980s, ECLAC has been able to maintain a steady, if restrained, drumbeat of criticism. Its views penetrate not only the front pages of Latin America's largest newspapers, but also the universities and into the inner circles of policymaking power in most nations. This is not the same as arguing that high policymaking circles follow ECLAC's recommendations—for presently they do not. Yet, ECLAC's voice is indeed heard, and there is reason to believe that in some circumstances it serves as an influence holding in check the most ardent advocates of a free market "solution" to Latin America's current crisis.

The opportunity to observe ECLAC as an institution has been quite rare. One recent account of its inner workings, however, is quite illuminating. In 1956, the prominent British economist Nicholas (later Lord) Kaldor traveled to ECLAC headquarters in Santiago, Chile, in order to conduct a brief study of Chilean tax policy. According to Gabriel Palma and Mario Marcel (1989: 246) who have written about Kaldor's encounter, "it is important to point out that Kaldor's analysis . . . did not follow the mainstream of ECLA thought. . . . While the latter located the essence of the LDCs' [less developed countries] economic problems *outside* the LDCs, . . . Kaldor emphasized that the key problem for Chile's economy [lay] *inside* it—basically, in the absence of a really *progressive entrepreneurial class*." Kaldor made an important discovery: Chile's low rate of capital formation was not directly attributable to its status as a poor nation! The notably low level of private savings (and capital formation) was a function of the Chilean bourgeoisie's extraordinarily high propensity to consume. Kaldor's comparison of the Chilean and British upper class is telling:

The most important difference is that in Chile the personal consumption of property owners appears to take up 21.2% of national resources, [but] in Great Britain it appears to take up only 7.4%. Since in Britain the category of property owners includes a relatively large number of small rentiers (which does not appear to be the case in Chile) the implication is that the proportion of natural resources engaged in producing goods and services for the luxury consumption of the well-to-do is at least three to four times as high in Chile as in Britain. . . . The proportion of gross property income allocated to personal consumption is only 30% in Britain whilst it is over 60% in Chile. British property owners, in addition to paying 42% of their gross income in taxation, save (on balance) a further 27.4%, whereas Chilean property owners who pay only 16.5% in taxation, save only 22%. Or, starting from the gross disposable income after taxation, British property owners appear to have saved 48% of their post-tax income and spent 52% whereas the Chileans saved 26% and spent 74% (Palma and Marcel 1989: 250, citing Kaldor).

Kaldor's findings were never published by ECLAC in spite of its commitment to do so. After various delays, ECLAC announced in 1959 that it could not publish because there was then an election in Chile—ECLAC did not want to appear to be a partisan organization. The transparency of this pretext was embarrassingly obvious, for it does not explain why the study was not published well before the election—or after.

Kaldor's policy conclusion, perhaps naive, was that the elite had to face much higher direct taxes—particularly the landholders who, then and now, have managed nearly to exempt themselves from direct taxes. Such a policy, according to Kaldor, would allow wages to remain the same, while providing the state with a source of income that it could plow into necessary capital formation.

ECLAC has remained remarkably silent on the question of direct taxation of the rich in Latin America, even though, as Kaldor pointed out, "the Chilean capitalist class was the weakest link in the country's economic structure and the productive mobilisation of the resources wasted by this sector deserved to be a first priority in the formulation of economic policy" (Palma and Marcel 1989: 250). There is, it seems, only one way to interpret ECLAC's remarkable encounter with Lord Kaldor and its subsequent relative quiescence in pursuing a policy that would indeed seem to sever the "weakest link" in Latin America's economic structure: ECLAC is able to occupy only a particular, limited, critical space.

Structuralism vs. Institutionalism: An Encounter with Veblen

In his masterful study *Imperial Germany* (first published in 1915), Thorstein Veblen took up the question of "late starters" in the development process. He wrote extensively on the United States from this perspective, and in a much more limited way on Germany and Japan. His work rarely touched on the colonial nations, and then only indirectly. It is not, therefore, immediately obvious that Veblen's insights into the development process are applicable to Latin America; but on closer inspection, an argument can be made for their relevance.

It seems never to have occurred to Veblen to argue that the causes of economic backwardness essentially derived from outside the social formations he examined. Since it would be the weakest of all possible assertions to claim that Veblen suffered from analytical myopia—he was charged with many faults, but never this one—it would appear worthwhile briefly to explore his frame of analysis. Backwardness, to Veblen, was a condition that arose from a lack of mastery of the "industrial arts." The industrial arts entailed a distinct way of producing with modern technology under the rhythmic discipline of the machine; above all, they constituted a historically unique form of human perception and interaction. Under capitalism, a "modern," "materialistic," and "mechanistic" form of human interaction replaced the "romantic," "ritualistic," and "spiritual" forms of perceiving and interacting that had characterized the "principles of conduct, articles of faith, social conventions, [and] ethical values" prevailing in feudal or "autocratic" (e.g., precapitalist) societies (Veblen 1934: 259). If a society introduced or assimilated "the industrial ways and means offered by the technological knowledge and the material sciences" (Veblen 1934: 252) of the advanced nations, then the "servile aristocratic bias" (251) that had penetrated and defined the sociocultural patterns of the backward nations would slowly but steadily be dissolved.

Veblen did not believe that such a position was either fanciful or mechanistic. His study of Germany bears up quite well, even today, in illustrating his perspective and readily demonstrates that there were certain important advantages that accrued to "late starters." Most important among them were "the merits of borrowing and the penalty of taking the lead." In Germany, Japan, Britain, and the United States, Veblen found that nations could "borrow" technology, science, and machinery—that is, one could borrow central components of what I have earlier referred to as the sphere of production—but *only to the degree that the borrowing nation was able culturally to assimilate the advances of the industrial arts.* The culture that needed to borrow would never be able to do so in an unlimited or unconstrained manner. It would have to alter itself in such a way as to make it compatible with an industrial and mechanized form of social organization.

Resistance would come from every level: the religious authorities; the aristocracy; the peasantry; and the artisans. All had certain "vested interests"—material and "spiritual"—in the prior social arrangement. The fundamental question became one of determining if there were an agent or process that would lead to the inculcation of the machine culture, one that could thoroughly or partially transform a feudal, autocratic, or "dynastic" social formation. The arts and sciences of a technologically developed culture could essentially be stolen, and Veblen did not believe that these processes could be readily contained once created. The ultimate barrier was not to be found, then, in external institutions of production—such as, today, transnational corporations—but in the internal institutions of the backward society.

Veblen's work is replete with references to dichotomies. He often described two sets of social forces that existed simultaneously but in direct contradiction to each other. For example, the captains of industry were to be contrasted with the captains of finance, the former exhibiting tendencies to organize production in accordance with the logic of the machine culture, the latter attempting to grasp whatever opportunity existed to extract a rentier's profit from the manipulation of existing production systems, but never, in any case, advancing the industrial arts.

There is no argument that development must either occur or not. It all depends on whether the forces that advance the industrial arts are able to overtake the prevailing cultural and social interests that perpetuate the status quo. Once started down the path toward development, the society nevertheless must continually face the possibility that it will again slip into backwardness or stagnation because of the presence—and even further enhancement—of retrograde elements that are part of its cultural composition. At best, Veblen posits a fragile form of development wherein new possibilities of retardation arise at every turn. What propels the society seems to have more to do with the suppression or diminution of retarding influences, rather than the integration of some new, "missing" element.

On the positive side, beyond the introduction of a set of institutions that nourishes technological advance, Veblen would include the state and a managerial elite. Both of these "agents" have to exhibit a proclivity toward the industrial arts. Veblen tended to express this in somewhat negative forms. Thus, in the case of the state, he emphasized the need for one that would not "hinder the pursuit of knowledge" (1954: 224).

In addition to the points discussed above, Veblen emphasized a number of elements that might well be taken into consideration regarding the possibilities of a reinvigorated neostructuralist analysis:

1. In *Imperial Germany*, Veblen described the "dynastic state," a specific form that inordinately relies upon militarism and a "warlike animus" to maintain social cohesion. In terms of the prevalence of what might loosely be termed a "military caste" in several Latin American social formations, one finds some parallels with Veblen's analysis. Neostructuralism, in concert with a new emphasis on internal factors that impact upon, and determine opportunities for, development, must examine the particularities of Latin American militarism—and how such a retarding factor might be displaced over time.

2. Although far from alone in this regard, Veblen made the distinction between "industry" and "finance" of paramount importance. The work of the ECLACistas has tended to be insufficiently orientated toward this theme; only recently has ECLAC come to give this matter the attention it warrants. For example, Fernando Fajnzylber (1989: 70–71) has decried the fact that a rentier elite, particularly in the 1980s, has displaced industrial capitalists at the pinnacle of economic power and has stressed the consequence of this shift in terms of undermining social forces that would expand the technological base.

3. On many occasions, Veblen emphasized the pervasiveness of what he termed the "predatory animus" that existed simultaneously with its opposite, the "instinct of workmanship." The former inspired all rentiers as well as most states; the latter was nurtured by an industrial culture that had successfully adopted the mores of the industrial arts. By drawing the distinction between "predatory" and other economic activities, neostructuralism could probe an important area that has been largely neglected by the structuralists. Alternatively, as mentioned earlier, neostructuralist research needs to proceed by way of drawing and maintaining a distinction between activities and policies that develop the sphere of production and those that would constrict and control the sphere of circulation.

4. While the structuralists sometimes have highlighted the role of pervasive monopolies in their voluminous work on inflation, the role of Latin American oligopolies in determining the nature of socioeconomic reproduction has not received the attention it deserves. Veblen's emphasis on the retarding role played by large business concerns generally has found no parallel in ECLAC's work, except, of course, when the structuralists have turned their attention to transnational firms. This research, however, has moved forward to the exclusion of studies that would analyze the role played, politically and economically, by the powerful "groups" of family-dominated firms within the Latin American social formations. These "national groups of economic power" normally have combined assets that allow them to play an economic role equaling and often exceeding that played by the transnational firms.

5. Neostructuralism will have to emphasize the key role of ideology in perpetuating a perspective that disparages the need for a "tool-using" mentality. Recently, it appears that ECLAC has come to view such a shift in ideology as entailing "the modification of the elite which gives birth to the values and perspectives which are diffused into the wider society" (Fajnzylber 1989: 166).

6. Veblen closely examined the social processes and traits that led to a "submissive" mentality in precapitalist societies. Timidity has been a noticeable trait in Latin America throughout the 1980s. Even as program after program of "stabilization" has failed, "unemployed workers, dismissed civil servants, and financially embattled business people have accepted their sacrifices with surprisingly little protest" (Handleman and Baer 1989: 14). ECLAC has not developed a body of research to explain and analyze the scope, causes, and depth of the Latin American embrace of fealty, passivity, resignation, loyalty, nationalism, and chauvinism. How these characteristics interpenetrate the economic foundation of the Latin American social formations and how they define or influence the scope of policymaking are fundamental issues that must be explored if neostructuralism is to point the way forward in the 1990s.

The Neoliberal Ascendancy

The neoliberal ascendancy began in 1973 when the ideas of F. von Hayek and Milton Friedman were adopted as the guiding principles behind the new government in Chile. The right turn in Chile could no longer be viewed as an aberration after the Cancún, Mexico, conference of 1981, which brought together a selection of leaders from the North and the South to discuss a New International Economic Order. ECLAC had long been in the vanguard of those in the UN organization, and elsewhere, who had urged a fundamental redistribution of global economic power. When the Cancún conference ended with the resounding rejection of the South's agenda, ECLAC suffered a historic defeat. From that moment onward through the 1980s, neoliberalism gained Latin American adherents at a rapid pace.

The ascendancy of neoliberalism is to be linked above all to an open attack on the fundamental ideas of ECLAC. A representative—but far from unique—example of this sustained attack is to be found in the manner in which the head of the World Bank's Latin American division depicts that region's economic crisis, and the means of overcoming it. S. Shahid Husain wastes no time getting to what he, and the Bank, take to be the causes of the debacle of the 1980s—too much preoccupation with accumulating capital and too little emphasis on efficiency. In the Hayek-Friedman vocabulary, *efficiency* and *markets* are synonyms. Without markets, the neoliberals proclaim, relative prices become distorted, which means that too much is spent on the wrong things (e.g., wages), while too little income flows to the correct areas (e.g., profits). This has occurred because "governments expanded their role and ownership in most aspects of economic life" (Husain 1989: 2). As a consequence, "public agencies and enterprises became hosts to inefficiency, waste and vested interests." But, it is asserted, "private entities could have functioned quite efficiently" (Husain 1989: 2).

Husain reserves his strongest criticism for a scarcely veiled attack on ECLAC's theories of ISI: "In industry, import substitution and limits on external competition [that is, policies of assertive industrialization, and] import licenses . . . ultimately created closed, rigid and high-cost structures which could not grow any more" (1989: 2–3). What, then, should Latin America do? Or, more directly, what is it that the World Bank will demand that Latin America do now that it must inordinately rely on multilateral institutions—most particularly, the Bank—for external credit (Cypher 1989)? The Bank's prescription is simple: First, "get prices right" by eliminating all subsidies and letting market prices prevail; second, privatize all public sector enterprises; third, balance the public sector's budget (slowly); fourth, diversify exports; and, lastly, continue to use external debt as a basis for expansion (Husain 1989: 3–4).

Husain's discussion, such as it is, makes no mention of a host of problems that have contributed to the crisis of the 1980s. High on this list[10] would be the introduction of global monetarism in 1979, which sent real interest rates soaring, thereby greatly increasing the long-term cost of external debt. This roughly coincided with the virtual elimination of new sources of credits—except the IMF, the World Bank, and the U.S. Agency for International Development (USAID). Then, too, there was a precipitate drop in the terms of trade for many exports; manufactured products faced growing protection from the advanced nations. Latin American elites turned to financial speculation with a vengeance in the 1970s and also, with minor exception, bled their nations white with capital flight in the 1980s. In short, whatever the importance of the factors that the Bank highlights as the source of the crisis, the list of factors omitted from its treatment vastly outweighs the few that are included.

Nor is there the least evidence that the World Bank remedy is working. While the Bank acknowledges that the 1980s have been disastrous for Latin America, Chile is viewed as an example of success. Husain emphasized the annual growth rate (6 percent from 1986–1988 according to the World Bank) and the deregulation of the economy—the latter presumably causing the former. How well Chile has performed seems to be linked, largely, to how the term "performance" is utilized. For example, behind only Bolivia, Chile has led Latin America in open urban unemployment in the 1980–1987 period with a rate of 22.5 percent (Gómez Contreras 1988: 12). Between 1982 and

1987, the purchasing power of the minimum wage fell 40 percent, and, on average, minimum monthly income was well behind that achieved in Venezuela, Argentina, Mexico, Uruguay, and Brazil. From 1960 to 1973, when Chile utilized many aspects of ISI policies, real growth for the entire economy averaged 4.4 percent per year. From 1973 to 1987 the figure was 2.6 percent (Gómez Contreras 1988: 12). Chile's deindustrialization has been dramatic; annual real growth of industrial output averaged 5.5 percent from 1960 to 1973, but only 0.8 percent from 1973 to 1987. By almost any balanced, objective criteria the Bank's and the government's neoliberal program in Chile must be termed a failure.

In spite of a plethora of data, such as the above, which can be found in virtually every case where the Bank and the IMF have relentlessly championed neoliberal programs of "structural adjustment," the Bank has pledged to continue its "aggressive" policies with "substantial" new lending in "close coordination" with the IMF and the IDB (Husain 1989: 5).

While the World Bank's case for the success of neoliberal programs in Latin America cannot withstand even the most perfunctory examination, it and the IMF believe that the success of the Asian export economies demonstrably proves that ECLAC's ISI policies have been shown to be inferior to "free market" models of development. There is now a considerable body of literature that attempts to debunk this myth, to which should be added a recent contribution by Shahid Alam that compares the export-oriented policies with ISI programs in Latin America. While the former have been repeatedly held up by the Bank and the IMF as paragons of virtue because of their presumed lack of "statist intervention," Alam finds that both Korea and Taiwan were every bit as "interventionist" as were the ISI nations. In fact, he argues, to carry through the policies of state-guided export promotion that existed in these two nations, the state had to be more capable, in a qualitative sense, than in Latin America. That is, in the ISI case there was more tolerance for error; the nations that were highly linked to the global economy through trade had to carry through policies in a less-forgiving, more-complex environment (Alam 1989: 143).

Because of this, Alam believes that while the Latin American nations attained "tolerable success" in many instances with ISI policies, they will not be able to duplicate that success if the Bank, the Fund, and the Latin American elites consolidate their neoliberal initiatives. Their promarket, antistatist policies stand in direct contrast to the history of the "successes" they seek to duplicate. While the Asian nations have built relatively successful "interventionist states"—and used them as the fulcrum to industrialize their nations—the elites of Latin America seek to duplicate this model while dispensing with the chief vehicle used for its achievement.

Toward Neostructuralism?[11]

If there is to be a renewal of Latin American thinking about development, it will of necessity have to take place beyond the confines of the UN organizations. ECLAC is faced with the fact that some of the most outspoken advocates of the Hayek-Friedman "free market" model are to be found within the Latin American elites, at the World Bank, and in the IMF. Since the two latter institutions are the dominant "development" organizations of the United Nations, ECLAC has been placed in a delicate predicament. An outspoken attack on the failed policies of the Bank and the Fund might risk the dismembering of ECLAC.

Neostructuralism may have to confront an even greater difficulty than the lack of a comfortable institutional base. Structuralism could find, among its champions, ascendant elements of a new industrial bourgeoisie throughout much of Latin America. Today only, scattered elements of this social stratum stand willing to support a reinvigorated ECLACista strategy. As the case of Chile indicates, while neoliberal policies may deeply damage certain industrial interests that had previously nurtured close ties to the state under ISI policies, and while such policies may lead to a profound deindustrialization of the economy when the domestic market plummets because of neoliberal wage compression tactics, these same interests may openly support neoliberalism (Cortazar 1989: 59). They have done so, first, because a higher priority has been placed on the destruction of populist policies than on short-term industrial profits, and second, because throughout Latin America the distinction among industrial capital, bank-commercial capital, and landholding capital was particularly blurred in the 1970s. A wave of mergers and intermarriages led to more broadly based "national economic groups of power" that held all three forms of capital.

During the 1970s, as the advantage tilted toward speculation in finance and real estate, industrial pursuits were downgraded. With the tilt toward neoliberalism, rentier interests in banking, commerce, and landholding have welded new alliances within a state apparatus that champions monetarism. It is now more difficult, but not impossible, to locate a fraction of the economic elite that would champion a strengthened and rationalized ISI policy. Meanwhile, many industrial interests have forged a marriage of convenience with the neoliberal policymakers because privatization affords them a unique opportunity to obtain large, state-owned industrial concerns at prices well below the value of the assets being sold. Furthermore, the state may prove to be a valuable ally in obtaining financing for privatization. Some industrialists recognize that the neoliberal program to destroy the protective institutions of labor—above all, unions—only serves to limit the internal market. Others, however, see the cheapening of labor as the one advantage that Latin American industry may have in the export-oriented development strategy that has been imposed by neoliberal policymakers with the fulsome support of the Bank and the IMF.

When ECLAC doctrines were most highly regarded in Latin America, in the 1940s and 1950s, the populist coalitions that emerged in several nations were able to shift the distribution of income and the priorities of policymaking toward the industrial elite (and the working and middle classes) because the sectors that were relatively slighted by these policies generally enjoyed the benefits of a rapidly expanding economy. Such a situation cannot, in all likelihood, be duplicated in the foreseeable future. Thus, neostructuralism will, of necessity, be much more confrontational than its earlier counterpart. In order to force through new policies oriented toward the expansion of the internal market it must successfully face down (and outmaneuver) its ideological opponents and an array of vested interests.

First on the list are those who have devoted so much of Latin America's wealth to the most shallow pursuit of speculation—neostructuralism will have to confront the issue of capital flight. Stringent controls on the movement of liquid funds across national borders must be a matter of the highest priority. Brazil has had some notable success in controlling capital flight, and neostructuralists will have to find what is transferable in the Brazilian innovations. At the same time, there is a need to practice assertive diplomacy on the question of capital flight. A principal objective of neostructuralism should be to use various international fora, such as the United Nations affords, to campaign for cooperation from the major central banks of the advanced nations, which have the regulatory capacity to monitor capital flight. The *haute bourgeoisie* of Latin America will strongly resist the loss of one of their most powerful political weapons. Only a strong nationalist-populist movement will find it possible to check the capital flight phenomenon, but it will have a certain "moral authority" to do so.

Neostructuralism will have to confront another institutionalized prerogative of the elite in Latin America: the capacity to slough off virtually all forms of direct taxation. A populist campaign to reveal the inequities of the tax system could serve as the basis for a fundamental reorganization of the sources of state revenues. Neostructuralist policymakers can facilitate a transition that would place tax reform on the policy agenda by conducting in-depth studies of the tax systems of Latin American nations. There is no royal high road to achieving tax reform. At best, gains here will be small, slow in coming, and bitterly contested. The benefits, aside from the question of social justice and boosting the morale of the middle and working classes, would be threefold: First, the public sector deficit could be cut, perhaps eliminated; second, the need for external funds (international loans) could be greatly reduced (ECLAC, as their suppression of Kaldor's research in Chile demonstrated, was too coy on the question of tax reform and too receptive to the idea that development policies would require extensive foreign borrowing); third, tax reform will shift the distribution of income, particularly if it cuts into the massive internal deficits that transfer income from working- and middle-class taxpayers to the rich who hold the internal debt, and thereby serve to increase the internal market for basic wage goods. This last will help consolidate links between a fraction of industrialists and those who propose populist strategies. As the distribution of income shifts, relatively fewer luxuries are imported and lavish foreign travel is curtailed. A tax reform that distinguished productive from speculative activities—and raised taxes on the latter—would be another important step in the right direction.

Neostructuralism would exist in an international environment radically changed from that of the early post–World War II years. In the 1990s the United States will continue to play the role of the declining hegemon. Splits in the power structure of the global politicoeconomic system, which can be exploited by adroit policymakers from weaker nations, could afford some relief on short-term questions such as the foreign debt. In the longer term a fractured global structure of power should work to the advantage of the Latin American nations across a broad range of international issues in trade, investment, and finance. With clear U.S. hegemony no longer conceivable, the international organizations, such as the IMF and World Bank, may be restructured in accordance with the expanded voting powers of nations such as Japan and those of the European Community. This, along with repeated examples of the failure of neoliberal experiments in Latin America, may facilitate a transition within the "development" institutions toward more heterodox policies of development.

Finally, in this brief and not exhaustive list, neostructuralism will have to confront a profound crisis in agriculture and in the ecosystem. Structuralism's emphasis on industry will have to be tempered by well-articulated policies that use the needs of the agricultural sector and the limits of the ecosystem as the fundamental basis for expansion of the internal market. The centralizing, urban, and industrial biases of the state apparatus in many nations will have to be challenged by new doctrines of development.

It would be a simple matter to dismiss the above as nothing but an idealistic "wish list."[12] To do so, however, would be to assume that the current crisis in Latin America is sustainable—or that the neoliberal policies that are ravaging the region can be perpetuated. Veblen certainly maintained that the general populace had a large quotient of tolerance for abuse. Neostructuralism's role, it seems, would be to articulate a coherent and reasoned program of nationalist-populist development that would serve to displace this tolerance (and the timidity and resignation that have accompanied it) with a measured enthusiasm for change.

Notes

The author gratefully acknowledges the assistance of Robert Devlin, James Dietz, and Cristóbal Kay for access to research materials. None are in any way responsible for the use of these materials.

1. The "CEPAL manifesto" was an early monograph (1950a) by Raúl Prebisch; James Street has written a concise study of Prebisch's role in the creation of the structuralist school (1987c: 649–659).

2. Dependency formulations have been expressed in varied forms, as Cristóbal Kay (1989: 125–196) has noted. While some of these formulations are quite subtle and sophisticated they nonetheless share two premises that I emphasize here. First, external factors and forces constitute the point of departure; these factors and forces are presumed to play prime causal roles in the "dependent" social formation. (Although some writers who have been lumped into the dependency group emphasized the interactive nature of the internal and external factors and forces, it nonetheless remains the case that the dependency writers look outside the social formations of Latin America for the sources of prime causality.) Second, no internally generated policy can fundamentally alter the determinate socioeconomic condition of the "dependent" social formation.

3. Friedrich von Hayek's influence in current Latin American policymaking has not been widely discussed. His "Austrian School" emphasis on the tender mercies of the *haute bourgeoisie* has resonated within the higher circles of power in Latin America. According to this approach, which singles out individual incentives as the prime moving force behind the economic system, a nation must be extremely circumspect in taxing the economic elite lest they lose their precarious grip on their entrepreneurial ethos and slide into indolence. Generally, this has been interpreted as a call to eliminate virtually all direct taxes on income and wealth—but not the subsidies the state provides to the elite. Friedman's influence has been well documented, particularly in the case of Chile from 1973 onward. Raúl Prebisch (1981b: 151–174) wrote a restrained critique of their ideas, but the role of these two ideologues of supply-side/monetarist economic policymaking in Latin America has not received sufficient attention given the extensive application of their doctrines in the 1980s.

4. This term is used by Peter Evans (1989: 207–238) in a recent case study of a dispute over the control and direction of the Brazilian computer industry. He describes those who have explored the issue of assertive industrialization as having adopted a "post-dependency/bargaining approach" (233). Here, the emphasis is on interdependence, and on the possibility of the state's playing a crucial role in industrial policy in spite of the desires of the advanced nations to dominate industries that have a high growth potential.

5. I have not attempted to review every manuscript published by ECLAC, a daunting task well beyond the limited resources at hand. Rather, somewhat eclectically, I have relied upon the following materials to inform my critique: Kay (1989), Prebisch (1950a, 1981a), Cardoso, Pinto, and Sunkel (1969), Bernal Sahagun (1980), Cardoso (1979), and Rodríguez (1980). In reality there is nothing that can be designated as the "ECLAC structuralist model" per se because ECLAC allowed its researchers some latitude and freedom in expressing their ideas. Thus, it is possible to locate a "left" ECLAC position and, perhaps, other gradations. I am not concerned with such subtleties here,

although I would readily grant their importance in a more refined and exhaustive treatment of the subject. I also recognize that my methodology risks overlooking some crucial aspect of ECLAC's analysis (for example, I have made no attempt here to treat ECLAC's work on inflation).

6. I refer here to the overused argument that the Latin American nations must export in order to import capital goods and some intermediate goods, in order to sustain the reproduction of the social formation. This is a truism—up to a certain point. The question, of course, is where is the point? While the composition of imports varies from nation to nation, and over time, it is not immediately obvious that exports are used purely or even largely for the purpose of sustaining the production base of the Latin American economies. Rather, as is well known, exports can be used to gain foreign exchange, which in turn is used for capital flight. In addition, foreign exchange is widely utilized to sustain the Latin American elite's voracious appetite for foreign travel to the center and to import the luxuries that these nations produce.

7. This point would seem to be contested by Kay's recent study of the structuralists. He maintains that "while the unequal terms of trade were not the cause of the periphery's poverty, they reduced the surplus that could be available to overcome it" (1989: 35). However, Kay contends that the differentials between productivity growth in the center (the result of the assumed ability of the center's nations to retain the benefits of productivity change, while the nations of the periphery pass on the benefits of their productivity increases to the advanced nations through lower prices of export commodities) "and the gains from trade explain the rising gap in incomes between centre and periphery" (34). What he seems to argue, then, is that the perpetuation and relative expansion of poverty in the periphery is due to the transfers related to foreign trade, but the underlying cause of relative backwardness arises from "a sizeable low-productivity precapitalist sector [that] continues to survive in the periphery" (29). It is not clear what Kay—or other interpreters of the ECLAC school—would like to do with this formulation. In Kay's case, he seems to be arguing that the underlying cause (or causes) of backwardness lies in the disarticulated production base of Latin American social formations. Yet, he glides over this point in a few phrases, devoting the rest of his analysis (for the most part) to the dynamics of international trade and drawing an all-too-subtle distinction between fundamental cause and perpetuating cause. In the final analysis, it is the latter that gets analytical attention; the former is occasionally raised—often in the most couched terms—and quickly dropped. This becomes argument by caveat— at best a tendentious approach. Given these ambiguities, I maintain that the work of ECLAC should be evaluated in terms of the context in which its ideas were propounded. This context is one wherein, at best, the internal causes are acknowledged as being fundamental and then virtually ignored. Prebisch, for example, seemed to collapse the perpetuating cause into the fundamental cause, or even to deny the distinction in favor of the external factor as the fundamental cause. The following statement serves as an example: "For each peripheral country, the type and extent of its linkage with the center depended largely on its resources and its economic and political capacity for mobilizing them. In my view, this fact was of the greatest importance, since it conditioned the economic structure and dynamism of each country" (1984: 177).

8. By *sphere of production* I mean the complex interaction among tools, technologies, labor power and skills, production organization, management

skills, knowledge of machinery and technologies, and research and development that is oriented toward increasing the output capacity of this sphere.

9. *By sphere of circulation* I mean the social processes and organizations that transfer and maintain account of commodities that have been produced. This sphere entails the social processes of trade (wholesale, retail, foreign), finance, consumption, and the accounting of such social processes.

10. This is a far from exhaustive list, and many factors were of an external nature. Two others of fundamental underlying importance should be added. First, as mentioned earlier in the text, the disarticulation of the production base was most noticeable in the distinct paths taken by the industrial and agricultural sectors in the 1950s, 1960s, and 1970s. The extremely low level of productivity growth in the latter sector led in many cases to chronic and growing basic food imports, some of which were funded by governments' international borrowing throughout the 1970s. Here, then, is an important internal cause of the crisis of the 1980s. Alternatively, the impossibility of continuing debt-financed growth in the 1980s made manifest an underlying chronic disproportionality in the productive base. Second, the ISI model of development excluded an emphasis on science and technology and, most important, the construction of an indigenous capital goods sector. This condemned the Latin American nations (with some exception in the case of Brazil) to a situation of chronic reliance on capital goods imports and payments for the use of technologies. Without a "coherent" and integrated productive base, the ISI models inevitably entered into crisis. Again, however, debt-financing in the 1970s served to disguise a deeper reality. For a more considered discussion of these and related factors, see Cypher (1988).

11. I have not attempted to extend my discussion of technology in this section because this issue is discussed in detail in Chapters 9 and 10. Nonetheless, it is perhaps worth repeating that in my view the Achilles' heel of structuralism was its tendency to downplay the possibilities of technological autonomy and development in Latin America. Neostructuralism will have to confront the cultural and economic impediments that hinder fundamental progress in this area.

12. I have discussed, in extreme brevity, only the most fundamental issues that neostructuralism must address. Other matters of basic importance would include, most particularly, the land reform question and planning. Regarding the latter, ECLAC's emphasis on development banking is worthy of emulation: In both Mexico and Chile, to mention but two examples, the major state-run development banks established a broad range of fundamental industries. Their string of successes is an impressive tribute to the strategic policies of ECLAC.

Part 2

Failures of Past Development Strategies: Lessons for the Future

5

Latin America's Debt Crisis, the International Monetary Fund, and Financial Reform

Ronnie J. Phillips

> *As through this world I've wandered,*
> *I've seen lots of funny men,*
> *some will rob you with a six-gun,*
> *and some with a fountain pen.*
>
> —Woody Guthrie

Two closely related issues have dominated the economic news in recent years: debt and financial instability. An enormous increase in public and private debt has made the United States the largest debtor nation in the world. With the ongoing savings and loan crisis, for the first time since the 1930s a run on the banking system is a possibility. At the same time, LDCs, especially in Latin America, have also faced these twin problems of debt and financial instability and, as a consequence, have been caught in a spiral of debt, capital flight, depreciating currencies, and inflation. Latin Americans are told by their governments and/or the IMF that their problems can be solved only through an increase in savings and a reduction in the current standard of living. This typically involves an elimination of government subsidies for basic commodities, as well as wage freezes and other reforms intended to reestablish global competitiveness.

The problems of international debt and financial instability are endemic to the current global financial system, based on fractional reserves and deposit guarantees through a lender of last resort. Fractional reserve banking with deposit guarantees creates a vast amount of debt that, if it cannot be repaid because of slow economic growth, necessitates a general reduction in the standard of living. The stockholders of financial institutions with the government guarantee do not absorb the full costs of any loss; rather, losses are distributed over the taxpaying population. The attempts by the IMF to serve as an international lender of last resort thus have failed and will continue to fail because their faulty premise is that an increase in *real* savings—that is, a reduction in current consumption—is a prerequisite to restoring growth. What is actually necessary is financial reform along the lines proposed by Henry Simons (1948), among others, to separate the depository and lending functions of banks.[1]

Fractional Reserve Banking

Latin America, like most of the Western economies, has a financial system in which banks issue liabilities that are accepted as money backed by government money (currency), government debt, or private debt. In addition, the nominal value of bank money is guaranteed by the government, either 100 percent or very close to it. If a bank fails, the creditors are paid by the government from its tax revenues. The minor variants of this basic structure, although not without interest, are of little consequence for the current analysis.

Every student who takes a course in economics and studies the financial system learns that, in the U.S. economy, money is debt. She or he is taught that whenever the banking system receives an injection of new reserves, the money supply will be expanded by some multiple of this initial increase in reserves. The argument in favor of fractional reserve banking is that it does not require someone to save or to reduce present consumption so that another may borrow. Money that was not previously saved can be loaned because of the money multiplier. In the basic definition of the money supply (currency plus checkable deposits), the banks are able to lend a percentage of their checkable deposits, although the creditor may view the balances not as savings but as balances held for transactions purposes, that is, to be spent. The unique magic of fractional reserve banking is that it allows *both* the depositor and the borrower to spend the money balances that are created.

Few discuss the history that led to fractional reserve banking. The brief story that is usually told is that banking goes back to the warehouse function of the goldsmiths, who discovered that their paper liabilities, nominally redeemable in gold, circulated as money. As long as all depositors did not redeem the banknotes at the same time, the goldsmiths could "safely" hold less than 100 percent gold reserves. Thus, fractional reserve banking was born. Some may regard this evolution as responding to the demands of the invisible hand. Further analysis reveals, however, that banks often emerged to meet the needs of a sovereign who required an alternative to direct taxation in order to finance a war, and in the United States, it is no coincidence that national banks were established in 1863, when the needs of government were great in financing the Civil War. A similar evolution in banking could be found in the case of the Latin American countries (Tamagna 1965).

The argument that fractional reserve banking would provide for the proper money supply is based on the "real bills doctrine," also known as the commercial loan theory of banking. This doctrine has provided the basis for guiding our thinking on monetary problems from Adam Smith to the present day. The real bills doctrine reasons that, as long as banks make loans for bona fide commercial reasons, an automatic system exists for the expansion and contraction of the money supply. However, making loans on the basis of nominal magnitudes introduces instability into the macroeconomy since both the demand and supply of money depend on income. The system is unstable where the responsiveness of the demand for money is less than the responsiveness of the supply of money to an income change (see Girton 1974: 58; Mints 1945: 30–34). Fractional reserve banking does not create, through the market mechanism, the "correct" amount of credit necessary for the expansion of business. The real bills doctrine is the core fallacy in fractional reserve banking.[2]

Although there had long been banking panics, it was not until the 1930s that it was recognized that the money-as-debt system had severe problems. Cloaked in the guise of keeping "mom and pop" from losing their life savings, the system of federal deposit insurance was adopted in the United States and other countries. This effectively socialized the costs of fractional reserve banking while keeping the profits private. The banks were happy, although some initially opposed federal deposit insurance, and the government was able to shore up a banking system that held large amounts of government debt. Fractional reserve banking is not "natural" in any sense other than that it is a humanly created institution that evolved as a result of bankers' private interests, the public's need for a convenient money, and the government's need for an alternative means of financing its expenditures.

Thorstein Veblen (1904: 103–104), writing about the banking system at the turn of the century, noted:

> So that all advances made by banking houses or by other creditors in a like case—whether the advances are made on mortgage, collateral or personal notes, in the form of deposits, note issues, or what not; whether they are taken to represent the items of property covered by the collateral, the cash reserves of the banks, or the general solvency of the creditor or debtor—all these "advances" go to increase the "capital" of which business men have the disposal; but for the material purposes of industry, taken in the aggregate, they are purely fictitious items.

What Veblen meant by this was that the loan activities of the banks, whereby they risked depositors' money, did not go toward increasing industrial output; rather, they merely raised the nominal value of capital available to business and generated instability (see Phillips 1988b). Since bank loans were made on the basis of the nominal value of business capital, a further expansion of loans took place, leading to a further increase in the nominal value of business capital, and so on. When the divergence between the value of the nominal business capital and its actual industrial earning capacity became, in Veblen's words, "exceptionally wide," and "the overrating is presently recognized by the creditor and a settlement ensues," the price of capital falls and the loan expansion stops. Such a process generates financial boom and bust (Phillips 1988b: 173).

Financial instability can be analyzed in a simple (IS-LM) framework that incorporates the assumption of liability management on the part of bankers. This model has been set forth by Fernández (1984, 1985) and Kahn (1986) and utilized by Phillips (1988b). When applied to a national economy, the balance sheets of the commercial banks are consolidated. The liabilities of the banks are considered money and the exchange rates between bank monies are fixed. Where a unit of account such as the dollar has been established, the exchange ratio between bank monies is nominally set at one to one. In extending the model to an international context, the same assumptions hold; that is, fixed exchange rates among national currencies.[3]

There are two markets: capital/money and goods. "Money" in this model is limited to the liabilities of banks, or inside money. This assumption is appropriate since the bank in this model is really the central bank of an LDC and therefore cannot create outside money. It is assumed that all investment funds are borrowed from banks and its income goes to capital. The balance sheet of the banking system is thus:

Assets	Liabilities
$\dfrac{y}{r}$	$\dfrac{\overline{S}}{P}$

where y is income, r the real interest rate (y/r = real earning capacity of the bank assets), $\overline{S}$ is the nominal value of bank shares, which is guaranteed by the government or the IMF when it functions as lender of last resort, and P is the price index. For simplicity, assuming net wealth is zero in equilibrium, assets must equal liabilities. The liability management assumption is that banks will respond to a decline in their net wealth (negative net wealth here) by raising interest rates to attract depositors.

$$(5.1) \qquad \dot{r} = \alpha \left(\frac{\overline{S}}{P} - \frac{y}{r} \right) \qquad \alpha > 0$$

For the goods market we can use either a fixed price or a flexible price model. If output is fixed for simplicity at the natural rate, y^n, then

$$(5.2) \qquad \dot{s} = -\beta(y_d - y^n) \qquad \beta > 0$$

where $s = \overline{S}/P$, and in the fixed price model

(5.3) $$\dot{y} = \Gamma(y_d - y) \qquad\qquad \Gamma > 0$$

where y_d is a function of income, y, and the interest rate, r. Although this model assumes s is exogenous, Fernández (1985) analyzes the situation where $s = f(y)$.

In an IS-LM framework, we can graph (5.1) and (5.2) (see Figure 5.1). The arrows indicate the dynamic path of adjustment (see Kahn 1986: 10–16).

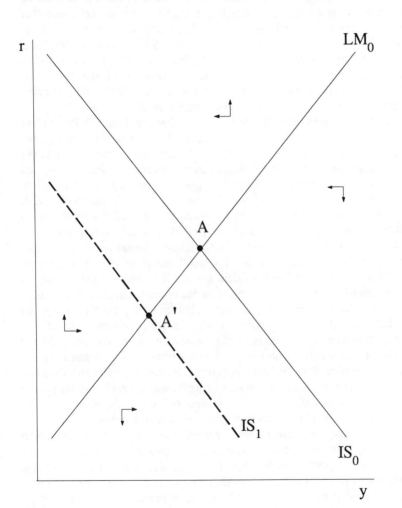

Figure 5.1

Now consider a downward shift in the IS curve caused by a fall in government expenditures. Under the assumption of liability management, an explosive situation of a rising interest rate and falling income can occur. Note that with a normal LM curve, this situation would lead to falling income, an excess supply of money, and a falling interest rate as the economy readjusts to a new equilibrium at A'. For a country, liability management can be a response to capital flight (see Fernández 1985).

The problem of fractional reserve banking is that with a guarantee on the nominal value of deposits, equilibrium must return to $y/r = \bar{S}/P$. The question is whether a return to equilibrium is possible from a fall in income that leads to rising interest rates under liability management. Another possibility for returning to equilibrium is to alter the nominal value of shares, $\bar{S}$. This is in fact the Simons solution to the instability of fractional reserve banking that has been discussed by Fernández (1984), Kahn (1985), and Phillips (1988b). In Figure 5.1, the path of adjustment under the Simons solution would be along the LM curve from point A to A' since at every instance $y/r = \bar{S}/P$, for a perfectly functioning market.

It became apparent in the 1930s that the fractional reserve system had considerable difficulties in a period of large declines in economic activity, and in the 1980s the problems have resurfaced. Under these circumstances, banks have a strong incentive to hold excess reserves in anticipation of bank runs and unworthy borrowers, leading to a decline in the money supply and a loss of confidence in the banking system. The remedy for bank runs in the 1930s was federal deposit insurance, which enabled the costs of fractional reserve banking to be socialized and, therefore, passed on to the average taxpayers. For large depositors, the gain in receiving taxpayer guarantees of their money exceeds any possible tax liabilities. For small depositors, it is quite possible that, in the event of a large bailout, tax liability will exceed the higher nominal returns they receive as a consequence of federal deposit insurance. In the United States, for example, the recent plan for bailing out the savings and loan industry will require approximately $1,000 per person over a number of years. The economic question is whether most individuals have received more than $1,000 in benefits with insured deposits from higher interest rates and lower immediate risk. In Latin American countries, where the financial system is less available to the mass of people, and the revenues are paid in the form of an inflation tax, it is even less likely that the majority of the people have benefited from government guarantees of deposits.

The lender-of-last-resort system seemed to work for many years, at least in stopping bank runs, but it has long been recognized that the banks faced a "moral hazard" problem in that there is an incentive to increase the riskiness of their loan portfolios in order to appropriate an effective subsidy to risk-taking provided by non–risk-based deposit insurance. This helped set the stage for the debt crisis of the 1980s.

In the 1970s, when the banks experienced huge inflows of funds from the oil-producing countries with current account surpluses, they were again faced with the problem of potentially large excess reserves. If they had continued to accumulate reserves, the economic downturn of 1974/75 might possibly have been deepened and lengthened. However, given the incentives in the financial system and the global competition from the unregulated Eurodollar market, the banks responded in what appeared to be a reasonable way: by making loans to sovereign governments that, because they had the power to print money and to tax, would not default. The banks became, according to William Darity and Bobbie Horn (1988), "loan pushers." During this period banks designed loan packages that attracted borrowers who were formerly denied access to international credit altogether, or at least denied such large amounts (Darity and Horn 1988: 17).

The current debt situation can be contrasted with what happened in the nineteenth century. James Street (1985a: 403–404) points out that, historically, debt problems have been resolved through default, unlike today when default would imperil the continuity of sovereign governments and the survival of large banks. With the possibility of defaults by countries, an international lender of last resort becomes necessary, and the IMF has undertaken many of the functions of a global lender of last resort.

International Debt and the IMF

The IMF plays a crucial role in the relationship between the banks and the debtor countries. It must resolve the contradictions of the fractional reserve banking system by means of its conditional loans, which are primarily intended to reduce the overall level of risks to the banks by increasing the likelihood of loan repayment. The IMF serves as an international credit rating agency and provides standardization of loan conditionality. Competition among banks results in varying conditionality, or perhaps no conditionality, on loans, and the IMF, by imposing a rigid program on each country, can standardize these terms. Secondarily, the IMF programs impose the costs of debt reduction on the taxpayers and consumers of the debtor countries. The loans are to be repaid by an increase in real savings; that is, by a reduction of current living standards in the face of a slowdown in real economic growth. Third, the IMF loans represent the socialization of the costs of bad debts over the taxpayers of all member countries. The IMF accomplishes this socialization through its ability to reallocate credit and through new allocations of Special Drawing Rights.

When the petrodollar recycling problem emerged in the early 1970s, IMF Executive Director Johannes Witteveen noted the limitations of relying on private banks, which "are not in a position to make their lending conditional on the pursuit of appropriate policies by borrowing countries" [*IMF Survey* 1974: 134]. The role of commercial banks created an enormous problem for recycling petrodollars, and it is for this reason that Witteveen and others argued that the IMF should take a preeminent role in their allocation. Witteveen argued that the recycling process would be an enormous task, and that adjustment would not be accomplished quickly or easily. The problem of excess demand in the early 1970s would be reduced as a result of the oil price increase, but appropriate policies would be extremely important to slow inflation [*IMF Survey* 1974: 136].

The shift from the immediate financing of the balance of payments deficits to a long-run global strategy of adjustment through austerity was announced in the fall of 1976 by Witteveen. Although the IMF had previously used adjustment programs, it is with the oil crisis that the number and length of the programs increased dramatically through increased surveillance and new conditionality in the standby arrangements. Witteveen commented that such arrangements were more desirable because the IMF, with its "more autonomous character," would be better able to impose conditionality on loans [*Fortune* 1977: 102]. The plan was for the IMF to mediate between the borrowing needs of the deficit countries and the desires of the surplus countries to ensure that the money lent would be repaid. With its standby arrangements, the IMF sought to impose the discipline that a national government, or private bank, was unable to undertake.

The essential elements of these adjustment programs were to allow market forces to operate in commodity and currency markets, to increase competitiveness through devaluations, to pursue real wage reductions through deindexation, to impose monetary and fiscal restraint, and to promote an open economy. The stated goals were to promote economic growth and reduce inflation. The results can be seen in Table 5.1. In four of the five most heavily indebted Latin American countries that were under IMF programs, inflation accelerated over the period 1983–1985. At the same time, growth was uneven at best, and certainly well below the very rapid rates of growth some countries had experienced in the past. From 1980 to 1985, real wages fell in four out of five of the heavily indebted countries. Only Argentina registered a modest 2.4 percent rise in the real wage by the end of the period. In Chile the decline was about 7 percent; in Brazil, 16 percent; in Mexico, 31 percent; and in Peru, 40 percent (IDB various years).

One expectation of IMF stabilization programs was that national savings as a percentage of income would increase because of higher economic growth and positive real interest rates. As can be seen in Table 5.2, the savings rate either fell (Argentina, Brazil, Chile, and Mexico) or rose only moderately (Peru). It cannot be argued that savings were dramatically stimulated by the stabilization programs. With respect to interest rates and savings, a recent study by Rossi (1988: 125–126) concluded that for South America a

Table 5.1   Rate of Inflation and Rate of Growth of Real GDP in Five Latin American Countries, 1982–1986 (in Percentages)

	1982	1983	1984	1985	1986
Argentina					
Inflation	165	344	627	672	90
Growth	–4.9	2.8	2.7	–4.5	5.5
Brazil					
Inflation	98	142	197	227	145
Growth	0.9	–2.5	5.7	8.3	8.2
Chile					
Inflation	10	27	20	30	19
Growth	–14.0	–0.7	6.3	2.5	5.7
Mexico					
Inflation	59	102	66	58	132
Growth	–0.6	–5.3	3.7	2.8	–3.8
Peru					
Inflation	65	111	110	163	78
Growth	0.9	–12.0	4.8	1.6	na

Source: IMF, *International Financial Statistics*, August 1988.

1 percent rise in the real interest rate would reduce consumption one one-hundredth of 1 percent, hardly a strong stimulus to saving. Coupled with slow economic growth, the prospects for increasing national savings seem remote.

Manuel Pastor (1987: 169–170) notes that, while it is difficult to blame the IMF exclusively for all of Latin America's economic woes, nevertheless, "it is fairly clear that, under generalized IMF control, the region seemed to have behaved in ways reminiscent of the typical program country of the pre-crisis period—inflation had accelerated and redistribution away from poorer groups had almost certainly occurred." By the mid-1980s, many countries had begun to move away from the IMF's standard programs and to implement "heterodox" stabilization schemes that included such things as incomes policies and indexation (see Blejer and Cheasty 1988).

Despite its greater "autonomy" in dealing with countries, the IMF has been unable to make a significant contribution to solving the debt crisis. Despite huge social costs, Latin American governments have been unable to reduce their debt burdens. The IMF, working from a strict monetarist model that straitjackets its policy recommendations, is unable, or unwilling, to alter its basic austerity programs. Because these programs have been a failure, the IMF's "seal of creditworthiness" is largely meaningless. In addition, because of the small size of its resources relative to the private banking sector, the IMF has not been able to socialize enough of the costs to reduce significantly

Table 5.2   National Savings as a Percentage of GNP for Five Latin American
Countries, 1981–1984

	1981	1982	1983	1984
Argentina	14.4	13.6	13.6	12.8
Brazil	19.3	18.3	17.8	17.8
Chile	8.7	1.4	4.8	3.7
Mexico	24.9	23.4	27.2	24.5
Peru	14.2	15.5	15.0	15.0

Source: Inter-American Development Bank, *Economic and Social Progress in Latin America 1985*, p. 39, Table II-3.

the debt burden. At present, the IMF may in fact be playing an inhibiting role to the extent that it promises to socialize the costs and therefore help the banks to reduce their losses. If the banks wait for the IMF to do so, and if the debtor countries can cut deals with the IMF, the adjustment can be redistributed toward the global taxpayers of the countries who are members of the IMF. The Federal Deposit Insurance and Federal Savings and Loan Insurance corporations in the United States can neither fully monitor member banks nor bail out large-scale defaults. The IMF faces the same problem with respect to its member countries.

Solving the Debt Crisis

A real solution to the debt crisis involves a restructuring of the global financial system along the lines suggested by Henry Simons (1948) of separating the depository functions of banks from their lending functions. Although such a restructuring might take many years to achieve, if it is ever possible, developments in the global debt market have provided the means to a Simons solution to the debt crisis. This solution has recently been formulated by Roque Fernández (1987). With the emergence of the secondary market for Third World debt, the debtor countries are potentially in a situation greatly to reduce their debt burden by repurchasing their own debt on the open market at a fraction of its original value. The costs will then be paid by the banks' stockholders, in the first instance, and the U.S. taxpayers if the banks' equity capital is exhausted.

Fernández presents the following simple model to illustrate his proposal. The government budget is:

$$(5.4) \qquad g + rb + a = t + (1-x)rb + d$$

where g is government expenditures; r is real interest rate on the external debt; b is the stock of external debt; a is amortization payment on the debt; t

is tax revenues; $(1-x)$ is portion of the external debt that is refinanced (note that rb is the portion of external debt that is paid or not refinanced); and d is government borrowing from the domestic financial system. Note that if a is 0, the country is not paying down the stock of debt at all; if x is 0, it is not making an interest payment; and if x is 1, the country is paying all of its interest expense.

If we suppose that the country makes use of the secondary debt market to amortize its loans, then the change in the stock of debt, Db, will be

$$(5.5) \qquad\qquad Db = (1-x)rb - za$$

where z is the ratio of the nominal value of debt to its value in the secondary market. Thus, for example, if the external debt is selling for 80 percent of its nominal value, then $z = 1.25$. By making use of the secondary market, the country is able to make a larger reduction in the stock of debt than it would if it made the amortization payment on the nominal value of the loan, a, to the bank. The banks, however, will incur a loss on the debt they are selling in the secondary market, a loss they are evidently willing to accept.

How will the countries raise the funds necessary to purchase the debt in the secondary market? Fernández suggests that the revenues be raised through an inflation tax that the monetary authorities are able to impose as a consequence of their monopoly in the issuing of money. Hence, the balance sheet of the central bank in flow terms would be

$$(5.6) \qquad\qquad d + DF = m\pi$$

where d is defined as above, loans to the government, and DF is the change in net foreign assets. These assets are acquired through the central bank's issuance of the monetary base (which is also the money supply since, by assumption, the money multiplier is equal to 1). The revenues available to the government are thus the real money stock, m, multiplied by the rate of inflation, π, assuming no growth in real income or velocity.

The change in net foreign assets, DF, assuming no private capital flows, will be determined by the balance of payments identity

$$(5.7) \qquad\qquad DF = ne - xrb - a$$

where ne is net exports.

By using (5.4), (5.5), (5.6), and (5.7) we can investigate the fiscal implications of various options for paying the external debt. Assume, for example, that the government pays only the interest on the debt, but no amortization payment. Then, by substitution with $a = 0$ and $x = 1$, we have

(5.8) $(g - t) + ne = m\pi$

where we assume no increase in the debt through new borrowing (therefore $Db = 0$) and no change in net foreign assets $(DF = 0)$. Expression (5.8) indicates that the inflationary tax is used to finance the government deficit and to purchase foreign money to pay the interest (that is, $ne = rb$).

Consider a second option: The country wishes to make an amortization payment but no interest payment $(x = 0)$. Maintaining the assumption that $DF = 0$ and $Db = 0$, then we have by substitution

(5.9) $(g - t) + \dfrac{rb}{z} = m\pi$

Thus, when $z > 1$, the case when the debt is selling at a discount in the secondary market, there is a fiscal advantage for the government in the use of its inflationary tax revenues. Both of these examples require net exports to be positive; otherwise the country must find other means to finance its debt, such as debt-equity swaps.

Under these assumptions, then, from (5.5) we have that $rb = za$, and $ne = a$; therefore

(5.10) $b\dfrac{1}{z} = \dfrac{ne}{r}$

which indicates that the real value of the stock of debt, evaluated at the secondary market price, is the discounted value of net exports. In other words, Fernández argues, the price of the external debt in the secondary market, $1/z$, reflects an evaluation of the economy's ability to meet its external commitments.

Fernández goes on to evaluate the negotiation options for debtor and lender under the assumption that the debtor countries are willing to engage in debt-equity swaps. In terms of our definitions, this merely means that the country, if it does not have a net export surplus, can export equity shares. In equation (5.7), net exports is replaced by a term, e, which includes net exports and domestic shares in firms acceptable to foreign investors and (5.10) becomes $br = ez$ where $z > 1$.

Given this basic model, Fernández (1987: 24–27) then examines various options available in negotiations between the bankers and the debtor countries. Suppose that the objective function of the lenders is represented by the change in the stock of debt

(5.11) $-Db = za - (1-x)br = Dc$

which is the revenue that the banks will receive assuming the use of the secondary market as discussed. The process of negotiation can be viewed as a game in which the bankers wish to receive an outcome in which $x = 1$ to maximize their revenues. The debtor countries, on the other hand, may be satisfied with merely paying the interest on the loan and no amortization ($a = 0$) in order to minimize their annual payments. Note however that if $x = 1$ and $a = 0$, the debt is not being paid off and the banks are receiving no revenue. Fernández notes that though this situation may be an equilibrium, it is not an optimum outcome. A solution to the debt crisis through the use of the secondary debt market requires negotiation between debtor and creditor. However, the negotiation occurs from a starting point different from that of the financial system, which insists on the repayment of the nominal value of loans. The Simons-Fernández formula utilizes the market system to solve the immediate crisis and points the way toward a reform of the system to prevent its recurrence in the future. Simply put, the nominal value of the loans would no longer be guaranteed to the creditor. The secondary market has emerged to do this implicitly, and full scale reform of the global financial system would make it explicit.

The Simons-Fernández Solution and Financial Reform

The emergence of the secondary market provides a means of leverage for the debtor countries to reduce their debt burden. In essence, the secondary market enables the value of the debt to fluctuate with the real capacity of the economy to pay the debt. The problem facing the banks is that they carry the loans at their nominal value on their balance sheets when, in fact, they know that the market value is lower. They cannot carry the loans at their market value because of the implied decline in net worth that would result. For the debtor countries, there are still costs, but they are greatly reduced by the use of the secondary market. In addition, debt-equity swaps would involve giving up ownership of real resources in the economy to reduce the debt. However, these costs, if reallocated through the secondary market, will still be less for the countries.

The secondary market solution provides the key to avoiding crisis in the future. Clearly, the nominal value of debt must fluctuate with the real capacity to pay that debt. This would be the situation if banks could lend only funds raised through issuing ownership shares and could not use depositors' funds, guaranteed by federal deposit insurance, for loan purposes (see Fernández 1984; Phillips 1988b).

The costs of the present system must be paid, and the question remains: Who will pay? Bankers and politicians reply that the taxpayer must bear the burden. If this is indeed the case, then taxpayers should see that reforms are made to avoid the same problem in the future. The fractional reserve system, whereby the money supply is backed by debt, will tend toward extremes of excessive holdings of reserves, as in the 1930s, or inadequate holdings of reserves, as in the 1970s and 1980s. An equity-based system of the type proposed by Simons would never face either problem; the supply and demand for loans would be separated from the supply and demand for money.

The proposals for an international debt facility through the IMF can play a role here. However, if the international debt facility is established to resemble federal deposit insurance, then the costs will be socialized globally and distributed over the world's taxpayers. There will be no incentive for banks or countries to change their behavior if they do not have to pay the full costs directly. If an international debt facility is established, then the funds must be raised through selling ownership shares, and the costs of default paid by those who are being adequately rewarded for taking the risks.

A financial system that was equity-based would see "fictitious credit" greatly reduced, if not eliminated. However, the argument that the abolition of the fractional reserve system would result in a fall in the amount of funds available for loans does not logically follow. Some loans might not be made, that is certain, but would the Third World be worse off today if they had not had the bank loans of the 1970s? If one argues that they would be worse off, then what is the debt crisis about? Reform of the financial system does not guarantee that development will be renewed, however. The problems of an appropriate strategy of development will remain.

Notes

I am grateful to Dino Francescutti for translation of the articles by Fernández, although any errors of interpretation are my own.

1. The proposal to separate the depository and lending functions of banks enjoyed wide support in the 1930s. Among those who publicly supported it were Irving Fisher (1945), Lauchlin Currie, Richard Lester, Gardiner Means, and Paul H. Douglas. Legislation was introduced in the U.S. Congress in June 1934 by Senator Bronson Cutting of New Mexico and Congressman Wright Patman of Texas to require 100 percent reserves on checking accounts (see Phillips 1988a). At least three Nobel Prize winners in economics have supported versions of the proposal: Milton Friedman (1960); Maurice Allais (1948); and James Tobin (1985, 1987).

2. The real bills doctrine is part of the popular folklore of bankers, government officials, and the average citizen. Economists, as they have done for two hundred years, continue to discover new theoretical rationalizations for its "soundness." Recently, the debate has reappeared in articles by Sargent and Wallace (1982), Laidler (1984), and McCallum (1986).

3. The assumption of fixed exchange rates is made for simplicity in analyzing financial instability. An interesting and important issue is whether free competitive banking under fractional reserves is a stable system. The view

that free banking is inherently unstable has been questioned by a number of writers, but discussion of this issue goes beyond this chapter. It should be noted that a return to fixed exchange rates occurs regularly in the discussions on international monetary reform and that, although recent history has experienced more flexible exchange rates, much of the last 175 years has seen fixed exchange rates.

6

The Evolution of Argentina's Policies Toward Manufacturing Exports

Hugh Schwartz

The institutional theory of the development of newly emerging societies . . . draws upon the same basic conceptions of the nature of human behavior and the process of social change that have characterized the institutionalist interpretation of the evolutionary history of modern advanced industrial economies. Development is . . . a complex cultural process rather than a stable system of counterbalancing forces regulated by a fluid and self-adjusting market mechanism . . . . The forces inhibiting social progress . . . are rooted in institutional . . . patterns of behavior that are present in all societies, but seem to be particularly obstructive in the cultures of many less economically developed countries.

—James Street (1987a: 1861)

Argentina was one of the most prosperous countries in the world in 1940, with perhaps the sixth-highest level of per capita income—and was projected by a prominent Australian economist to rise to second-highest by 1960. As it turned out, though, by 1960, the country's per capita income had slipped badly in relative terms and, by the late 1980s, was only the thirty-fifth– to fortieth-highest in global terms.[1]

Explaining what has happened in Argentina during the past forty years or more—and *why* it has happened—has occupied the attention of many economists and other social scientists. Certainly, much of Argentina's decline seems to be associated with the character and magnitude of state intervention in private enterprise. Key public policy decisions included, first, the decision to transform a particularly open economy, based largely on agriculture and grazing, into one emphasizing inwardly oriented industrialization. This focus continued even after economic growth had slowed and despite the successes of some, more recently industrialized, countries that had accelerated their economic growth by fostering a more outwardly oriented industrialization.

Finally, even when shifting gears in the mid- to late 1960s, incentives to export varied greatly from time to time and from product to product. While incentives provided major windfalls for some activities (probably at great costs for the economy as a whole in many cases), they often were inadequate for other activities fully to offset the overall bias of public policy stimuli and favor production for the local market. Further, and perhaps just as important for private decisionmaking, when there were occasionally clear incentives to export, they often were insufficient to convince producers that such a redirection of policy signals was likely to last.[2] Often they did not last, and the inconsistency created an environment that discouraged initiative and investment.

Argentine policies affecting industrialization, too, have so gyrated that it is no wonder that the share of manufacturing production exported has generally been low, that the value of industrial exports has fluctuated widely, and that the resulting level and composition of industrial exports may be better explained by the nature and maturity of the country's ISI, and the low and uneven rates of expansion of the local market, than by the relative incentives to export.[3]

The magnitude of the shifts in the incentives to export and, indeed, to invest in facilities capable of manufacturing products high enough in quality and low enough in cost to lead to profitable export activity, has been documented.[4] Moreover, vehemently expressed comments by producers testify to the impact of the often dramatically fluctuating incentives on exports in individual cases. Why then proceed any further, especially if one is an economist? Are not the economic policy implications clear enough? I maintain that it may, indeed, be advisable to extend the analysis.

A Brief History of the Argentine Export Experience

Argentine exports of manufactures date to the late nineteenth century, if account is taken of products that enter into the national accounts as manufacturing industry. Some processing has long been added to the products of agriculture and grazing, and there were notable increases in the proportion of industrial value added in the exported products, first and temporarily during World War II, when Argentina exported clothing, shoes, and some other products on a much larger scale than before, and then, on a more lasting basis and a larger scale, in the period beginning the mid-1960s. Somewhat more than half of Argentina's exports were products that figure in the national accounts as manufactures as of the late 1950s to early 1960s, with natural resource–based products, such as processed and semiprocessed foodstuffs (especially meat products) and leather goods, accounting for nearly 90 percent of the total.

There was a major diversification into products not based on traditional Argentine agricultural inputs during the 1970s. Metallurgical and metalworking products increased from less than 1 percent of all industrial exports in 1961 to nearly 19 percent in 1973, attaining a share as high as 29 percent in 1975 before declining slightly to 18 percent in 1979. Chemical products (increasingly, petrochemicals and petroleum derivatives) increased their share of total manufactured exports from 5 percent in 1973 to 21 percent by 1981. These increases, particularly of those products not based on inputs of traditional raw materials, appear to have resulted largely as a spin-off of ISI, as suggested by Teitel and Thoumi (1986). That may or may not have been anticipated from the outset in the case of the products based on local agriculture and grazing, but it certainly must have been an unsurprising development in retrospect.

However, the evolution of exports was quite unexpected in the case of those products based primarily on industrial inputs (many imported) and was recognized by few economists until several years after it was under way. As these exports materialized, most foreign (and a good number of domestic) observers assumed that Argentine production costs were high; exports destined for other Latin American countries were assumed to be under regional common market or free trade preferences reflecting trade diversion, or, independent of their destination, these exports were simply taken as reflections of the difficulties of selling in domestic markets because of adverse economic conditions. The latter may well have been the primary factor in the case of the initial exports of petrochemicals, petroleum derivatives, and steel products, particularly given the recent completion of large, modern facilities, but many of the metalworking exports of the 1970s also appear to reflect the payoff to learning and specialization. For those product groups that experienced statistically significant export growth rates between 1971 and 1980 (resource-based products as well as others), the rate of growth was 18.5 percent.[5]

Regional trade preferences played a part in this growth, but well over half of the new intra–Latin American trade was in products not favored by the preferential agreements, and some of the favored products also were exported beyond the region, along with other products for which the principal demand was beyond Latin America. Some manufactured exports were initiated in moments of adversity in Argentina's troubled domestic market, but a good share continued even in times of more favorable conditions at home (or in times of major currency overvaluation). Overall, industrial exports appear to have made a significant contribution to the financial profitability of the exporting firms, a conclusion that is being examined more closely in an IDB study currently under way under the direction of Elio Londero and Simón Teitel.

While exports of some products continued to gain into the early 1980s—

most notably, vegetable oils, produced in large, latest-technology facilities—exports of most Argentine products slumped badly as the currency became sharply overvalued, and then the adverse effects of the international recession set in during 1982/83. There was relatively little rise in industrial exports even by 1984 despite the economic recovery of the relatively open U.S. market, which was effectively exploited by Brazil and Mexico, as well as a few of the smaller Latin American countries. Argentine exports of manufactures in 1984 were at or below the level of the mid-1970s in constant dollar terms ($4.572 billion in 1984 compared to $5.849 billion in 1977–1979, in constant 1984 dollars [ECLAC 1986: 29]). Metalworking products, conceivably the exemplar of ISI learning and specialization, were at only half the level registered in the late 1970s. An ECLAC study characterized this slump as:

> the reflection of a decisive process of deindustrialization that has characterized the recent situation in Argentine industry. The large subsidies and reimbursements on their exports, which sustained the primacy of these products in foreign markets, were not associated with a transformation and modernization of the productive base. On the contrary, as a consequence of applying policies that discouraged industrial activities, investment was insignificant, research and development efforts were abandoned, and the country remained isolated from the international technology revolution affecting industrial production (1986: 62).

Less than 5 percent of the output of products not based on traditional raw material inputs was exported in 1984 (ECLAC 1986: 145). Indeed, except for a few years, exports as a percentage of output also were extraordinarily low for some traditional raw material–based manufactures such as shoes, handbags, and dairy products. Preliminary estimates suggest that given the impetus of increased incentives to export, many nontraditional industrial exports increased significantly in 1987/88, but only to levels slightly above those of 1978/79.

While an ISI that produced a certain number of winners appears to have been the principal factor in explaining Argentina's manufactured exports, it can be asked whether the particular form of Argentina's ISI led to nearly as sound a process of industrialization or to as significant and lasting an increase in manufactured exports as might have been desirable (which is not to argue that economic success, even comparable to that of the countries of Southeast Asia, would have required as rapid a rate of growth in exports of manufactures as in the case of the Asian economies, with their poorer resource base and their generally smaller domestic markets). Moreover, the conclusion that Argentina's long-run pattern in manufactured exports does not appear to have been very much influenced by export incentives is a troubling one.[6] The extraordinary instability of those incentives must have played a major role—

particularly the dramatic swings in the real effective exchange rate as the currency shifted from highly overvalued to undervalued, and then back again—and probably a twofold role. First, the swings in incentives were very large; second, for some producers, there were delays of several weeks to several months in perceiving their full magnitude and in assessing how best to reorient production.

The Basic Viewpoint

It is my contention that institutional and behavioral realities have played a role worth noting in the evolution of Argentine manufactured exports (a similar theme can be found in Di Tella and Dornbusch [1989]).[7] I suggest that these factors help explain why more such exports did not develop earlier, and why there was such a collapse in the export of products based on imported inputs in the 1980s. There are at least five categories we should consider:

1. Argentine institutions in the areas of education, science, and technology, and Argentine attitudes toward education
2. The Argentine life-style, including what might be characterized as a tendency to rely on Providence
3. The strong nationalistic strain that pervades much political thought and, particularly, expression in Argentina
4. A significant (though now possibly declining) national tendency toward intransigence, particularly political intransigence
5. Psychological factors affecting both private and public decisionmaking, ranging from more apparent kinds of factors such as motivation to less-obvious and less-analyzed, but equally important, factors such as the sometimes imperfect way in which information is perceived and judgments are made[8]

Argentine educational institutions were probably the strongest in the developing world for much of the twentieth century and also were more accessible to the public at large than they were in many industrialized countries through the end of World War II, and even somewhat beyond. This, along with considerable attention to technical and scientific instruction, constituted strong support for the kind of industrialization that could substitute efficiently for imports and that could have contributed, and in some cases did, to manufactured exports, especially in the late 1960s and the 1970s. But financial support for public education declined from the late 1960s on, as did support for other public institutions important for Argentine technological development. In addition, there were years in the 1970s when the universities became more politicized than before. It is possible that the adverse effects of these factors on the country's export potential have not been fully felt, even at this point (see Chapter 10 for further discussion of this issue).[9]

The Argentine life-style has probably had mixed effects. Proportionately, more Argentines traveled abroad than did citizens of most developing countries during the 1920s and 1930s, the 1940s perhaps, and probably beginning again after 1955. These travelers developed many foreign contacts and a great deal of familiarity with foreign tastes and foreign products, and, in some cases at least, foreign technology. These aspects could have contributed to an increased export orientation. On the other hand, the powerful inclination toward consumption left less for investment,[10] which, in turn, meant insufficient amounts for the large investments that export-oriented projects in some industries would have required. (This is not to deny that, on a number of occasions, conflicting public policies also affected the capacity and willingness to invest and may even have been the most important deterrents during certain years in the last four decades, but they were not the *only* deterrents.)

Related to the Argentine outlook and life-style is the assumption that the economic prosperity of the late nineteenth and early twentieth centuries can be explained in large measure in providential terms. Survival and moderate comfort came more easily in Argentina than in many other developing countries. Providence was regarded as having as much importance as hard work, and there was a tendency to expect that the country's rich soil and favorable climate would generally lead to good harvests that, in turn, would usually take care of everything—including the foreign exchange needed for essential raw materials, intermediate goods, and machinery for industry. There were few exultations, either in Argentine literature or in the popular press, of yeomen farmers who toiled long hours to clear fields and later rose to great prosperity, or of hardworking mechanics who subsequently emerged as leading manufacturers. Rather, the life-style that most seemed to capture the admiration of the populace, at least through the first four decades of the twentieth century, was that of well-to-do ranchers (in some cases, descendants of those awarded land grants and, in others, sons of those who gained after the Indian wars of the nineteenth century) who resided much of their time in well-appointed, largely European-furnished apartments and townhouses in Buenos Aires and other leading cities.

Also admired was the imagined independence and rough-hewn comfort of the no-longer-really-existent gauchos, who possessed the skills necessary for survival in the wilderness but tended to be best visualized as gathered around a fireplace, playing a guitar and relating tales. Such admiration for other-than-entrepreneurial types, even though hardly universal, may well have influenced the attitudes of young people growing up and delayed the evolution of a competitively oriented, export-driven industrial sector.[11]

Whether or not the strong nationalistic strain that pervades much political expression in Argentina reflects a reaction against an international orientation, the fact is that highly nationalistic attitudes can be found on the political right, left, and center, and this has contributed to strong support for an essentially autarchically oriented ISI, with public policies reflecting a marked antiexport bias. Strong nationalism in Japan and South Korea, on the other hand, has not had this effect at all, but that may well be due to major differences in their resource bases. It was often exclaimed, at various social levels in the late 1950s to early 1960s, for example, that Argentina has meat, wheat, petroleum, steel, an educated population—"*¡tiene de todo!*"—everything presumably necessary for successful economic development, even on a relatively autarchic basis. In Japan and Korea, the more limited resource base may help explain the insistence of nationalistic authorities on favorable economic performance, especially the ability to export, as a condition for protection and assistance from the state (on Korea, see Amsden 1989).

Differences in the nature of the political and economic influence of foreign powers immediately preceding the Asian states' industrialization drives also may help explain the dissimilar impact of nationalistic tendencies. Exploring the possible role of cultural differences is best left to experts in other disciplines, but I draw on the political scientist O'Donnell for one important insight. He concludes that Argentine governments have been "colonized" by civil society, and thus there has been a lack of state autonomy. To the degree that this is true, the Argentine state, unlike those of Japan and Korea, would not have had the authority to implement the conditions for protection and official assistance that were undertaken in the Asian countries. Indeed, this lack of state authority in Argentina, emanating primarily from the frequently shifting coalitions of those who made up the government, led to "difficulties in imposing the authoritarian 'solution' that seemed to offer a chance of extracting Argentine capitalism from its political and economic spirals" (O'Donnell 1973: 25).[12]

The significant national tendency toward intransigence, particularly political intransigence, appears to be a manifestation of the "to a friend everything, to the rest, little" mentality noted by Lanus (1988), and has been accentuated by the considerable political significance of so many disparate forces—rural interests, large manufacturers with market power (abetted by high levels of protection from foreign competition), labor unions, the military, the church, and the urban middle class, split in turn into several different groups, all of these in various, often shifting, coalitions (which may, indeed, be a sign of the modernization process, as maintained in O'Donnell 1973). Economists have taken note of the stop-go policies and Argentina's changing economic incentives, and they have tended to explain such shifts in terms of overreactions, or mistaken reactions, either to balance of payments difficulties or to the general economic situation. Not enough attention has been given to the role of political intransigence in fostering policy changes.[13] This lack of willingness to compromise appears to be due to major differences in the outlook toward life in various respects and may not reflect underlying conflicts of economic interests alone, as many economists have assumed.[14]

The stop-go policies or, more accurately in the context of my argument, the partially intransigence-fostered stop-go policies—the policy changes brought on by attempts to impose one group's will in the context of political shifts, or the exercise of vetoes or blockages by those not quite strong enough to gain the upper hand—have led to a level of economic uncertainty that has discouraged even medium-term, private investments. They have been particularly inimical to export-oriented investments or investments of a dimension or specialization likely to lead to the manufacture of internationally competitive products.[15] The adverse economic effects have, in turn, contributed to increased emigration, especially of professionals and technicians.

While increased emigration may have been a factor in leading to the establishment of a few trading companies and to Argentine contacts abroad that have facilitated exports of Argentine products generally, in some cases it has meant that Argentines who might have produced at home, including for export, have become a part of foreign production efforts, adversely affecting the potential for Argentine exports on both the supply and the demand side. The emigrating members of Argentine production teams were less and less inclined to return, as Argentine instability continued and as they developed firmer roots in their new countries. Not all of those who were unfavorably affected by the stop-go policies emigrated, of course, but the policies—to which political intransigence contributed, it should again be noted—led to the dissolution (or partial dissolution) even of some production teams whose members remained in the country, many of whom drifted to other activities or who became sales representatives for imported products similar to those they formerly produced. The latter have moved increasingly to careers in service activities and, with the years, have dropped out of the potential group of those who might produce for export, if not immediately, then at some point in the future, after additional learning experience. This exodus has led to a loss of the economic value of knowledge accrued in the process of production, some of which is specific to the firms in which it is acquired.

Stop-go policies, in part explained by intransigence, have intensified social strife and led to changing values that have, in their turn, also undermined the development of manufactured exports. There has been an increasing emphasis on realizing gains in financial markets and an increasing tendency of bright young professionals, who might have gone into manufacturing, to make speculation the cornerstone of their activities, as the gap between prospective earnings in manufacturing and the financial areas has widened greatly, abetted at times by insider contributions to the successes of speculations. The extraordinary gains of certain speculations became difficult to repeat, however, and that, along with continuance of the conditions that had made speculation more attractive to begin with, led to more incidents of misrepresentation and fraud. This was particularly widespread in the responses to various investment promotion mechanisms, with the result that the incentives did not breed the kind of strengthening of the productive apparatus needed to develop competitive, export-oriented activity. In addition, the extremely favorable nature of certain incentives caused some serious-minded producers to refrain from responding to them because they assumed, often correctly, that countervailing political pressures would soon bring an end to the measures. The increasing risk and unreliability of market transactions provided a transaction cost stimulus to avoid markets, much along the lines outlined by Williamson (1985); this must have been particularly inhibiting to the more risky market transactions represented by many exports (with the major exception of intrafirm exports).

Psychological Factors[16]

For economists, the term *psychological factors* brings to mind matters of motivation, first and foremost. There seems to be a bimodal split with respect to the motivation to export. Some firms, particularly those bent on expansion, reacted to local instability and secular slowdown by concluding that there was a very great incentive to export (particularly in 1987/88). The shift in financial incentives has been so great in Argentina, however, that the risk and uncertainty factors that enter into profit maximization calculations have increased firms' tendency to think defensively, in terms of mere enterprise survival. This probably has had the effect of reducing the incentive to export, certainly insofar as new expenditures on equipment, design, and quality control personnel, or marketing systems would be needed to facilitate those exports. Other enterprises have been so impacted by the added risk and uncertainty prevailing at any one point in time, or that may prevail in the near future, that they no longer make careful calculations; rather, their approach is to assume that there is no incentive to export. This can be seen in the example of some firms that contend that they seek only to survive, and to increase the likelihood of that, they will consider sales only in local markets or in the closest foreign countries such as Uruguay and Paraguay, whose economies are, in fact, highly integrated with Argentina's. In these cases, it may not be that their motivation has changed, but that their perception of the relevant information has become more imperfect, or that the way in which they assess data has been different.

The net incentive to export manufactures and to invest in facilities that can produce exportable goods is a product of a number of policies—often a very large number. Exchange rates; export incentives; the effective rate of protection; quantitative restrictions; customs regulations; the effectiveness of governmental export promotion measures; tax provisions; credit regulations; wage and price control authorizations; governmental rulings on labor disputes; and changes in the investment in education and in the support of public institutions that aid producer efficiency and help producers apply newly developed technologies: all can affect the profitability of export activity and of investment in facilities that might be able to generate exports. Although at those times when there is a major overvaluation (or undervaluation) of the currency, producers are convinced that incentives are strongly unfavorable (or favorable), often it is quite difficult for some to discern the balance of incentives at any given point in time—this apart from the difficulty of gauging what incentives might be twelve months ahead.

Taking the effective rate of protection alone, it is common to find businessmen who are unaware of the range of the effective rate of protection for their products or those they could produce. This may not seem surprising to economists who have made estimates of effective rates of protection, but, somehow, we do not seem to realize its full implications. Moreover, the effective rate of protection is but one component of the incentives to export, and the frequent unawareness of it suggests that except when incentives to export are exceedingly favorable (or unfavorable), they are not likely to be well perceived by many of those whose behavior they are intended to influence.[17] I state this as a fact, but since there are always some producers who seem to perceive signals well, I must concede that it is a contention that needs to be tested, something that I have attempted to convince one international institution to do in another country and that might well be verified for Argentina as well.

In part, the multitude of signals is the result of the sometimes large number of entities that make policies affecting the incentives to export (or to invest). Fewer "cooks in the kitchen" and a greater inclination toward one-stop export centers might help.

The manner in which enterprises assess this imperfectly perceived information also can affect their inclination to export. Sometimes, and not only in the case of small and medium-sized firms, use is made of calculation proxies—rules of thumb or judgmental heuristics—rather than the more sophisticated maximizing techniques taught in economics and business administration (see Schwartz 1987). This "second-best" approach to calculation occurs even among those who are familiar with the optimization techniques, as psychologists have demonstrated (see especially Kahneman, Slovic, and Tversky 1982); it occurs with respect to the entire universe of business decisions, and so, a fortiori, with respect to those affecting the decision to export.

Decisions based on rule of thumb are at least somewhat different from those maximizing calculations would elicit. The implications of this for exports needs to be determined empirically, but insofar as judgmental heuristics such as anchoring (that is, overweighting recent data observations) are used, or reinforcement reasoning processes are relied upon, it implies that there will be a lower level of exports than would result from unbiased calculation.

The significance of perception, judgment, and motivation at the governmental level cannot be overestimated. It is not only whether the incentives to export or to invest in facilities capable of producing exportables are perceived and assessed well by private producers, but how well the bottlenecks they are intended to overcome are perceived and assessed both by entrepreneurs and by public sector officials who design policies to deal with them.

Some weak responses of manufacturers to public policy measures are attributable to producers' difficulty in "reading" the signals initially, or to errors in interpreting them. However, other weak or unexpected entrepreneurial responses may arise from biases in government officials' judgments, resulting from the techniques they use to analyze data—techniques that often involve those same rules of thumb or judgmental heuristics, rather than more rigorous processes of economic reasoning taught in universities and specialized public administration training programs. Government officials may have problems with: the valuation or "reading" of the relevant technological, market, and public policy data; assessment of the way in which those same data are understood and valued by manufacturers; the way in which they formulate judgments about the nature of the key problems or leading development opportunities, the response that can be expected from industrialists to alternative policy options, and the policy options selected and the results they are expected to encourage.[18] Still further complications may arise from the motivations of official decisionmakers, not the altruistic, or—to take the other extreme—the self-interested and personally maximizing, global objectives sometimes assumed to guide their actions, but, rather, the particular objectives that actually turn out to apply in individual situations and actions.

Perception and judgment considerations must be particularly serious in those countries in which government salary levels are so much lower than those in the private sector that the middle levels of government service have great difficulty attracting and holding qualified people—or in discouraging them from taking second and even third jobs. Moreover, the possibility of misperception or misjudgment is increased insofar as many officials charged with a responsibility for understanding industrial phenomena and providing elements that contribute to the development of the relevant industrial policy have limited contact with the manufacturing plants and production processes in question. This is particularly true of many economists working in ministries of industry and planning in many countries.

The Implications of the Argentine Experience

To the degree that the points outlined above are correct, there are underlying, not entirely economic, factors that affect the disposition and ability of producers to export, both directly, and indirectly through their contribution to stop-go economic policies. Estimates of the significance of factors such as political intransigence for the adoption of stop-go economic policies may help to reduce the frequency and magnitude of the swings—particularly since there is at least some doubt as to whether the intransigence is based on widespread philosophical differences.[19] It is possible, in any event, that the seriousness of the recent economic situation in Argentina may have administered a shock treatment sufficient to lead many individuals to act less intransigently than before. If so, this may reduce the number or magnitude of the stop-go policy swings.

Empirical studies may reveal that the institutional and behavioral factors, which are difficult and time-consuming to transform, may be much more an impediment to the functioning of some policies than to others. As an example, the continuance of strong, virtually intransigent views on the use of conventional tax policy to stimulate exports (for example, through export subsidies on the one hand and major tax relief for new, export-oriented investment on the other) may lead to counterproductive major swings in incentives, but certain forms of support to technological development (including even special tax-deduction incentives) do not appear to be quite as subject to differences in position and, therefore, to such swings in incentives.

The significance of psychological factors, such as perception and judgment, on exports is another matter and an important one. The inclusion in calculations of data on the way in which incentives are perceived by producers, and any major differences there may be between actual incentives and the way they are perceived, will provide information to policymakers that could cause them to alter either their policies or the degree to which, or ways in which, they are explained to producers. Information on the way in which producers process the information they perceive on export or investment incentives also could help point to the need for changes in the policies or in producer response to those policies. Similarly, periodic surveys that delve into producer perception and assessment of bottlenecks—going well beyond the lists of business complaints currently compiled in many countries— might prove quite helpful.

In addition, information on perception and judgment patterns at the government level could well explain errors in the design of government policy, which seems to be suggested by Nogués in the case of the Argentine economic cabinet of 1976–1981 (1986:46). With the approach I have outlined here, it would be possible for economists to provide analyses that are more likely to be acted upon, even by those with a heavily political agenda, and that are more revealing of problem areas than the current, usually aggregate evaluations of the response to incentives.

Let me close by returning to Mallon and Sourrouille's *Economic Policymaking in a Conflict Society* in which they judged political intransigence to be the key factor holding back growth of the Argentine economy:

> Even among Latin societies, Argentina has been considered the nirvana of intransigents, where "social forces confront each other nakedly, no political institutions, no corps of professional political leaders are recognized or accepted as the legitimate intermediaries to moderate group conflict, and no agreement exists among the groups as to the legitimate and authoritative methods for resolving conflicts." The judicial and legislative branches of government have traditionally been weak, so that fundamental decisions are made in the executive establishment "under the influence of pressure groups of importance that extend their heads directly into the governmental structure." This praetorian style of conduct allegedly reaches also into the management of private enterprise and labor unions and of relationships between them (1975: 166, citing Samuel P. Huntington and Kalman H. Silvert).

Mallon and Sourrouille maintained that the fundamental cause of the semistagnation and great cyclical instability of the Argentine economy was that policymaking was not properly adapted to the conditions of a conflict society (1975: 154); they called for a satisficing rather than optimizing, approach, a sequential, incrementalist, and flexible approach to policymaking (164, 166, and, especially, 167). At the same time, they maintained that a rate of growth at least two to three times as high as Argentina had been able to achieve in the generation ending in the early 1970s would be necessary to resolve the tensions of a conflict society, while at the same time preserving a pluralistic form of government (171). But, is such a high rate of growth feasible with a satisficing, incrementalist, and flexible approach as Mallon and Sourrouille advocated? And what happened to cause Sourrouille, a decade later, as minister of the economy, to become the principal exponent of such a different approach to economic policymaking? The phenomenon of political intransigence continues to be of great importance in Argentina, but a more overtly behavioral analysis of factors, such as proposed in this chapter, may provide a more promising way to get a conflict society back on the path to more-sustained economic growth and to achievement of the increased exports of manufactures that Mallon and Sourrouille, among others, have recognized as essential to that objective.

Notes

The views expressed here are mine and do not reflect those of the IDB, with which I was associated when I began preparation of this chapter. I am grateful to James Dietz, Dilmus James, Elio Londero, Julio Nogués, Francisco Thoumi, and Simón Teitel for comments on an earlier draft, and to Javier Villanueva for several suggestions at the outset, including one that I take a look at Lanus (1988), which deals with the historical evolution of characteristics particularly Argentine. None of the aforementioned should be implicated in my discussion or interpretation, however.

1. It should be noted that despite this slide in relative terms, Argentina's growth was better than 2.5 percent, on average, between 1946 and 1988, and nearly 0.7 percent in per capita terms, not much below that of the United States, as Di Tella and Dornbusch (1989: 1) note for the years 1946–1983.

2. Julio J. Nogués (1988b, esp. pp. 17–31) has prepared an absorbing but disturbing account of Argentina's complex export incentives programs.

3. For a careful analysis of Argentine manufactured exports in the 1960s and 1970s, which concludes that the exports were primarily natural resource–based or a by-product of an ISI that, through learning and increased economies of scale, increased their international competitiveness, see Teitel and Thoumi (1986).

4. See, for example, Ballestero and Thoumi (1988), who estimate that Argentine real exchange rates were the most unstable of those of all countries during 1960–1982, in a region characterized by generally unstable exchange rates, and who conclude that the exchange rate instability of the Latin American and Caribbean countries explains a substantial proportion of the high intra- and extraregional export instability. Nogués (1986: 47) contends that the 1976–1981 fluctuations in real effective exchange rates probably were more severe than in any developing country in the post–World War II period.

5. Among those products not based on traditional Argentine raw materials, growth rates of over 20 percent were achieved by nonferrous metals, printing, clothing, metal structures, nonelectrical and electrical machinery, professional and scientific equipment, auto parts, pulp and paper, and domestic electric appliances. Four product groups not characterized as traditional resource-based products reached exports of over $100 million by 1980: clothing, basic chemicals, and auto parts, among those in the rapid growth group; and iron and steel (which had a growth rate of 12.2 percent [Teitel and Thoumi 1986: 470–471]). Note that some successful exporters benefited from substantial subsidies, among these metallurgical and chemical enterprises, which were owned by the Argentine military (Nogués 1988b).

6. See Teitel and Thoumi (1986: 477–485). Incentives do appear to have played an important role for certain products at certain points in time, though; for example, for metalworking and leather products in the first half of the 1970s and, perhaps, for naval construction products for much of the period (but see Nogués 1988b).

7. Di Tella and Dornbusch (1989: 14) write (emphasis added):

It is impossible to read these pages without a sense of deep frustration at the sight of a country, rich in natural resources and with a reasonably well trained population, sliding decade by decade behind most other countries either more or less developed than herself. The economic reasons for the brief successes and the failures can easily be seen: the excessively lenient fiscal policies, the extreme inward-looking strategy, the persistent overvaluation of the peso, the strong distortion of the relative price vector, the lack of export consciousness affecting both staples and industrial goods, the lack of economic criteria in state investments, the extreme lack of confidence in the price mechanism, the perverse interference with the economy, the continuous changes in policies, etc. *However, all this is not enough to provide an explanation. It is necessary to scrutinise the political and cultural attitudes of the country and the way in which they are clearly reflected in the economic performance to find the deeper reasons behind the phenomena described in these pages.*

8. For an examination of problems of perception and judgment in entrepreneurial decisionmaking, in part in Argentina, see Schwartz (1987).

9. In the full quotation excerpted at the outset of this chapter, Street characterizes technological knowledge and instruments as the "propelling force of economic growth."

10. In *La causa argentina*, Lanus (1988), who appears to come from Argentina's upper social classes, devotes special and not altogether flattering sections to Argentine attitudes toward consumption and Argentina's orientation toward Europe (see the sections titled, "Una suprema vocación: el consumo" and "El trasplante europeo").

11. For a view of the possible importance of cultural factors in explaining the evolution of modern industry in East Asia, see the April 1988 Supplement of *Economic Development and Cultural Change*, especially Ruttan's article.

12. The authoritarian "solution" refers to the concept of bureaucratic-authoritarianism with which O'Donnell is associated. See also Nogués (1988b: 24), who refers to the increasing tendency of export subsidies to be particularized to specific ports, regions, and even firms as "a growth in the economic and political power of corporative groups accompanied by a diminishing power of the state."

13. I would have thought otherwise, but Carballo de Cilley (1987: 59) reports, on the basis of interviews with 1,005 respondents in five major metropolitan areas, that most Argentines regard themselves as having rather centrist political positions. If so, then the intemperance toward the views of others is more difficult to explain but may be a consequence of two generations of rapid growth without having to work too hard or compromise very much on matters of principle. Other factors may enter, too, in helping to explain the inclination toward political intransigence; e.g., some of the struggle may have evolved over efforts to gain what was perceived, differently by different groups, as equal treatment before the law. Actually, some

Argentines deeply involved in the political process claim that political intransigence has eased in recent years.

14. The intransigence growing out of other than economic considerations was a major factor in explaining the extreme repression of the 1976–1982 period. Intransigence reflecting primarily economic considerations also had led to violence in 1973–1976, but of a much lower order of magnitude. Mallon and Sourrouille (1975) stressed the debilitating role of political intransigence in their important work but attributed it almost entirely to underlying conflicts of economic interests.

15. Estimates of investment for the economy as a whole, which may be almost as relevant for long-term industrial production as are those for industry alone, indicate that net investment increased an average of less than 3 percent a year during 1970–1974 and less than 2 percent a year during 1975–1979, and declined an average of more than 1 percent a year during 1980–1984 and more than 2 percent during 1985–1987. Gross investment in equipment and tools (destined primarily but not exclusively for industry) declined an average of nearly 10 percent during 1980–1985 but appears to have increased at an average of 15 percent during 1986–1987, before declining again in 1988 by more than 3 percent (calculations based on Argentina, Central Bank 1980–1988). Export-oriented investments in products not based primarily on domestic raw materials may have been fostered by the recent Argentine-Brazilian accords more than by anything else to date, according to official spokespersons. It is necessary to verify the details of such investments, however; certainly the accord had little to do with recent large investments in steel and paper, and probably petrochemicals as well. The fiscal deficit and the factors contributing to that have, of course, also tended to inhibit investment, and particularly investments likely to lead to internationally competitive products.

16. Pioneering work on the possible application of psychoanalytic concepts to decisionmaking, including entrepreneurial decisionmaking, can be found in Kets de Vries and Miller (1988) and Zaleznik (1988).

17. This assumes that the measures are well enough publicized so that producers are aware of them to begin with. The accuracy with which information is perceived is yet another problem, and one that economists have generally ignored even though differences in the way in which data are perceived can lead to efforts to solve problems that are variants of the ones actually confronted. Interviews with key decisionmakers in more than a hundred well-reported, successful, small and medium-sized metalworking enterprises in Argentina, Mexico and the United States revealed that many of them tended to err by 10 to 15 percent in ascertaining the minimum cost of the steel—their most-important raw material—they would require, and errors concerning the cost of machinery often were more than 20 percent. Equally notable was the limited awareness of many producers, especially in Argentina and Mexico, of the applicability of certain, relatively new technologies to their manufacturing processes. Moreover, in Argentina, in 1976/77, following upward revisions of the formerly negative real rates of interest (but to levels that still left them hovering around zero), many small and medium-sized metalworking firms seriously misperceived the real level of those rates and their continued attractiveness in the light of expected profits. In Mexico, which had not experienced a currency devaluation in twelve years, the initial reactions of some very successful firms to the September 1986 devaluation revealed that they had great difficulty in understanding the likely consequences

of the policy changes for their industry. In many types of situations, the differences in perception and judgment varied dramatically according to the professional training and experience of the producers, and according to the frequency with which they were confronted with relevant data.

18. For the view that leading economic ideas play an important role in the perception and judgment of decisionmakers as to how the world works and what the correct policies are, see Nogués (1988a).

19. See Carballo de Cilley (1987); perhaps her finding may have resulted from the particular framing of the questions.

7

Technology, Ceremonies, and Institutional Appropriateness: Historical Origins of Mexico's Agrarian Crisis

William E. Cole

It is interesting to note that except for a short period after World War II, the high point of Mexican agriculture occurred half a millennium ago at the zenith of the Aztec Empire. During the colonial and postindependence periods, the more productive forms of ancient, indigenous agricultural technology largely disappeared and the institutional structure was, for the most part, replaced by emergent forms. By 1910, what remained of the ancient agricultural systems were ceremonial vestiges and the least productive of the technologies, e.g., slash and burn. Mexico, then, presents a case wherein intercultural[1] technology transfer destroyed indigenous technological capabilities that had been millennia in the building. Throughout the postrevolutionary period, official Mexican policy toward agriculture has been marked, on the one hand, by efforts to recapture central aspects of the institutional form of the ancient systems and, on the other, by attempts to infuse modern technology into the system. The institutional form, of course, is the *ejido* land tenure system upon which the twentieth-century agrarian reform efforts have been based.[2] What is attempted here is a historical analysis of Mexican agriculture using the tools of the Veblen-Ayres school of institutional economics. This approach, I believe, is in the spirit of James Street's argument (1980: 245) that "in Latin America, institutionalists [should] investigate the reasons for the disappearance in the colonial period of the native innovative spirit characteristic of the Aztec and Inca civilizations and the subsequent failure to revive it in modern times."

The Tools of Analysis

In his contribution to what are known as the paradigmatic volumes of the *Journal of Economic Issues*, Street [1987a] summarized and analyzed the several paradigms of institutionalist thought as they relate to the study of

103

economic development. In one component of that work, he expanded the Veblen-Ayres paradigm to cover the panorama of Third World economic problems. Because it is especially relevant for historical studies, what I shall call the Veblen-Ayres-Street paradigm should serve us well in the present analysis.

At the heart of the Veblen-Ayres-Street approach is the "technology/ ceremony dichotomy." Those two forces are said to be in confrontation, with technology a dynamic and progressive protagonist, while ceremonies are "static, resistant to and inhibitory of change" [Ayres 1962: 174]. Ayres "emphasized that technological progress consisted of a combination and recombination of existing . . . tools, machines, instruments, processes, and conceptual devices, always in association with skilled human manipulation and cognitive attention" (Street 1987a: 1867–1868). Unto itself, this process of combinations and recombinations is seen as inherently dynamic. Street (1987a: 1867) further points out that "Ayres paid particular attention to the historic role of social institutions in either obstructing or permitting technological advance." Being past-bound and change-resistant, ceremonial behavior, in the best scenario, slows the pace of progress and, in the worst, may thwart it altogether. Thus, institutionalist theory defines development as the successful assimilation of new technology and, therefore, "attributes retarded growth in the Third World to the dominant influence of archaic social institutions and the consequent failure to utilize available technical knowledge and skill" (Street 1987a: 1861).

Foster (1981: 908) adds to the analytical model used here by pointing out that both technology and ceremony are "common to all institutions." This fits with Veblen's contention that technological and ceremonial behavior live together in "some sort of symbiosis" and Ayres's (1962: 110–111) statement that "technical activities are almost inextricably blended with activities of another sort." Foster (1981: 908) carries the analysis further by adding that "every institution serves to bring the activities to bear in a contributory way on the [technological] function, which is the collaborative activity of the group. . . . On the other hand, every institution serves a completely different kind of function: it serves to differentiate between groups in invidious terms."

Functioning economic institutions are therefore seen as organized around a technology but also as containing ceremonial aspects that are inextricably woven with the technological. In the Veblen-Ayres-Street view, progress will take place by successfully introducing a technological improvement into the institutional milieu. Successful introduction depends upon the degree of change-resistance put forth by the ceremonial factors. Furthermore, the rate of progress will depend upon the degree of ceremonial resistance. It therefore follows that when we encounter a society with a relatively high level of economic performance and one that has improved steadily over historic time, we have also found a set of institutions in which the ceremonial aspects support, or at least do not inhibit, economic progress. Conversely, a long record of stagnation and decline implies that the ceremonial components of the institutional systems have negated or strangled technological dynamism. It should now be instructive to refract major highlights of Mexican economic history through the prism of the Veblen-Ayres-Street paradigm.

Ancient Agricultural Systems of Mexico

The splendor of both the Mayan and Aztec civilizations, the architecture, the ceremonial trappings, and the level of learned achievements, all bespeak agricultural systems capable of producing a surplus. The ample surplus is implicit in letters written by Cortés in which the market at Temixtitan was described as "twice as large as that of Salamanca" and the market for cloth said to be larger than the great silk market of Granada (Schell 1986: 43).

In pre-Hispanic Mexico, there were probably at least as many agricultural systems as there were separate and distinct societies. Many of the systems have been studied and can be usefully organized under three categories: (1) slash and burn; (2) systematic fallowing of permanent fields; and (3) irrigation and/or terracing (West and Augelli 1966: 233). While each of these systems was more productive in terms of output per hectare than the subsequent plow culture of the colonial period, at least one of the systems utilized by the Aztec and probably one of the Mayan systems were extremely productive; the *chinampa* system of the Aztec and the "raised field" system now thought to have characterized much of Mayan agriculture. Both are types of irrigation agriculture. Until recently, it was supposed that the Mayan civilization had been built upon the foundation of slash and burn agriculture. Propelled by satellite photographs, however, recent explorations make it clear that a very productive raised field system deserves the credit for sustaining the great civilizing accomplishments of the Maya.

Because it has been more widely studied, I will focus upon the chinampa system of the Aztecs, which has been authoritatively described as "one of the most intensive and productive ever devised by man" (Chapin 1988: 9). Palerm (1973: 37) describes the system:

> The chinampa is a small artificial island built in the shallow waters of a freshwater lake. First a suitable construction site is found, where the waters are shallow and there are no strong currents. Next, the perimeter is marked off with willow stakes and sticks; usually a long rectangular shape. . . . Layers of aquatic vegetation, dirt, and mud are deposited within the rectangle until the chinampa surface is 20–30 cm above the water level. The chinampa does not require irrigation. Since it is narrow and surrounded by water, filtration provides sufficient

moisture. Neither does it require fertilizing. . . . In the chinampas we find the most advanced systems of crop rotation and mixing, as well as the most intensive use of nurseries and seed plots. The chinampas produce all year, year after year.

The system produced staple crops such as maize and beans as well as vegetables, fruits, and flowers. Sources of animal protein were plentiful in the form of fish, salamanders, frogs, and a wide range of aquatic fowl. The plots were so prolific that up to four crops per year were obtained (Chapin 1988: 9–10).

Chinampa agriculture was centered on lakes Chalco-Xochimilco and Texcoco in the central region, known as the Valley of Mexico (Sanders, Parsons, and Santley 1979: 279–280). It is believed "that the dense rural population and the large cities in the Valley of Mexico in preconquest times were based mainly on the tremendous amount of food produced on [the] intensely cultivated plots" of that system (West and Augelli 1966: 236–237). By the time of the conquest, the chinampa system had grown to considerable size, with those at Chalco-Xochimilco, for example, covering about 120 square kilometers (Chapin 1988: 9). It is noteworthy that the urban developments that preceded Tenochtitlán, some of which served as its building blocks, had been based on earlier forms of irrigation technology. At the time of the conquest, chinampas represented the latest stage in Mesoamerican agronomic development.

While the technologies of irrigation, terracing, soil preparation, crop rotation, et cetera, were very sophisticated, the agricultural implements that were utilized with them were extremely simple and of remote origin. The dibble stick with a fire-hardened point was widely used throughout Mesoamerica, and the *coa*, a hoe with a triangular blade, was used extensively in central Mexico in conjunction with the full range of systems of land use. In some areas, such as Michoacán, the blade of the coa was made of copper; in most instances, however, it was fashioned from hardwood (West and Augelli 1966: 233). The fact that the system was highly productive while the implements were simple in the extreme has very important implications for this analysis. For one thing, it is obvious that the technology was not implicit in the simple physical tools but was almost entirely in the form of knowledge.[3]

That we may fruitfully use our proposed analytical approach, some mention must be made of ceremonies and institutions of the time. The variety of institutions, even economic ones, and the attendant ceremonies were so extensive and complex that only a few will be mentioned here. I will, however, highlight that institutional aspect that has crucial importance for present-day Mexico: the traditional tenure system of ancient origin. "Throughout most of [preconquest] Mesoamerica, the landholding village was at once the basic unit of settlement and the principal form of land tenure" (West and Augelli 1966: 237). In central Mexico, where land was cultivated in permanent fields, each village was divided into wards, called *calpullis*. In turn, each calpulli had a tract of land from which agricultural plots were assigned to each family. Each family had a usufruct, which was as close as they came to a concept of individual ownership of land. It is a crucial point for this analysis that the ancient Mexicans did not have a Romanesque concept of private property (Rincón Serrano 1980: 22).[4]

A few general comments about the social structure will help to place the tillage and tenure systems in broader perspective. In describing Aztec society at the time of the conquest, Soustelle (1955: 37) says: "The Mexican community had become differentiated, complex and stratified: the different sections had widely differing functions, and the authority of the ruling dignitaries was very great. The priesthood [was] high in honor and importance. . . . Trade now dealt with a great volume of valuable merchandise, and the influence of the traders was increasing." Although the social structure was differentiated and stratified, "no impenetrable walls separated the classes and . . . the humblest life was not without its hope" (Soustelle 1955: 72). A common man (*maceualli*) had a right to a life interest in a plot, his children could go to the local school, he had a vote in local elections, and "if he were courageous and intelligent he could rise out of his class and become honored and wealthy" (Soustelle 1955: 70–71). When the Spaniards encountered the military chiefs and high administrators who attended the Aztec emperor, they believed them to be the equivalent of the hereditary nobility at the court of the king of Spain. That belief, based upon their European viewpoint, was clearly incorrect. Military leaders, administrators, and judges were chosen through a system that placed a high premium on merit. "The ruling class continually renewed itself, taking recruits from the general body of the people; and this was its great strength" (Soustelle 1955: 45–46). Contrarily, it was the Spanish system of inherited status and power that served to debilitate development in New Spain, a point that should become clear shortly.

Slavery existed, but it was not of the unremitting nature familiar to much of the rest of the world. Mexican slaves could own property, including slaves, could purchase their own freedom, and their children were born free.[5] Marriages among slaves and freeborn were not uncommon.

The important role of religion and, within that, the central role of human sacrifice are among the most widely studied aspects of Aztec society. The subject, of course, is extremely complex and is mentioned here only to enrich our picture of the broader society within which the technology and tenure systems in question were operated. Soustelle (1955: 94) says that "religion told [the Mexican] his duty, ruled his days, coloured his view of the universe and of his personal destiny." And yet, it was a religion flexible enough to incorporate into its pantheon the gods of other peoples with whom the Aztec had come into significant contact. That fact is eminently highlighted by the Aztec's expressed willingness to admit Jesus to their holy cadre.[6] One could say that such flexibility stood in stark contrast to the Spaniards' rigid, inquisitional adherence to their particular brand of monotheism. Of one thing we can be sure, given the sizes of the ruling and sacerdotal classes, and the splendor with which the official court and the religious ceremonies operated, large agricultural surpluses were required. A sizable portion of that surplus came from the nearby chinampas that were developed and operated by Aztec villagers.[7]

Agriculture in Colonial Mexico

At this point, three principles of the Veblen-Ayres-Street institutionalist approach concern us. The first principle holds that technological advance takes place through new combinations and recombinations of existing elements of technology; the second is that technological progress spreads in inverse proportion to institutional resistance; and third, the chances for new combinations are increased when a new frontier is penetrated. When a cultural frontier has been successfully penetrated by an alien society, the opportunities for technological advance may be particularly propitious, for two reasons: The power of local custom (ceremonial behavior) may become severely weakened; and the successful vanguard may be sufficiently far from its own centers of power and custom as to greatly lessen their impact. Thus, a frontier permissiveness allows the dynamism of technology greater rein, with technological synergism drawing upon both host society's and alien society's components. Street (1987a: 1884) put it thus: "A frontier is a region that offers the space for expansion of population in movement, for a rupture with old institutions, and for the application of techniques brought from other regions to achieve an accelerated rate of development. Given the increased cultural contact, and the special challenges posed by frontier conditions, new combinations and adaptations of useful knowledge are almost certain to occur."

Spaniards who came to Mexico brought with them new technologies, new varieties of animal and plant life, and new customs and beliefs. Among the new implements, of course, was the plow, and among the imported animals was the ox to pull it. It was a combination that was working wonders in European agriculture. Firearms, of course, constituted another imported technological advance. Furthermore, the temporal and religious authority within the Aztec Empire had been crushed by the conquest, which, ostensibly, should have severely reduced ceremonial resistance to change. At first blush, it might appear that we have a case before us for which we can predict flourishing economic progress based upon a spate of technological innovations.

The long colonial period in which the plow system of tillage largely replaced the chinampa, other systems of irrigation, and terraced fields would offer us a good test case only if we were to assume the plow to have been a technological advance. Unfortunately for the analyst, such a case would not be easy to make. It is said that even today on lands where either of the technologies could operate, hoe cultivation can produce about twice the output per hectare of plow cultivation (Wolf 1959: 198). The fact of the matter is that each of the competing systems has peculiar advantages and disadvantages.[8] The coa could not successfully work the relatively flat valley lands that featured fertile but heavy soils with a thick cover of heavily rooted grasses. It was in those conditions that the plow could make its mark. The coa, on the other hand, is particularly well adapted to the lighter soils and sparser vegetation of the slopes, the area where the plow is singularly destructive. Apparently, if the two systems could have been topographically restricted to the respective areas to which each was well suited, a productive agricultural economy might have been possible. Unfortunately, however, the triumph of Spanish institutions, albeit on the strength of military technology, carried with it the demise of indigenous technology as well as institutions. The result would include eventual plowing of the slopes and their destruction through soil erosion.

The decline of the highly productive indigenous systems can be attributed to circumstances other than direct competition with the plow, including population decline and the colonial style of urbanization in Mexico City. The drainage of Lake Texcoco is associated with the urban buildup of colonial Mexico and resulted in destruction of most of the chinampa plots.[9]

It was the escalating mortality rate, however, that caused early, rapid, and broad-based changes in both the tillage and tenure systems. Estimates of the population of Mexico on the eve of the conquest run between 10 million and 25 million persons (Frank 1979: 23–24). By the close of the sixteenth century, the indigenous population numbered about 2 million, their ranks having been largely decimated by the diseases that accompanied the invaders (West and Augelli 1966: 258). The problem was straightforward: There were not sufficient Indian farmers to produce surplus enough to sustain both the Spanish population and the Indians who were utilized in the mines and as servants, if the extant tribute system remained their major source of food and fiber. In the early colonial period, the redistribution system whereby a surplus was extracted to sustain the Spaniards and their Indian labor force was known as the *encomienda*. Strategically located villages were given "in trust" to individual, highly ranked Spaniards with the stipulation that each "trustee" support Christianization of the native population. In turn, he was owed a tax or tribute in the form of agricultural production. Quite literally, therefore, the decimation of the indigenous population threatened decimation of the incipient colonization project. Suddenly, labor was the scarce factor of production. At this new juncture, a labor-saving and land-extensive technology was called for, and the European plow was there to answer the call. Chevalier (1963: 60) tells us that in 1597 alone, twelve thousand plows were imported.

An ancillary problem contributed to the successful introduction of the plow. A major concern of the newly arrived Spaniards was the provision of wheat for the bread to which they were accustomed. Attempts were made to have the wheat grown by Indian villagers utilizing their traditional systems, but, "whether because of ignorance or disinclination, the crops obtained by the natives were in general quite poor" (Chevalier 1963: 51). Because of the strong demand for wheat and the niggardliness of supply, some of the conquerors turned to farming, not as tillers, but as owners and supervisors. New words for agricultural enterprise came into being: *estancias de labor* (plow land) and *estancias de pan llevar* (wheat land) (Chevalier 1963: 66). Some of those units formed the basis for the later development of the great haciendas. There was no shortage of good land and, given that the indigenous communities tended to avoid the heavy soils and grasses of the valleys, those especially fertile areas were open for these new institutional forms.

Although a number of Spaniards received land, all of them were disinclined to perform useful work upon it. That trait, which constrained the mobilization of an effective labor force, was based in the fact that, no matter what his station had been in the Old World, each New World Spaniard thought himself to have the qualities of nobility (Simpson 1962: 95–96). Consequently, throughout the colonial period, mobilization of a supply of labor would be the dominant problem for the Spaniard, and it is not surprising that he put a peculiarly ethnocentric interpretation on it. As would occur later with European colonists in Africa, the problem was viewed as rooted in the values and attitudes of the indigenous population. Specifically, the Indian was deemed to be without a work ethic. When we recall the New World Spaniard's imperative against the personal performance of useful work and reflect on the achievements of the ancient Mexican societies, the viceroy's words of 1594 may appear to some readers as incredible: "Inasmuch as Indians and work are natural enemies and they avoid it as far as possible, obviously not one would work if he were not forced to do so and all would be lost. The Indians will never work or hire themselves out, even ten percent of them, unless force is used" (quoted in Chevalier 1963: 67). That argument was made in an attempt to convince the Crown and clergy to desist in their efforts to establish a system in which the labor force would be "free to choose its own tasks and adequately recompensed in wages" (Gibson 1964: 223).[10] By that time, the encomienda system had degenerated to the point where excessive tribute was exacted in the forms of both produce and labor.

A compromise between the forces pushing for a relatively free labor market and those defending encomienda was the *repartimiento*, a system under which the colonial government was permitted to conscript labor for use on the estancias. This system was highly regulated and "followed the procedures of the indigenous coatequitl," or Aztec system of labor conscription (Gibson 1964: 227). Each of the subject villages was given a labor quota that village officials were responsible for delivering. Hours of work, distances traveled, and wages were subject to regulation. Wage payment represented an innovation in the Aztec system; in pre-Hispanic Aztec society labor outside of one's plot or household "had been prescribed and carefully regulated" (Gibson 1964: 220). In addition to work on their own properties, pre-Hispanic Indians performed periodic unrecompensed labor services on common properties and buildings. There is widespread evidence that such work was generally carried out with what appeared to be a sense of contribution, merriment, and sometimes great rejoicing. Where the Indians had appeared to derive special satisfaction from monotonous labor, the European view had been formed in societies where such work was considered onerous. It is not surprising, therefore, that the Spaniards created a work atmosphere in which the "Indian peoples lost the sense of joyous participation and adopted an attitude of resignation. Labor tended thus to move from the social, moral, and spiritual categories, in which the Aztecs had placed it, into the economic and physical categories of Europe" (Gibson 1964: 220–221). Putting it within the framework of institutional economics, it might be said that the labor institutions that were appropriate to Aztec technological and belief systems were not nearly as effective when put within the alien system of technology and beliefs.

Although the regulations undergirding repartimiento were designed to protect Indian workers, the system was widely abused. As demand for labor outpaced supply, the pressures for abuse increased. "Spaniards sequestered laborers, beat them, refused to pay them, seized their food and clothing to prevent escape," et cetera (Gibson 1964: 233). "Private payments, bribery, and fraud frustrated efforts to reform the system" (Gibson 1964: 235). Nevertheless, the official desire continued to be the creation of a system of wage labor in which the Indian would be a relatively free bargaining agent. In 1632, a viceregal order banned repartimiento, and tendencies that were already under way to promote wage labor were accelerated. Quickly, and not surprisingly, the system was subverted. Labor was attracted to rural estancias "by advancing sums that the Indians could never pay back" (Chevalier 1963: 69). By the seventeenth century, "serfdom through debt" had become the institutional foundation of the hacienda, and the system thus became the institutional form that encapsulated the plow technology and a new, hybrid set of ceremonies. The ceremonial structure featured a leisure class of Spanish lineage and an underclass of Indian and mestizo workers. Within a couple of generations the descendants of foot soldiers had become a new, landed gentry.

By the end of the colonial period, the population of Mexico had grown to between 6 and 7 million, still significantly lower than immediately prior to the conquest. The plow culture was then probably utilizing more land than had been required to feed and clothe the much larger preconquest population and, in the course of doing so, destroying the fertility of much of the soil: "In the late colonial period, when Indians and mestizos began to employ the plow on low slopes, sheet erosion and, finally, serious gullying of the soil ensued. The consequence is that extensive highland areas, from central Mexico into Central America, have been lost to agriculture" (West and Augelli 1966: 270–271). It will be recalled that the ancient hoe culture had been appropriate for the sloping terrain, preserving the integrity and fertility of the soil as well as producing more output per unit of land.[11]

New technologies had replaced the old, and new institutional forms had replaced the old. The force of the ancient beliefs had been broken, and even a new race of people, the mestizo or "mixed blood," was becoming important. Nevertheless, many scholars have remarked on the low levels of productivity of the hacienda system that had come to pass. Instead of the dynamic cultural frontier predicted by theory, in which new combinations of technologies would flourish, it appears that a less-sophisticated agricultural technology supplanted the highly productive technology of pre-Hispanic Mexico. However, an obvious explanation for the observed failure is found within the Veblen-Ayres-Street theory itself. Stagnation occurred because some ceremonial features were sufficiently change-resistant to overcome the dynamic potential inherent in the mix of technologies. A normal tendency might be to look first to the ceremonies of the host society. Thus, one might speculate, for example, that the Aztec institutional structure was the barrier to change. To do so, however, one would have to downplay the fact that the formal institutional structure of Aztec society and even the principal trappings were destroyed, and assume that a sufficient residue of the ceremonial system remained intact as to thwart the potential synergistic development of new technologies. Surely, however, there are few historical examples of equal destruction of the institutional structure. How much more of a weakening of the ceremonial grip would be required to permit "idle curiosity" to bring about "new combinations and recombinations" of the technological elements of the two cultures? Prudence suggests looking elsewhere for an answer.

An answer is found when we investigate the ceremonial and technologi-cal aspects of the institutions of the New World Spaniard. The Spaniard took with him to New Spain the seeds of the foods of his accustomed Iberian diet and the artifacts and knowledge composing the technology for cultivating them. In these and other aspects, the New World Spaniard sought to build a society that replicated that of the Old World, of which his was a political extension. A major aspect of the new society was different, however. The presence of a conquered people permitted and encouraged all Spaniards to assume the roles of persons of noble heritage, always valuing abstinence from physical work. We have, then, the phenomenon of a transcendent culture made up almost exclusively of persons who shun pursuits that would put them in intimate contact with the elements of technology. Moreover, those persons to whom most of the roles of useful work had devolved were denied access to education, credit, and social mobility, to the extent of being forbidden by law to own horses. It would have been surprising if technological advance had occurred in such a repressive cultural milieu. The villains, therefore, were not among the institutions of the Aztec, but rather among those of the Spaniard. Thus, the wheat, cattle, sheep, plow, and wheeled wagon all came to the New World to be used there in much the same way as in the Old World, for century after century, without undergoing significant technological innovation. The singularly prominent innovation was in the institutional artifact known as the hacienda and even that was not altogether dissimilar from the feudal manor.

While the colonial Mexican frontier does not furnish us with an example of progress as described by the Veblen-Ayres-Street paradigm, we have, almost in passing, touched upon such a case: the preconquest penetration by the semibarbaric Aztec of the relatively highly civilized regions of central Mexico, which occurred relatively late, during the fourteenth century. The established people of the lake region looked upon the invading warriors "with the contempt of the civilized for the barbarian," referring derisively to the Aztec as "Chichimec from Aztlán" (Wolf 1959: 130). The established people of Middle America had built their civilization upon a long series of technological advances, the most important being the discovery of the maize seed and its subsequent improvement from a wild grass to a prolific centerpiece of an advanced horticulture system.[12] That endeavor, according to Simpson (1962: 12) "was one of the most important achievements of mankind anywhere." And it was only one of many technological accomplishments. Simpson (1962: 12–13) tells us further:

> The intelligent people of Middle America discovered and invented many valuable things. They took the small bitter seeds of a species of lupine and from them developed the infinite varieties of beans that we know. A small wild squash under their patient hands became a pumpkin. A morning glory with a thick root was metamorphosed into the sweet potato. The "Irish" potato, tobacco, "Sea Island" cotton and the ordinary "Egyptian" cotton, . . . a great many useful herbs, the fibers of the maguey and henequen, cochineal, a native indigo and Tyrian purple, and the techniques of cultivation and manufacture of all these things, were Indian discoveries and inventions.

The agrarian economies of Mesoamerica had been millennia in developing prior to the invasion of the "barbarian" Aztecs of the north. What transpired was not the destruction of the extant culture, but the flowering of a new and vibrant one. Out of this cultural penetration arose a dynamic fusion. The great city of Tenochtitlán that awaited Cortés was the apex of that dynamism; the city's markets displayed the agricultural surpluses and the extensive manufactures of the advanced craft industries he described (Wolf 1959: 140). Horticultural expertise was taken to its apex in the chinampa system, itself based upon a sophisticated system of dams, locks, and dikes for controlling the waters. Both public administration and commerce developed into more complex and efficient systems after the arrival of the Aztec. The results were lacustrian cities featuring architecture, administration, municipal services, and levels of consumption that struck the invading Europeans as marvelous. Clearly, this was an Ayresian example of progress under frontier conditions.

With the colonial period, however, we have a case in which intercultural and intercontinental technology transfer resulted in destruction of indigenous technological capacity and its replacement by an imported technology so encapsulated in a pernicious ceremonial system that any latent progressive potential was nullified. We now have some substance for an answer to Street's proposed quest for "reasons for the disappearance in the colonial period of the native innovative spirit characteristic of the Aztec."

The Postindependence Period

The three-quarters of a century following independence in 1821 saw an acceleration of trends that had been at work throughout the colonial period. By the turn of this century, the decadent, inefficient hacienda system stood transcendent, with some eight thousand such units accounting for 40 percent of the land surface of Mexico. Silva Herzog (1952) reports that 840 of these could be classified as true haciendas in the sense that several of their major features paralleled aspects of the self-contained feudal manor. Ninety-six percent of rural families had no land in 1910, and most of them were virtual serfs on the large estates (West and Augelli 1966: 312). This last surge in growth of that technologically backward system was the result of a misguided attempt to transplant foreign institutions to Mexican soil. The alien institution was the family farm, based upon the Roman concept of private property or ownership in fee simple. The language used to justify this attempted transformation of the remaining communally owned villages into private properties was that of economic liberalism. The ostensible aim was to create a Mesoamerican yeomanry, a sturdy class of independent property holders, in the image of the English and French revolutions (Wolf 1959:

246). As a centerpiece of the reform, the elimination of communal properties and ecclesiastical holdings was supported by the Constitution of 1857. Subsequently, when titles for the land they had traditionally worked were given to villagers who had no cultural basis for a concept of property ownership, the "pieces of paper" were often purchased by unscrupulous hacendados to add to their already large holdings. Equally unscrupulous judges ruled against those villages protesting the outright usurpation of their lands. Where king and church had once acted to weaken the voracious tendencies of landed whites, in independent Mexico no such bulwark stood between the villages and that insatiable appetite for land and labor. Furthermore, the church, now defenseless, was, in essence, coerced into contributing its considerable properties to the hacendados. Thus, the attempt to modernize rural Mexico by placing land in a market system had the perverse result of greatly strengthening the forces of backwardness. More land was usurped by haciendas during the nineteenth century than during the entire colonial period.

The haciendas were large, rarely smaller than a thousand hectares and usually much larger. Most of them were self-sufficient, earning handsome returns from marketed output in times of economic boom and, in times of depression, turning inward to provide for the subsistence of both owner and worker. Under the hacienda system, much of the arable land was left uncultivated "because [ownership] was based as much on social prestige as on economic production" (West and Augelli 1966: 312). The system and its results were described by Cole and Sanders (1970: 16–17):

> The hacienda was an inefficient economic unit, and in organizing human resources and encouraging the growth of individual talents it failed miserably. The hacienda was characterized by absentee ownership with the owner [often] residing in the capital city or Europe. Production techniques were inefficient; traditional methods of cultivation were used with the same kinds of seeds used for the same crops year after year; the large work force was under utilized and inefficiently directed. Little or no effort was made to exploit new opportunities in technology or crops, and vast areas of the estates were allowed to lie unused.

The degree of inefficiency was such that maize and other cereal grains had to be imported during the years preceding the revolution.

In the vernacular of institutional economics, the entire period from 1821 to 1910, between independence and the revolution, could be characterized as one in which no significant technological advance took place in the agricultural sector. The changes were in the institutional structure and had to do with social stratification (invidious comparison). In the clash of institutions, those of the Spaniard finally won complete victory over those of the Aztec. That victory carried with it the demise of the remaining vestiges of a technology and social system that had once produced a surplus to support a huge population living in a complex civilization. Not only was the victorious technology less productive, it had become intertwined with a value and belief system that thwarted change.

The Revolution and Beyond

There is no doubt that the deplorable agrarian conditions played a decisive role in the revolution that began in 1910. Significantly, the revolutionary armies of Emiliano Zapata and Pancho Villa were largely composed of dispossessed peasants. "Land for the landless" became a major goal of the revolution, and its fulfillment was augured in Article 27 of the Constitution of 1917, which provided the legal foundation for land reform. The principal vehicle of reform became known as the ejido system. The term *ejido* refers to a system whereby villages hold lands in common, with ownership devolving upon a population center. The governing body of that center divides the arable land into parcels, with the usufruct for a parcel given to each of the heads of household in the village. The reader may be struck by the similarity of the ejido system to a system of Aztec origin. In fact, the ejido system represents an intentional attempt to emulate features of the calpulli. The term *ejido* has a Spanish derivation, having been the word used for the untilled common lands of Spanish villages (Rincón Serrano 1980: 21), but the central feature of the "new" tenure system—common ownership with individual usufruct—was definitely of ancient Mexican origin.[13] The return to the communal tenure system of the precolonial period was motivated by a desire to insure that peasants' land could never again be taken from them by powerful and/or unscrupulous persons. There seems little doubt that had reform been based upon the conferring of titles in fee simple, the incidence of landless labor would have reasserted itself as the dominant feature of agriculture in less than a generation.

The desire for land was so overwhelming that some type of land reform was undoubtedly a necessary condition for the creation of political stability. Furthermore, at the time of the constitutional convention and during the years immediately following the revolution, it was expected that the reform could be carried out by expropriating idle lands from the haciendas and large estates, "leaving their owners' genuine agricultural activities virtually untouched" (Lamartine Yates 1981: 142). By combining landless labor with idle land, an increment to total rural output was assumed to be inevitable.

In addition to the major changes in land tenure that were taking place, equally important technological changes were in the making. "[Movements toward] technical change began about 1930, involving the introduction of modern European and North American techniques, such as large-scale irrigation, mechanization, the use of commercial fertilizers, and the planting of improved crop strains" (West and Augelli 1966: 312). These were to be the first major technological changes since the dubious introduction of the Spanish technical artifacts. Moreover, President Lázaro Cárdenas (1934–1940) took measures to orient the technical change toward the ejido sector.

As a part of Cárdenas's agrarian reform, other measures were taken to complement the distribution of land to the landless. For example, the National Ejidal Credit Bank (BNCE) was established in 1935 to provide the *ejidatarios*[14] access to the credit needed to make their plots productive. The ejido tenure system served to make the individual ejidatarios ineligible for loans from private banks. The land, being imprescriptible, could not serve as collateral for loans.[15] As a part of the new banking system, experts and facilities were included to provide technical assistance to those ejido villagers who were awarded credit (Mogab 1984: 205). Credit, technical assistance, and the incentives implicit in the usufruct were thought to constitute the ingredients of genuine agrarian reform. Success would require overcoming the vast technological ignorance that resulted from centuries of rural stagnation. In other words, it would have entailed nothing short of a reversal of the process of underdevelopment that had been under way for centuries, a truly monumental task. The massive and persistent effort that would have been required never materialized.

The Mexican Miracle

In the 1940s, following a change of presidents, the nation's development strategy was shifted to a new vector, bringing with it crucial changes in the official approach to the agricultural sector. Modernization became the overall theme and industrialization became the lever for accomplishing that goal. Henceforth, agriculture would be expected to play an important but secondary, instrumental role. The urban growth implied by the industrialization goals meant that the agricultural sector would have to produce a steadily growing surplus. Prospective food shortages could be expected to cause prices to spiral and food imports to mushroom, either response being inimical to industrial progress. Furthermore, in its support role, agriculture, or at least a portion thereof, would have to modernize. Sufficiently rapid growth of food and fiber output, it was reasonably assumed, could not be expected as an automatic market response from illiterate smallholders utilizing traditional techniques on unimproved lands.

The succeeding two decades of growth in agricultural production have often been characterized as a "miracle." Between 1940 and 1959, agricultural production more than tripled; at 1950 prices, agricultural crop output was 2,739 million pesos in 1940 and 8,700 million pesos in 1959 (Cole and Sanders 1970: i). Livestock production almost doubled during that same period, rising from 1,526 million (1950) pesos in 1940 to 2,888 million in 1959. The average annual rate of growth of crop production between 1942 and 1964 was 5.1 percent, with the comparable rate for livestock production being 3.6 percent (Hewitt de Alcántara 1978: 100). Furthermore, that growth was accomplished while the agricultural labor force was declining in relative importance. Where, in 1930, some 68 percent of the labor force was in primary activities (agriculture, livestock, fishing, and forestry), that proportion had declined to 54 percent by 1960 (Nacional Financiera 1966: 46). This latter fact suggests the increasing use of labor in industrial activities, an accomplishment in keeping with the strategy of modernization through industrialization. Industries and urban centers were growing apace and the agriculture sector was succeeding in its support role.

Land reform was not abandoned, but its importance was downgraded. Between 1940 and 1970, there was a redistribution of 19 million hectares of land of decidedly poorer quality than that distributed under previous stages of the reform (Esteva 1983: 341). The revolutionary rhetoric about land reform continued, but agricultural progress was the result of two major technological developments: irrigation and the improved seed varieties of the green revolution. Crucially, these two developments were concentrated in northern Mexico. Important points of note are that that region was sparsely populated and represented something of a cultural melting pot because of its location along the border between Mexico and the United States. Thus, the northern deserts provided land where water could produce fertile soils with seemingly magical swiftness. And, importantly, on those lands productivity would not be hobbled by millions of illiterate holders of small ejido plots. It was both an internal frontier in the sense used by Street and a cultural frontier according to Ayres's usage.[16] In other words, technological change could thrive.

As we have seen, Mexicans have been preoccupied with water since pre-Columbian times. The country's northern reaches are inhospitable deserts, the mountainous regions feature rapid runoff that promotes erosion, and the lowlands are often swampy and tend to flood. It is not surprising, therefore, that the ancient Mexicans developed considerable expertise in the arena of hydraulic resources. However, between the period of conquest and the twentieth century only a few works were constructed, and those by missionaries and private individuals (Greenberg 1970: 10). For practical purposes, that expertise gained over centuries prior to the conquest had been lost. By 1940, however, much of the lost ground had been regained, largely on the basis of imported technological know-how.

The first steps were taken on the road back to technological competence in irrigation when, in 1908, the dictator Porfirio Díaz spent 35 million pesos on improvement of irrigation and, in 1913, the National Agricultural School introduced training in the principles of irrigation (Greenberg 1970: 10). The thrust of that incipient renewal of interest in irrigation was interrupted by the revolution (1910–1917). After a measure of political stability had been restored, the Bureau of Irrigation was created in 1921 as a dependency of the Ministry of Agriculture; it mainly engaged in organizational work and resource inventory before being succeeded by the National Irrigation Commission in 1926 (Orive Alba 1970: 62–63).

The young Mexican engineers who staffed the National Irrigation Commission were generally well trained, usually in the United States. In the early stages of the commission's work, highly qualified engineers from the United States were hired on a fixed-term basis to work on the Mexican projects, with the young Mexican engineers serving initially as apprentices (Orive Alba 1970: 71–72). The training undergone by the Mexicans focused on the technology of large dams in relatively arid regions; also, that was the area of expertise of the expatriate senior engineers.[17] During the 1930s, the commission gained significant experience in the construction of irrigation works so that, by the advent of the new development strategy of the 1940s, it was ready to play its key role. Indeed, its staff developed an enviable reputation for professionalism, an accomplishment that stands as a model for the successful international transfer of technical knowledge.

In 1946, the commission's status was elevated to the cabinet level as the Ministry of Hydraulic Resources. If we properly view that ministry's reservoir of knowledge and experience as Mexico's technological capability in irrigation, it should not come as a surprise when we see that the bulk of postwar efforts would be on large-scale irrigation projects in the desert regions of northern Mexico.[18] In a basic sense, the decision to focus on the north was strongly influenced by the nature of the technology that had been transferred to Mexico two decades earlier.

The fact that about 90 percent of Mexico's arable surface requires irrigation if it is to be used efficiently (Kolbeck 1967) would appear to imply that irrigation expenditures could have been utilized effectively almost anywhere in the country; it is therefore a matter of great consequence that most of the investment in irrigation went to the northern states. For example, during the three presidential terms covering the period 1941 through 1958, 45 percent of expenditures for new irrigation construction were concentrated in only three states: Baja California; Sinaloa; and Sonora. Significantly, only about 6 percent of the nation's population resided in those states in 1960, and they accounted for only 6 percent of the agricultural labor force (Secretaría de Industria y Comercio 1964: Table 25). Not only did the bulk of the population reside elsewhere, more than 95 percent of the ejido farmers were also found elsewhere (Secretaría de Industria y Comercio 1964: Table 27).

For the other technological component of Mexico's agricultural development strategy, there was very little indigenous expertise. In 1940, Mexico had to import maize just as it had been forced to do in every previous year of this century. Wheat was also imported. In the land where in ancient times maize had been turned from a wild seed into a prolific and nutritious staple, yield was currently only eight bushels per acre. In the United States, at that time, the yield was four times as great on the average, and one hundred bushels per acre was not uncommon (Stakman, Bradfield, and Mangelsdorf 1967: 56). Not believing that the extant situation with staples could sustain an industrialization policy, the government moved to import a technological solution. The Rockefeller Foundation was recruited by the Mexican government to cooperate in a program that enabled a number of U.S. agricultural specialists to work with a small number of Mexican agricultural experts to improve seeds and techniques for the production of maize and wheat. Known later as the green revolution, the work of this group followed the techniques developed in the 1930s in Iowa and other parts of the midwestern Corn Belt. After much experimentation, several hybrid maize seeds and synthetics were developed and a rust-resistant wheat strain was perfected.

The varieties that were developed were appropriate for the newly irrigated land of the north—they required ample water at carefully regulated intervals as well as a package of chemical inputs that necessitated measured and timely application. Theoretically, it would have been possible to concentrate upon producing varieties with other prominent characteristics—for example, drought- or disease-resistance. Surely, one factor that influenced the choice of varietal types was the previous experience of the group of imported experts. That experience, of course, was imbedded in their fund of knowledge. That maize could be grown on irrigated land in the north with similar chemicals and mechanization as in Iowa, and wheat grown with techniques similar to those used in Kansas, was surely no coincidence. For one thing, the fact that average farm size was much larger in the north augured well for mechanization.

Other factors must also have helped push the Mexican government in the direction of a northern strategy. The amount of infrastructural resources that would be required was less in the north; to concentrate resources in central and southern Mexico where the millions of ejidatarios with their small plots were concentrated would have been very costly. The necessary roads, credit facilities, and marketing facilities would have been difficult to provide and would have constituted a high opportunity cost to the industrialization strategy. It should not be surprising, then, that most of the agricultural credit also shifted to the northern states. Moreover, other aspects of agricultural development, such as extension services, were disproportionately provided in the north. It was on the basis of that concentration of resources that Mexican agricultural production grew for almost two decades at unprecedented rates. Irrigation allowed new land to come under cropping, the improved varieties provided for significantly larger than average output per hectare, and government subsidies helped to finance the affair.[19]

Largely on the basis of developments in the north, Mexico's maize acreage increased by some 45 percent and wheat acreage by about 72 percent between 1944–1948 and 1959–1963 (Cole and Sanders 1970: 78–80). Respective yield increases were 27 percent for maize and 53 percent for wheat. The fact that these are national averages masks the remarkable nature of the results realized in the north from the technological change, especially in the case of maize.[20] While Mexico's wheat production had traditionally concentrated in the north, maize was grown in every corner of every state.

The miracle had a dark side, however. It has been shown that the purchasing-power value of the output (output adjusted by the domestic terms of trade) of small-scale ejido farmers fell between 1940 and 1950, whereas that of large-scale, modern farmers grew by more than 200 percent (Cole and Sanders 1974: 37). Furthermore, it was the success of the farmers of the modern sector that helped to depress the prospects of subsistence sector farmers. A fair critique of postwar agricultural performance up to 1965 would find that industrialization and urbanization were well supported by an abundance of output at reasonable prices. The main group that did not share in the successes of the strategy were the small-scale farmers, largely ejidatarios, who made up the bulk of the agricultural labor force.

Agricultural Problems After the Miracle

Comparative production data for the period 1965–1970 are instructive. The real value of agricultural crop production grew at an average annual rate of only 1.2 percent as compared to an annual population growth rate of more than 3 percent. On the other hand, livestock production grew at an average annual rate of 5.6 percent over the same period. Measured in terms of crop production, the miracle was over, and its demise reflects two important factors: First, the country had run short of "free land" that could be made magically fertile by turning the irrigation tap; second, some land that had been used for staple crops was being turned to cattle production. Henceforth, growth of total agricultural output would have to depend largely upon increases in yield. Furthermore, given that many farms in the modern sector were pushing their technological frontiers, the yield increases would necessarily have to come from technological improvements in the backward ejido sector.

By 1970, almost half of all agricultural land was held by ejidos and almost two-thirds of all farm families were classified as belonging to ejidos. Most of the ejido lands were created in the central and southern regions where population densities are very heavy. Poverty-stricken and often illiterate, a majority of the peasants receiving use rights to a plot had neither the knowledge nor the capital to allow them to utilize modern technology. They were left with the seeds and techniques that had become their tradition with the imposition of the colonial plow culture.[21] Given the overwhelming ignorance of modern technological alternatives and the high levels of illiteracy, the prospects for market-induced technological progress have never been bright.

The situation was not viewed as hopeless, however. A sizable minority of ejidatarios were motivated to change and sufficiently literate to assimilate new technology. They faced daunting institutional barriers, however. The output of the individual ejidatario is limited by the size of the land input and by the yield. While ejido land cannot be legally rented, an ejidatario could theoretically rent private land in order to expand holdings. In practice, however, no such land is available in the vicinity of most ejidatarios. The ability to increase output is therefore limited to yield. Moreover, most sources of yield increase require capital improvements; for example, to be able to use improved seeds would likely require some expenditure on irrigation, either a tube well or some conduit connecting to a larger system. However, because the ejidatario does not own the land, such expenditure cannot be recouped if he or, after inheritance, his children should quit the land. Furthermore, certain capital improvements as well as most forms of mechanization require, to be efficient, more land than that encompassed by the average ejido plot. Finally, as previously mentioned, the fact that the plots are imprescriptible has made it impossible for ejidatarios to obtain private credit to finance improvements. That same fact has made it difficult for public credit institutions to collect loans made to ejido credit societies, which, in turn, has debilitated that national effort (Fernández y Fernández 1959).[22]

The postmiracle period has been marked by several attempts to overcome the peculiar problems of the ejido and increase yields in that strategic component of the agriculture sector. During the presidency of Luis Echeverría, a sizable number of projects were developed that centered upon collectivization of ejidos. The principal objective was to agglomerate parcels so that improved seed varieties, water management, and mechanization would be economically feasible. Technically, individuals still retained usufruct title, but land was farmed as a conglomerate. In order to assure adequate technical expertise, the relevant banks supervised the operation of the projects. And, to insure the participation of the individual ejidatarios, a daily wage was paid for work performed, with the *pueblo ejido* family heads sharing in any profits resulting from the operations. Barkin (1980: 264), investigating a major example of these schemes, says that the Plan Chontalpa in no way justified the huge investment made in it. He argues that the system of wage payments and outside decisionmaking turned the ejidatarios from agriculturalists into a proletariat (1980: 268). At the bottom (*eslabón más bajo*) of a "top down" decisionmaking system, the ejidatarios had little role other than carrying out assigned tasks. If technology is largely composed of knowledge, there was little chance of effective technology transfer. Reporting broadly on the several hundred collectives that were created, Lamartine Yates (1981: 238–399) says that "in the worst . . . income fell below what individual ejidatarios had obtained when on their own, in the best it marginally improved on their previous performance."[23]

Possibly the most interesting of all of these experiments were several attempts to combine the ancient chinampa technology with the ejido system. In the Veblen-Ayres-Street paradigm this might be seen as the combination of an ancient ceremonial form and ancient technology into a single, present-day institution. Obviously, we should keep in mind that the communal tenure system of the calpulli was only one aspect of a very complex society. The ejido-chinampa projects had financial backing from the Mexican government and the World Bank, and the early stages of the efforts were reported by Gómez-Pompa and associates (1982) who, at the time of their report, were hopeful of success for those ventures.

Technicians who have studied both the ancient chinampa and current vestiges of that system, together with modern agronomic engineers, helped to design systems ostensibly appropriate to the lowland tropics. Machinery was used to remove rain forest cover and to create raised fields surrounded by permanently circulating irrigation water; the ejidatarios were taught to grow cash crops that were exotic to them; labor was organized in collective fashion for the same reasons as given above.[24] Later, Chapin (1988: 15) reported that nowhere in Mexico has the attempt to transfer chinampa technology been successful. The reasons for lack of success were many, including inappropriate tools, inappropriate plant varieties, and lack of knowledge. More important than all else, however, was the fact that the ejidatarios failed to cooperate with the supervisors of the systems. The technicians had "overlooked the wider social, economic, and political context in which the farmer lived, and therefore had no notion of how their model might adapt within that context" (15).

Speaking of the chinampa technology of pre-Hispanic times, Chapin (1988: 16) gives us what could be the preface to a Veblen-Ayres-Street explanation of the institutional setting of the time. "In Pre-Hispanic times, the chinampa system thrived in the Valley of Mexico because the social, political, economic, and environmental circumstances were favorable." At this point it will be instructive to recall Ayres's argument that technology and ceremonies are inextricably intertwined. In other words, in practice one can never find an example of pure ceremony or pure technology.[25] Calpulli and chinampa were not, in and of themselves, ceremonial and technological systems of the Aztec; each was some of both. While calpulli and chinampa were undoubtedly interacting companion parts of the agricultural society of the Aztecs, they both were integral and essentially indivisible components of a larger sociopolitical mosaic. When the modern variants of calpulli and chinampa were combined as the organizational forms for selected pilot projects, the complexity of the question of institutional appropriateness was undoubtedly not fully appreciated; otherwise, the failure of the attempted intertemporal transfer of institutional components would have been anticipated.

Policy Implications of the Institutionalist Analysis

Over the past several decades many analysts and policymakers have sought for a means to improve the productivity of the ejido system and the well-being of the ejidatarios. Does this analysis not suggest, however, that the central problem may lie with the ejido form itself? Historic memory of the rapid concentration of rural ownership following the privatization of property in the last century has, for many, made this an unthinkable conclusion.[26]

If, as the case appears, agricultural progress depends upon improved yields on lands now occupied by ejidos; if technology is fundamentally based in knowledge; and if rapid, effective dissemination of modern knowledge requires a literate population, the implications are awesome. If widespread improvement is to come from the ejido sector within the next decade or so, globally unprecedented levels of investment in adult education would be required. Given that previous governments have shied away from facing the opportunity costs of developing the ejidos, even in good times, would it be reasonable to expect the present government to make such a stand while grappling with the current, severe fiscal crisis? Beyond that, however, it should be noted that the present analysis would call into question the ability of such a policy to succeed. For one thing, we would have to recognize that literacy would also function as a carrier of the dominant and emerging values of the more-modern and more-articulate elements of society. It might therefore be unrealistic to expect that an educated rural community would nurture a communal mentality within the broader framework of a society whose modernizing urban sectors extol the values of private property and individual initiative. If we put the matter in the context of Neale's (1987: 1178) statement that "most of what people do is governed by the institutions of their society," we see the ejidatario caught between conflicting value systems.

More broadly, however, it could be expected that the debilitating aspects of the ejido system would serve to thwart the introduction of modern agronomic techniques regardless of the level of investment in education. The imprescriptibility of the land severely circumscribes the possibilities of establishing an effective formal sector credit system.[27] For most individual ejidatarios, it also removes the possibility that plot size can be increased by purchasing or renting additional land to take advantage of scale economies.

And, in any event, the absence of ownership weakens the incentive to make capital improvements.

It may therefore be a propitious time to concede that the intertemporal transfer of the ejido as an institutional form has not succeeded. While it may, at one time, have been instrumental in preventing the renaissance of the inefficient and detested hacienda system, it is apparently an inappropriate component for the complex set of institutions that make up modern Mexico. It seems obvious that the conversion of ejido plots to private properties would overcome many of the bottlenecks to progress. Such a scheme would constitute a unique form of privatization, simultaneously representing a variant of classical land reform that is characterized by the slogan "Land to the tiller." While undoubtedly some ejido land would be purchased by private farms currently in the modern sector, it could be expected that the dynamic units of the present ejido sector would also expand, once credit and additional land became available. In both cases, prospective increases in yield would boost national output.

An agricultural system based upon private smallholders would require strong public programs to support improvements in yield. The need would be especially strong in the areas of research and extension. Furthermore, the expected improvements in yield would redound to the benefit of most of the poor in Mexico, not just those who remain as landholders. National self-sufficiency in agriculture would stabilize food prices and free a sizable amount of foreign exchange for the importation of capital goods. The resultant rising incomes in agriculture would redound to increased demand for consumer and producer goods. All of this would serve to promote employment opportunities, and rising government revenues could support investment in education and medical care, for example. In other words, it is not necessary to see supporters of the suggested change as working against the interests of the poorest of the campesinos. To use a metaphor of John Kennedy, "A rising tide lifts all boats."

Any fears that giving ownership to the tiller would lead to new waves of urban-bound migration are probably unfounded. It should first be acknowledged that most of the rural-urban migration streams of past decades have originated in the regions with the largest concentrations of ejido populations. Moreover, a major factor influencing that movement has been the paucity of rural employment opportunities. It is therefore entirely possible that an agricultural sector that has been invigorated by investment would employ more persons than it presently does. Employment could be directly in agriculture or in ancillary activities; in any case, there are no grounds for thinking that employment would decline.

Surely, it is not credible to think that the ejidatarios themselves present a fundamental obstacle to the conversion of each usufruct to a title in fee simple, an act that would immediately increase each one's personal wealth.

The major obstacle is the fact that the dominant political party, the Partido Revolucionario Institucional (PRI), has maintained an elaborate institutional structure that has traditionally helped it to capture the support of most ejidatarios at the ballot box. The many levels of offices of power and prestige within that structure provide the ceremonial resistance to change. There is evidence, however, that in the recent elections ejido support for the PRI was considerably weakened. If the PRI hopes to recapture that support, something progressive will have to be done in the ejido sector, and, as we have seen, options are limited.[28]

Possible privatization of the ejido sector should proceed at a measured pace, starting in ejidos where progressive potential is known to exist, with results there serving to enlighten others. If it were tried on a wholesale basis at the outset, the results could be disastrous. The likelihood is that speculative urban investment would quickly move into the rural land market and mop up much of the potential return on productive agricultural investment. There would also be the danger that some private holdings would become extremely large, with some of those being owned by foreign corporations. This suggests the possibility of legislated controls that might, for example, restrict investment to persons or firms already engaged in productive agriculture, and the establishment and enforcement of reasonable upper limits on the size of private agricultural holdings. In short, a successful shift to private smallholder agriculture could not take place on the basis of fiat alone; rather, it would require far-sighted legislation and careful administration.

Notes

1. What we have is analogous to the concept *international technology transfer*, but that phrasing is inappropriate in this case because of the colonial status of New Spain at the time of the transfer. Furthermore, "intercultural" is more reflective of the analytical content of the paradigm I will be using.

2. Although the term *ejido* has its origins in Spanish property law, Mexican reference is to the postrevolutionary creation of a system of use rights in lieu of ownership in fee simple. The system is largely patterned on the system of village ownership featured in the Aztec and Mayan empires. One subsidiary feature of the current system—availability of some common grazing land—does reflect Spanish origins.

3. To some significant degree, the technology was implicit in the physical structure of the chinampa beds themselves.

4. There were other types of tenure arrangements in ancient Mexico besides that of the landholding village (Rincón Serrano 1980: 22). Certain lands were set aside to provide maintenance for the royal family and palace staff; other lands supported the religious orders; and still other lands were dedicated to the support of the army in times of war. Finally, there were patrimonial lands of the emperor and noble families.

5. For a thorough discussion of societal change in the various indigenous societies over the long preconquest period, the work by Sanders, Parsons, and Santley (1979) is recommended, especially the chapter titled "The Village and Institutional Evolution."

6. Possibly, the Aztec felt an affinity for some of the more bizarre aspects of the religion of the invaders. The sacrifice of deity by deity central to Christian doctrine (John 3:16) and the ritual cannibalism implicit in aspects of the Roman Catholic mass are cases in point.

7. Part of the surplus came in the form of tribute extracted from other societies in central Mexico that had been subjected to the Aztec and that often utilized irrigation and/or terrace tillage systems. In both cases, the ability to produce a surplus is an indicator of the productivity of the technology utilized.

8. The indigenous Mexican systems of tillage were well adapted to the horticulture practiced by Indian farmers, whereas plow culture fit with the single-crop system of the Europeans. Regarding the indigenous system, "not only were maize, beans, and squash raised together; but a few tomato, chile and amaranth plants, and perhaps one or two fruit trees were scattered about" (West and Augelli 1966: 233). This type of horticulture was practiced on terraced slopes, in irrigated fields, and in chinampas. In less densely populated areas outside of central Mexico, a similar horticulture was practiced together with the slash and burn system.

9. This process was slow but steady. As late as the turn of this century, some boats were still bringing produce to market in Mexico City through the remains of ancient canals.

10. The official effort to create a relatively free labor market was apparently fueled more by a humanitarian desire to protect the indigenous peoples than by a need to promote economic efficiency.

11. Agricultural technology other than the plow also made its way to Mexico. The sugar mill is one such and it made its mark: Its voracious appetite for cane speeded the introduction of the plow, and the need for indigenous labor put further strains upon the traditional Indian villages. The introduction of beef and dairy cattle, too, and the attendant technologies for their care, had significant impact. Space, however, requires that I limit the thrust of this chapter to the impact of the plow culture.

12. Evidence from archeological and geological excavations indicates that maize has been cultivated in Mexico for at least five thousand years.

13. There are many aspects of community organization spelled out in the Constitution and subsequent enabling legislation, among them provisions for village governance, the creation of cooperative societies for credit, marketing, and so forth, the provision of land for schools, and the provision of common land for livestock. This last aspect had its origins in the Spanish ejido, or common land provided for each community.

14. The term *ejidatario* refers to the individual recipient of a usufruct for a plot of land within a pueblo ejido.

15. Earlier, in 1926, the National Agricultural Credit Bank (Banco Nacional de Crédito Agrícola y Ganadero) had been established to provide credit for ejidos and small private farmers. That bank, however, was reluctant to make funds available to smallholders of either variety, preferring to deal with the more creditworthy owners of large farms and ranches (Cole and Sanders 1974: 33).

16. Street (1977) was using "frontier" in the sense of unutilized national lands that could be opened to settlement on the basis of infrastructural

expenditures; the Amazon Basin was an example he used. Ayres (1962: 19–20), on the other hand, appeared to concentrate on the penetration of one culture by another to an extent that the rigidity of ceremonial systems is loosened in both.

17. This information came by way of oral communication from Adolfo Orive Alba, who was himself one of the early trainees and later became the minister of hydraulic resources during the crucial period of the 1940s.

18. Over time, the Ministry of Hydraulic Resources developed some significant expertise in small-scale irrigation, but its relative impact has been much less important than that of the large-scale projects. Expenditures to make desert lands fertile would redound to the benefit of very few ejidatarios.

19. A major subsidy was in the form of irrigation water provided at a small fraction of cost.

20. In 1977, Street (44) commented that "the transfer of genetic science . . . brought the Green Revolution to Mexico [with the result that] Mexico presents an outstanding exception to the general stagnation of agricultural development in Latin America."

21. Except for a few surviving anachronisms, the only viable ancient tillage system still in use was slash and burn, found largely in the tropical lowlands where vegetation grew quickly and population density was relatively sparse. It was not viable for most ejido settings, where, on average, plots were too small to permit sufficient fallow periods to maintain soil fertility.

22. The BNCE does not loan to individuals, but to credit societies that, in effect, are cooperative societies made up of the ejidatarios of a particular pueblo ejido. Even in this case, there is still no provision for securing loans with property. A large portion of pueblos ejidos have not organized such societies, and many that did so abandoned them because of mistrust that developed among members. Without the risk of loss of land, the incentive for repayment is considerably weakened and the intentions of hardworking ejidatarios are thwarted by the indolence of some.

23. Where there was an improvement, underemployment or unemployment resulted. However, because the managing technicians could not discharge surplus personnel, net returns had to be shared among workers and nonworkers in the collective village.

24. Chapin (1988: 13) says that pre-Hispanic Indians were thought by modern-day chinampa designers to have worked communally, which helped to confirm in their minds that such a system of labor would be appropriate today, if combined with chinampa. He points out, however (15), that such an interpretation was incorrect because families worked individual plots prior to the conquest. Chapin is correct in reference to the direct labor on crops; however, as described earlier in this chapter, all households did furnish labor for communal projects, such as roads, dikes, and canals. This latter aspect may have led recent planners to give undue emphasis to collective labor.

25. The conceptual tools "technology" and "ceremony" are themselves parts of an inextricable fusion of historical, social, political, and scientific phenomena. Even the terms *calpulli* and *chinampa* are unreal or artificial divisions of a complex totality, itself known artificially as the Aztec society.

26. Lamartine Yates (1981) is one analyst who has been openly critical of the ejido system. Earlier, Plutarco Elías Calles, postrevolution president, said that "the happiness of countrymen does not lie in a plot of land, if they do not have the necessary skills or tools to cultivate it. In this way we are

only leading them towards disaster by creating false hopes and encouraging their sloth" (Esteva 1983: 39).

27. In 1982, President López Portillo nationalized the private banking system. Even if the banking system is mobilized to provide massive credit to the ejidos, which it does not now do, we have seen that the nature of the ejido organization tends to work against accountability and repayment (as in the case of the BNCE).

28. The agrarian or campesino sector has official representation within the party, with an organizational hierarchy that stretches from the office of the presidency through state-level organizations right down to the level of the village. It is the membership of this hierarchy that stands to lose positions of power and prestige and who would therefore resist the proposed conversion. This hierarchy might be co-opted by keeping it in place to serve as a political network for the remaining small-scale farmers in the private sector. The possibility, not altogether remote, that the PRI would lose the next presidential election would remove this institutional roadblock. It is, of course, recognized that the campesino representatives of the PRI structure might use whatever tactics were available to recruit ejidatario opposition to such a transformation of the ejido as is proposed here.

Part 3

Strategies for Development:
Toward Renewed Growth
and Equity in Latin America

8

Reflections on Latin American Development

Osvaldo Sunkel

Empirical and Theoretical Background

In the mid-1950s when I had just graduated from university and joined ECLA, I had the opportunity to take part in and witness a series of comprehensive studies on economic development in various Latin American countries. These studies included exploring the prospects of the various nations in a long-term historical context, using a macroeconomic approach that stressed both the differential development of diverse sectors of the economy and, in particular, the way in which they fitted into the world economy.[1] This was an enriching experience for me, as it enabled me to see two very important things: on the one hand, the enormous variety of situations, circumstances, structures, institutions, sizes; that is, the enormous diversity of the Latin American countries. But, at the same time, my attention was drawn to the great similarity in the structural characteristics of their economies. For example, bananas for Costa Rica, the canal for Panama, tourism for Mexico, copper for Chile, and coffee for Brazil and Colombia were highly specialized foreign trade sectors that determined to a tremendous extent the economic activity of those countries. Each sector was controlled by foreign capital or landed oligarchies, and it was very difficult to obtain even the most basic data. In the case of Chile, it was necessary to invent a new concept—returned value—in order to distinguish the true contribution of the copper industry to the country's available foreign exchange, as distinct from the gross value of copper exports. The ECLA study was the first time that the canal had been formally dealt with as being part of the Panamanian economy.

I recall these facts because when we attempted to understand the structure and functioning of economies, we were obliged to do some imaginative mental gymnastics in order to perceive and interpret certain realities that were certainly never found in economics textbooks. Empirical observation of the

133

real historical situation of these countries and the efforts to draw up appropriate interpretations on that basis constituted one of the pillars of the type of thinking that ECLA was to develop around the extraordinary personality and contributions of Raúl Prebisch.

On the other hand, the theoretical pillar with which we worked was fundamentally the central body of classical political economy, to a large extent in the form in which it had been expressed and transmitted by Paul Baran (1957). Theoretically, the central element of the capitalist development process is the accumulation of capital and the concomitant increase in labor productivity. This increase in the productivity of labor is due fundamentally to the incorporation of technological innovations and increasing specialization of production. This allows both a rise in income and an increase in savings and investments. And, to the extent that it is possible to expand the accumulation process in that way and to incorporate—to use Prebisch's words—technical progress, and to use its fruits for new processes of this kind, a dynamic accumulation process is created that explains, in essence, the development of capitalism.

When one examines the Latin American economies of the late 1940s and early 1950s, one can see that capitalist accumulation had been taking place for several centuries and, of course, had been advancing very intensively during the second half of the nineteenth and first part of the twentieth centuries. However, although this process had resulted in dynamic export sectors that were increasingly productive and did generate surpluses, these economies were structured very differently from those that had developed in the countries where the Industrial Revolution had first occurred. The Latin American economies showed hyperexpansion in one sector—exports—while in others there was limited growth. Some sectors hardly existed. Certain geographical areas, linked to the exporting sectors, had reached a higher level of modernization and growth and were endowed with more infrastructure, whereas the rest of the country continued in a highly primitive state, virtually without infrastructure and marked by extremely wretched social conditions with colonialist institutions and large concentrations of agricultural land. In general, there was a deep-seated imbalance between the foreign trade sector, with its access to the international economy, and the rest of the economy.

What had happened to the process of accumulation, to expansion of the surplus and its trickle-down effects? The surplus was produced in the periphery but, for a host of reasons—among them foreign ownership, the overexploitation of labor, the absence of a domestic infrastructure and a national capitalist class, the lack of state control and participation, the decline in the terms of trade, and the inelasticity of international demand for these types of commodities—a large part of it from the export sector was not reinvested and fed through to the rest of the economy. Rather, it flowed back to the sectors from which it had sprung in the industrialized countries of the center. We can recognize here the historical specificity of what Prebisch called the peripheral countries, which afterward came to be known as the backward or underdeveloped countries or, later on, the developing countries. The name used gradually became more diplomatic, but the countries continued to be, relatively speaking, as underdeveloped as before.

In the 1950s, when the phenomenon I have just described began to be recognized, a whole series of theories on underdevelopment sprang up—theories associated with the names of Singer (1950a, 1950b), Rosenstein-Rodan (1944, 1957), Hirschman (1958), Lewis (1954, 1955), and Nurkse (1953a). Looking back on these theories, I think that their basic point of departure was the idea—doubtless inspired by Keynes—that there was a good deal of idle capacity; that the peripheral countries were not in fact using their available resources. The emphasis of all these theories was, fundamentally, on human resources. Lewis's 1954 article and Singer's contribution of a two-sector model, according to which one could bring about the industrialization of countries by transferring abundant labor from agriculture to industry, are representative of that trend. This element is also to be found in Prebisch's work (1944, 1950a) and in the contributions of Mandelbaum (1945), Rosenstein-Rodan, and Nurkse, who held, as an outgrowth of the same idea, that there was an insufficient domestic market because the available but idle production factors were not being used. Capital was the scarce and constraining resource, but it would be generated, in Keynesian fashion, by employing the idle factors. Furthermore, there was a sector in which there existed a process of accumulation that produced large surpluses: the export sector. What should be done was to harness the resources of that sector through state intervention and set up a wide-ranging investment program—what Rosenstein-Rodan (1957) called the "Big Push," others referred to as "balanced growth," and Hirschman (1958) designated "unbalanced growth."

At bottom, the argument was that the periphery displayed special characteristics very different from the neoclassical economists' assumption that all factors would be fully used. In the periphery, some factors (especially human and natural ones) were indeed widely available, but there was a lack of the physical capital that would make it possible to mobilize these resources. Financial capital—the flow of savings and investment—was also limited but could be obtained, it was claimed, by making better use of the surpluses already produced in the export sector and through direct foreign investment or financial aid from abroad.

It was in this theoretical environment that the ECLA development strategy was born, although to phrase it so may be attributing too much paternal responsibility to the association. A development strategy had already arisen in the 1930s and 1940s and had been put into practice; Prebisch and the ECLA set out to rationalize it. Many Latin American countries, faced with the international crisis of the Great Depression, had in fact started to apply the policies ECLA would recommend: They protected their economies; took resources from the export sector and reinvested them through state intervention in creating infrastructure, in promoting industrial development, in modernizing agriculture, and even in providing some basic social services in education, health, and housing.

The model for these activities had originated in the larger and slightly more advanced countries that had already achieved a certain degree of industrialization and had had an entrepreneurial class and a strong state in the period prior to the Great Depression—Argentina, Brazil, Chile, Colombia, and others. The crisis gave rise to a de facto strategy; in the 1930s, nobody rationalized theoretically the policies that these countries were applying. The more progressive social forces, opposed to the traditional landowning oligarchies, faced with an extremely severe crisis and brutal external constraints, reacted spontaneously to protect themselves against this catastrophe from abroad. It should be recalled that many of these countries had run up an enormous foreign debt in the second half of the 1920s; the violent contraction in the imports of manufactured goods and the suspension of debt service gave a big push to the industrialization and development process, which had started during World War I, received additional impetus from the depression and, later, from World War II, and spread to the other countries of the region. This historical process is what Prebisch and the ECLA economists, and many others I have mentioned, rationalized and structured. Rosenstein-Rodan and Mandelbaum, for example, came from Eastern Europe, where countries such as Hungary, Bulgaria, and Romania had undergone similar processes and where plans for reconstruction and industrialization were being worked out for the postwar period.

It is not surprising, in the light of such real processes, that a body of theory should arise. Theory is not invented in a vacuum; there are, of course, people in ivory towers who invent theories that have nothing to do with anything, merely in order to refute someone else's theory (which has nothing to do with anything either), and thus obtain promotion in the academic field, but the theories that really have some meaning are those that stem from a real situation, from an appreciation of problems and the forces of society that intervene in, participate in, and shape that reality. That is perhaps the main contribution of the development studies and theories that arose during the 1940s and 1950s. The main idea was that Latin America was caught in a historical trap, but that it could make a deliberate effort to promote its economic growth, could seek a better balance between the different sectors of production, could increase state intervention to foster the economy, could support social welfare and control, and could use the surpluses produced by the export sector.

This message was propounded in many Latin American countries, as it was in many other nations around the world, and gave rise to a development strategy and policy—ISI—that enjoyed enormous success in the 1950s and 1960s. Any statistics one may review will reveal that those decades were quite exceptional in Latin America's economic history (see Chapter 2); one has only to compare the present situation with that of thirty years ago, in whatever aspect one may wish to consider. In those days, access to information on the principal export sectors was limited; there was no notion of the interrelationships among the different sectors of the economy nor were national accounts available. No forecasts were made as to probable future prices of the main export commodity, what those prices depended on or what their domestic impact would be, or what the action of the state might be in the medium and long run. Once there was some degree of state participation in the surpluses produced in the export sector, investment resources could be allocated according to certain long-term development criteria, instead of letting market forces operate freely as had been the custom since time immemorial. Latin American nations as we see them today are to a large extent the product of such policies, are, in spite of all their problems, certainly something very different from, and much better than, what they were thirty years ago.

The Development Crisis of the Late 1960s and the Responses of the 1970s

In the late 1960s, the ISI strategy and its policies became the object of increasingly insistent and well-founded criticism. The development process that had been successful for more than two decades had started to show— alongside its success—some fairly serious defects. Diversifying industry through expanding the domestic market was assuming, more and more, the character of a subsidiary industrialization in terms of consumption and technological and ownership patterns, while at the same time the import substitution process was facing ever greater difficulties. Although it had been possible to set up an industrial sector and partially modernize agriculture, it had not been possible to consolidate a modern, industrial bourgeoisie or to diversify exports. Exports continued to be, to a large extent, primary products subject to price and demand fluctuations and instability, vulnerable to declining terms of trade. The objective of dynamizing, stabilizing, and diversifying exports had not been achieved. It had been assumed that industrialization would start with the domestic market and, from that springboard, would later give rise to an expansion in export products. Although ECLA economists and others pressed for policy changes in this direction, and some efforts were made, little was achieved.

Another notorious defect of the development strategy showed up in the labor market. ISI created a great number of new jobs with relatively high productivity in manufacturing, but it also pushed a large share of the labor force into urban centers plagued by underemployment and into jobs with very low productivity, thus generating the phenomenon of marginalism or, as it is now known, the informal sector. Segregation of the labor market made the historical problem of unequal income distribution—deriving fundamentally from the long-standing maldistribution and limited access to property and education—even worse. Neither was it possible to raise the rate of personal savings and investment to the level required, although state savings and foreign savings rose.

Toward the end of the 1960s increasingly strong criticism started to be heard from both the left and the right. The criticisms from the left were, fundamentally, from the dependence perspective. In brief, it was pointed out that ISI had resulted in an even greater dependence and polarization in Latin America. There was a new dependence, in addition to that deriving from the specialization of the export-producing sector. The entire industrial sector merely reproduced the consumption and technological patterns of the industrialized countries, through foreign investment, penetration by MNCs, and the demonstration effect. A good deal of the expansion, modernization, and growth of industry had been co-opted, so to speak, by an increasingly transnationalized sector.

As a counterpart to the left's interpretation, there was criticism from the right. The neoliberal, neoclassical critique asserted that the state was intervening too much, that its excessive intervention was strangling private initiative. Prices of agricultural products were overcontrolled and too low; the currency was overvalued; and there was too much protectionism—all of which meant inefficiency and an irrational allocation of productive resources.

Thinking on development thus divided into three streams: criticism from the left; complaints from the right; and a persistent favoring of the strategies that had been applied in earlier years. With the crisis that arose in the late 1960s and early 1970s there were, in practice, three attempts to modify development strategies. The choice of the left was toward greater socialization, an even more active, interventionist role for the state, exemplified by the Unidad Popular in Chile, the Velasco Alvarado administration in Peru, and similar short-lived experiences in Bolivia and Argentina. All these attempts came to an end for reasons that were more political than economic, with a strong component of external pressure, even though they left much to be desired in the economic field, too.

The choice of the right was to replace the new socialist or interventionist development strategy wherever it had been attempted. It was precisely in the countries where such a strategy had been tried out that the rightist choice, the neoliberal and monetarist option, had its most extreme, I should say its worst, expression: the countries of the Southern Cone—Uruguay, Argentina, and Chile. But to a certain extent, nearly all the other countries of Latin America were influenced by this neoliberal revision of the development strategy. Such rightist experiences in most countries had grave consequences: stagnation in basic production sectors; diversion of savings and investment into speculative activities, dismantling of the industrial sector; extreme external dependence; worsening of the social and employment problems; high concentration of income and wealth; and colossal debt, both foreign and domestic.[2]

The third strategy—the developmentalist choice—continued to be applied with certain corrections, particularly in the foreign sector, in Brazil, Mexico, and Venezuela, enabling these countries to continue to grow, in spite of the problems—particularly dependence and greater inequality—that had cropped up in the late 1960s.

For neoliberal and developmentalist strategists, the permissiveness of international financing that began in the late 1960s and accelerated in the 1970s made it possible to forget all the problems; one merely had to send off a telex to the international commercial banks. If the workers were demanding higher wages, a foreign loan would do the trick; if the military needed weapons, get a foreign loan; if the state technocrats had some new, gigantic project, if business needed financing for its investments, if there were problems in agriculture, if the neoliberal economists were opening up the country to foreign products and the liberalization of the financial market, borrow from abroad. The transnational private banking community, overburdened with petrodollar deposits, was more than willing to oblige; in fact, it was pushing loans very hard. And the international financial market was giving a clear and unmistakable signal: negative real interest rates. The result was devastating: $400 billion of foreign loans—of external debt—and an equivalent amount in domestic debt. Latin American countries now must bear this burden, in some cases as a consequence of continuing the ISI development strategy beyond its proper limits.

In other cases, the debt was a consequence of the introduction of new, neoliberal strategies, as loaded with dogma and ideology as they were lacking in the most elementary perceptions of trends and characteristics of the Latin American economies.

Neoliberalism vs. Development

In the decade and half when it seemed that everything could be fixed through foreign loans and that growth was assured, the concern for development and the theory of development ceased. Theory, strategies, medium and long-term problems and solutions were no longer discussed. The main concern became short-term equilibrium and efficiency, and planning was dismantled. The idea of the need for a long-term strategy was lost, because the economies had indeed grown and, during the 1970s, continued to grow.

Even the first oil crisis in 1973 did not stop the Latin American economies, the majority of which are net importers of oil, from growing with evident strength and intensity. Instead of immediately starting a process of structural adjustment, which only Brazil partially carried out, it was stated with pride that the apparent economic success was a demonstration of the degree of development reached by Latin American countries, the strengthening of their productive forces' capacity for accumulation and industrial development. They had shown that they could keep on growing in spite of the fact that the world economy was going through a serious recession and a large-scale energy crisis. The reality was simply that the external debt had made it possible to offset this new external imbalance, and the majority of the national economies, in a totally irresponsible way, continued to expand—at some time in the future things would work out somehow or other. I think that this is a good indication, a kind of practical demonstration, of the degree to which the long-term development horizon and conception of development strategy had been lost.

I recently toured several U.S. universities, trying to discover what the different economics departments are thinking with regard to development: I did not find anything. On the contrary, I discovered that development economics no longer formed part of the economics curriculum. I learned that in three or four departments well-financed chairs of development economics had been set up or had been offered funds, but that the faculty and administration had rejected the candidates for these chairs. There was either no longer any such thing as the economics of underdevelopment, or, because it could not be dealt with in mathematical formulas as the profession's academic canons now demand, it was ignored. *Since the problems of development are too complex to be dealt with in mathematical formulas, the problem of development is eliminated.* (This reminds me of the case of the husband who finds his wife making love to another man on the sofa and, in order to solve the matter, decides to sell the sofa.) There is no subdiscipline of economics dealing with underdevelopment; there are no special cases; there are no specific differences. All economies are interchangeable—Haiti, Brazil, Hong Kong, China, Switzerland, the United States, and Biafra. The problem is not that of adjusting economic theory to the problems of development, but of adjusting the underdeveloped economies to the neoliberal utopia. Faced with such an absurd situation, I think that we absolutely must go back to thinking seriously about development, not only for obvious theoretical reasons, but also for crucial practical and political ones. Latin American countries are at present subjected to strong conditionality by the international community. The IMF and the World Bank, which complement each other in the short and in the long term and represent transnational banking and ultraconservative governments, argue precisely that there is no such thing as an underdeveloped economy with special characteristics, and that the only thing to do is to apply the neoliberal model that has been tried with such disastrous results in so many countries: reduce state intervention; open up the economy; let the markets function; permit the free forces of business to express themselves; that is, make the economy more like the neoliberal textbook portrait.

This position, which the World Bank now defends with an ideological stubbornness and dogmatism similar to that which has characterized the IMF for so many years, derives to a large extent from a strange, empirical legitimation of this type of model that stems form the analysis of the four famous Southeast Asian countries—South Korea, Taiwan, Hong Kong, and Singapore. Balassa (1978, 1982), Balassa and Michalopoulus (1985), Little (1970, 1982), Krueger (1978a, 1978b, 1980), and others from the World Bank have tried to convince us, in an irrefutably empirical manner, that the only way to grow is through open international trade, the free play of markets, noninterference of the state in the foreign sector, and liberalization of the financial sector; that is to say, laissez faire, laissez passer. This interpretation is a misrepresentation of the success that the Southeast Asian countries have had in their industrialization strategies, since in none of these cases do we find anything to support such a thesis. What happened in those countries was rather the contrary of what the World Bank would have us believe. I would go so far as to say that events in South Korea and Taiwan provide good examples of the best ECLA developmentalist prescription. Of course, I do not refer to Hong Kong or Singapore, because these are city-economies and it is absurd to use them as an example of a development strategy for a country. It is like talking about the economic development of London as if that city were a country; London's expansion and its characteristics are explained not so much by the development of England, as by that of the British Empire. Similarly, Hong Kong cannot be explained without referring to China, Singapore without reference to Malaysia, and the whole of Southeast Asia without mention of Japan. Putting these very peculiar economies into the same bag with South Korea and Taiwan results from overlooking their structural characteristics, formative historical processes, and internal and international sociopolitical and cultural contexts.

South Korea and Taiwan, in contrast, are indeed interesting and valid cases. Immediately after World War II, the U.S. military administration carried out agrarian reform. Later, the United States injected an unusual quantity of resources into both countries because they were threatened by China and by North Korea. Thus, they were placed in a situation of "modernize or disappear," and the ruling classes, with U.S. support, used the state extensively as an agent for development. Taiwan's public sector accounts for approximately one-third of that country's output. Both nations' governments severely control consumption. For example, while they were exporting color television sets to the rest of the world, the local population was not allowed to buy them; it is only within the past few years that domestic consumption of some export products has been allowed. All necessary selective intervention tools were put into play: differentiated subsidies; specific incentives to achieve overall export targets (sometimes for specific products); and discrimination against certain imported products. South Korea utilized that whole paraphernalia of state intervention and had a conception of an overall development strategy, well coordinated and carefully thought out, with the aim of achieving both growth and the restructuring of the production system in order to develop industry.

Another small detail that is not referred to in the above-mentioned studies is the fact that South Korea and Taiwan developed through industrialization and not through the use of their "natural" comparative advantages. While in the first stages of industrialization, these countries followed an import substitution strategy, later this was continued only selectively; the emphasis changed to export strategies with a simultaneous careful control over foreign capital and the choice of technology, provision of strong incentives for developing an indigenous technological capacity, and exploration of world markets to determine which of the most dynamic segments of world demand could best incorporate their industry. In other words, the "young tigers" of Asia planned their expansion into the world market. Any resemblance between South Korean and Taiwanese strategy and the invisible hand of the market is purely and simply coincidental.

It seems to me extremely important that we should be very careful of this new ideological contraband that is being imposed on Latin America through the conditionalities of structural adjustment programs and through the rescheduling of external debt that, in Latin America, will give rise to something totally different from what took place in the Southeast Asian countries. If support were available to do what those countries did, it would be welcomed, but assistance is not being extended for that purpose; on the contrary, it is contigent upon agreement to dismantle, privatize, and/or hand over to foreign control the industrial machine that Latin American nations have created with such effort.

This does not mean that we should not be highly critical of the Latin American experience, especially of the ineptitude of efforts to diversify dynamically manufactured exports and to correct the scandalous social injustices. But these and other faults in the development of Latin American economies are not so much the consequence of the orientation of the development strategies proposed in the region; rather, they persist because Latin American countries *have not implemented the central and basic tenets of the developmentalist prescription.*

It is therefore urgent and necessary to revive the debate on medium and long-term prospects, on the choice of deliberate industrialization strategies, on improvement in the distribution of income, and to discuss new forms of insertion into the world market. For almost fifteen years we have been completely removed from such issues, and, in the last five or six years, we have been concerned only with the very short term and the external debt. Economic theory, particularly neoclassical theory and its monetarist version, but also Keynesian macroeconomics, are bodies of thought whose basic objective—I would say almost sole objective—is the analysis of short-term equilibrium. My reason for making such a categorical statement is that the analytical conception of these bodies of theory deals exclusively with economic flows, markets, and prices—with annual economic flows and their macro- and microeconomic equilibrium, and with how economic agents function in the market. The economic theory studied today is about macroeconomic equilibrium, external balance, fiscal balance and balance in the labor markets, relative prices, how markets clear and how they interrelate so that there will be no inflation and no underutilization of factors: all of this in a framework of annual economic flows, or even of biannual or quarterly flows.

Population growth, the use of natural resources, science and technology, consumption patterns, the structure of international relations, the power structure, the role of business and of the state, the institutional characteristics of property ownership, and the organization of the means of production are the subject of medium and long-term development. Economic growth depends on having—among other things—an innovating business sector with a long-term view, capable of taking risks in order to gain new markets instead of turning, for example, to speculation in the financial markets, as has occurred with the neoliberal experiments. Economic growth in Latin American nations depends on their technological creativity to make use of the natural resources they have available in sufficient quantity, which, thanks to exploitation and a total lack of ecological perspective, are now being rapidly destroyed. It also depends on our conception of the state's role and on appropriate agreements and arrangements among the state, business, and the labor sectors, arrangements that make conscious use of the market mechanism through deliberate action and with a long-term view.

Where, I ask, in any of the chapters of a conventional textbook, are such subjects discussed? Where do we find the international system described as being asymmetrical, systematically diverting a large part of the surpluses produced in international trade to the industrialized countries? Where do we find debate on the impact of technological change? Short-term macro- and microeconomic balance is important and necessary, but insufficient. Witness, for example, the case of Colombia, which has been very prudent and careful in this matter, which has been neither excessively developmentalist nor neoliberal, monetarist, or Marxist; it has always navigated pragmatically in the mainstream of economic policy and has taken its export strategy very seriously. Despite all of this, Colombia has not solved any of the basic economic and social problems that characterize it, as they mark the other countries in the region.

The task ahead of us, if the conditions imposed by the IMF and the World Bank are not to lead Latin America into even deeper underdevelopment, is to rethink the national strategies for medium and long-term development under the new conditions that have cropped up both in individual countries and in the international economy.

Confronting Debt and Development

The profound injustices and the economic and sociopolitical contradictions of the present short-term adjustment policies call for new and urgent debate on adjustment, recovery, and development policies. Latin America's development policies since World War II have been inspired by two main theoretical sources: post-Keynesian developmentalism and neoliberal monetarism. The present far-reaching crisis now places nearly all Latin American countries in a crucial economic policy dilemma: They must either submit to a severe recessive adjustment along monetarist lines, such as that which multinational financial capitalism is trying to impose, or recover and maintain sufficient freedom to be able to carry out policies for putting the economy back on its feet in the framework of a strategy based on the development of national and regional productive and social forces.

To service the debt or not to service it, that is the question. All Latin American governments declare that they want to keep up their payments, but many have not been able to do so and have left the matter in suspense for several months at a time. Nor have they been able to let the situation fester, because, in the majority of cases, governments have been obliged to negotiate agreements with the IMF, whose monetarist policies create a steep reduction of demand designed to produce trade surpluses. In exchange for this reduction, the fund facilitates the rescheduling of the debt with small contributions out of its own accounts and those of the creditor banks. In some cases, such agreements have managed to survive, but others have not been able to withstand sociopolitical pressures inside the affected countries. So, the short-lived cycle begins all over again; thus, the Latin American economies, and those of other developing countries, have for several years been "waiting for Godot."

The costs of servicing the debt and those of not servicing it are equally intolerable in terms of economic and social costs and the resulting political instability. The multinational banks and the developed countries are prepared to accept a temporary moratorium and prefer to provide bridge loans for short-term refunding, which shows that they are scared of a financial collapse. But, they do not dare to embark on any large-scale, long-term refinancing or funding, which shows that they have no confidence that dynamic international development will soon occur. Nor do they have any apparent faith in the debtor countries' capacity to pay; the admission of some of the biggest U.S. creditor banks that they would probably never get back a large part of their debts is eloquent in this respect.

We must avoid making disastrous choices but also must overcome the present decline; therefore, we must design an international and national strategy of greater scope and breadth. We need to draw up basic, common principles for creating a new set of public international institutions to support the development dynamization and stability of the international economy. Within this framework, each country could decide whether to reschedule its debt or not, according to its own circumstances, but in a context that would favor development, not hinder it. However, the suggestions that have been made toward this end, year after year, have received little response from the main industrialized countries. Even the initiatives proposed by the U.S. secretary of the treasury, although they constituted steps—albeit small steps—in the right direction, have been toned down or are being rejected.

The multinational banks, the governments of the industrial countries, and the governments and ruling classes of the debtor countries share responsibility for the exorbitant debt run up by the majority of Latin American countries. It will be impossible to service that debt if the economies of the debtor countries are reduced to stagnation, as this would probably lead them to default. It is indispensable that the cost of servicing the debt should be spread over all those responsible for it and those who have enjoyed its ephemeral benefits. At the international level, the multinational banks and the governments of the industrialized countries should assume their share of the burden by facilitating debt servicing through reductions in principal and interest. In addition, these countries should grant new, long-term credits at low interest rates so that the debtor countries' economies may be put back on their feet through new development strategies.

The deeper in debt the Latin American countries are, the more they need to reformulate their development policies at the national level, directing them toward four basic objectives: the concentration of available resources to satisfy the basic needs of the masses; employment; expansion and selective diversification of exports; and substitution of imports. Only a reasonable and sustainable part of the foreign exchange obtained from export earnings should be earmarked for servicing the debt; the rest should be reserved for importing essential goods, either directly or indirectly, for popular consumption, and for capital accumulation. The contribution of the debtor countries' privileged classes to the servicing of the external debt, for which they are partly responsible, should be enforced through restrictions on both imports and the production of nonessential consumer goods.

The adoption of measures favoring domestic recovery directed toward the application of a new development strategy demands new leverage in economic policy that the present IMF agreements do not allow. The monetarist prescription, one of whose main objectives is to maintain or obtain the opening up of the economy, restricts overall spending on consumption and investment to such an extreme that the demand for imports is reduced until a trade surplus is achieved, while, at the same time, resources are freed for increasing exports. According to my analysis (and that of many other people), this orientation is both wrong and too costly in economic and social terms. It is mistaken because the elasticity of productive factors is low, especially in a context of low investment rates. It is highly unlikely that the value of exports will increase rapidly and substantially, above all if there are no deliberate, medium-term policies at the national and international levels directed to that goal. This strategy is too costly in terms of employment and mass consumption because, socially speaking, it is more effective to modify the import function by imposing direct, selective, interventionist measures, by restricting imports through taxes, tariff duties, and import and exchange controls, and by distinguishing between the essential and the less necessary. Such discriminating measures make it possible to assure a level of investment, production, and essential consumption that would minimize the effect of the crisis on employment and the standard of living of the lower-income sectors. Although this policy involves a change in relative prices and doubtless raises prices, it does not (and should not) imply galloping inflation, as long as there is idle capacity and a tax policy that strictly limits the income and spending of the well-off sectors and promotes private and public savings, and as long as incomes policy avoids unjustified wage hikes.

Economic policy requires leverage sufficient to enable it to take measures that not only can put the economy back on its feet in the short term, but are part of a long-term development strategy that is founded mainly on the natural, human, and productive infrastructural resources with which Latin America is relatively well endowed, and which constitute the only solid and permanent basis for steady development. Obviously, unless the negative international context improves and unless there is wider support for proposals on reform in trade, finances, and investment, policies will have to be austere. It is necessary and urgent to admit that, perhaps, the governments of the developing countries may receive nothing of any great significance from the industrialized world or from the international organizations, and carefully to examine what this might mean in terms of recovery and the development strategies that might be conceived to cope with such a situation.

Recovery, Accumulation, and Democracy: A Heterodox Proposal

After seven years of draconian "adjustment" policies and exhausting renegotiations of the external debt, the indebtedness and crisis afflicting the majority of Latin American countries continues to be extremely serious. A precarious external equilibrium has been achieved at the cost of profound internal imbalances. In the short term, deep and unrelenting recessions have led to a great deal of idle production capacity, to the accentuation of inflationary pressures, and to drastic cuts in imports. In the medium term, employment, real wages, social services, and income distribution have worsened. In the long term, we have seen an acute decline in the capital accumulation process and, consequently, in production and technological capacity and in the viability of the economic and social infrastructure. The political costs of maintaining this recessive adjustment and the servicing of the debt grow exponentially; the supposed advantages of this course of action rapidly disappear; and the alternative—a populistic recovery policy—is more and more likely. In the absence of a better alternative, the force of the sociopolitical pressures already at work will inevitably tend to impose such a choice.

There is an immediate alternative to these regressive or populistic strategies for coping with the crisis: *total or partial suspension of transfers of domestic savings earmarked for the servicing of the debt.*[3] Notice that it is a question of suspending the transfer abroad, not the domestic savings effort. This would enable Latin American countries to have a considerable volume of foreign exchange available, depending on the precise burden of debt servicing in each country, the proportion of the debt that is suspended, and the severity of reprisals from creditor countries and banks. If only it were possible, through the action of these different factors, to return a large proportion of the potential volume of foreign exchange, the corresponding increase in imports would permit an annual increase of several percentage points in GDP in the different countries. In the present conditions, this would mean nothing less than leaving stagnation behind and entering a period of recovery and growth of per capita income. This is the essential thrust that is required to overcome the vicious circle of recessive adjustment and leap into the virtuous circle of expansionist adjustment.

Indeed, if an appreciable part of the foreign exchange earmarked for the servicing of the debt could be devoted to increasing real imports, it would be possible to increase investment considerably, from the extremely low level to which it has fallen to something approaching its historical level. Rising levels of investment would spark a steady increase in economic activity, employment, and income, given the existing idle production capacity. This, in turn, would make it possible to raise domestic savings to the level necessary to finance this higher level of domestic investment. Bear in mind that this is a truly Herculean task, since it is necessary to offset not only the steep decline in savings brought about by recession and adjustment policies, but also to replace the large contribution of foreign funds that were available up to 1981 but that became a massive net outflow of savings. Achieving this far-reaching structural readjustment in the savings-investment rate is possible in the short and medium run only if we follow the Keynesian prescription and if there is decided action on the part of the state. And that is feasible only if there is a suspension of all or a significant part of the service payments on the external debt. An increase in imports is essential in the present circumstances if the new, autonomous investments are to have any real and steady effect and make it possible to get back onto the path of development. Thus, in the short term the external constraint to recovery would be lifted and in the medium run so would the internal constraint on productive capacity and savings, leading to steady growth.

If, on the contrary, the available imports are used on the populist alternative of recovery through raising consumer spending, economic activity would expand in the short run but would not be able to keep up its growth in the medium run. It is likely that this is what happened with the Cruzado Plan in Brazil, when—having previously achieved external adjustment, which temporarily relieved the external constraint—an inordinate increase in consumption led to excessive domestic demand, an acute decline in the foreign trade sector, the suspension of interest payments on the debt, and a low level of investment. An increase in investment is required, furthermore, in order to speed up the transformation of the productive structure into tradable goods and to make this effort compatible with changes that can no longer be put off in the social field.

We must insist that the suspension of servicing the debt should not in any way mean a suspension of the effort to achieve a corresponding level of domestic savings. This is one of the main differences between my proposal and the populist one. The effort to suspend debt should be embodied in an institutional mechanism such as, for example, a national fund for economic restructuring and social development. All social sectors should be democratically represented on the board of the fund. The product of such a national savings effort might be earmarked exclusively for financing priority projects for coping with the most acute social problems, both short- and long-term ones, and for improving the production of tradable goods.

We find ourselves in an international "negative sum game," in which all, or nearly all, lose or at least cannot win. The debtor countries are the most affected; in particular, their working classes. But the creditor countries also lose or do not win. The drastic reduction of imports to the debtor countries affects the creditors' exports and the income and employment of the corresponding sectors. It also reduces the opportunities for direct investment, loans, and private funding, while at the same time reducing the payment of profits and interest from the debtor countries. Furthermore, the lower level of domestic economic activity, and of trade, investment, and flows of international financing has a recessive effect on the world economy and simultaneously contributes to acute instability and uncertainty.

Development Strategies: Some Lessons

The development of the forces of production directly focused on the satisfaction of the basic necessities of the masses and the elimination of dependence cannot be achieved through the massive introduction of the individualistic, consumeristic, transnational style of development that intensively uses imported capital, imported energy, and imported technology. This has not been possible either through the deliberate creation of so-called modernization (the post-Keynesian developmental prescription) or through the opening of the economy to international competition and indiscriminate privatization (monetarism), even within a favorable international context. The transnational style simply cannot be spread to all of Latin American society. In the best of situations, that of developmentalism, it can benefit a smaller or larger majority, depending on the country, but large sectors of the population will remain within a hopeless poverty. In the case of monetarism, the economic, political, and social concentration and polarization is much greater, the development and diversification of the productive structure is much less, and external vulnerability and dependence are overwhelming.

It must be recognized that true national and regional development will have to be based mainly on the transformation of resources and on the natural environment in which Latin America is relatively rich, incorporating the efforts of the whole population and the intensive use of existing production capacity and available infrastructure. Latin Americans (not alone among the peoples of the world) must also adopt styles of living and consumption patterns, techniques and ways of organization that are much more frugal and suited to the natural and human environment, with a very prudent and efficient utilization of the little capital available, especially imported capital. The explicit aim, of course, is to produce goods and services and accumulate the basic social capital required to improve both productivity and the standard of living of the masses. It should not be forgotten that, in this sense, Latin America has improved its potential remarkably in the last few decades. If many countries were able to progress dynamically in the 1930s, in much harder international conditions and with far fewer domestic possibilities, they should be much more capable of doing so now.

Regional cooperation must play a more important role in these domestic and international tasks by pumping new life into the institutions of regional integration that facilitate trade, payments, and investments among the Latin

American countries. Another very decisive aspect is to support all the possible forms of integration and cooperation both within the Latin American region and with the rest of the Third World. Finally, it would be impossible to exaggerate the importance of economic and technical cooperation of all kinds, especially the exchange of experience and information on all the subjects relevant to the new national and international development strategies proposed.

These proposals, at the national, regional, and international levels, imply radical political changes. In the final analysis, it is necessary that the predominance of trade and international financial interests, and their respective local multinational bases, should be replaced by broad national coalitions representing the majority of the sectors of society, whose priority is to fight poverty, expand employment and economic activity, and achieve a more progressive distribution of income and educational, health, and housing services. Such changes occurred in many countries after the crisis of the 1930s, and the present crisis may well act as a spur to similar shifts. But, it is not a question of history repeating itself; today, there are new sectors of society that did not exist before or that were excluded from, or overlooked by, earlier development policies. These include, among others, the vast numbers of urban poor and the peasants who live in extreme poverty, new contingents of young people who have received some education, women who have now entered the labor market, and the large number of highly qualified middle-class people, all of whom would have to be represented in the drawing up and implementation of the new development strategy that is now needed to overcome the crisis. Perhaps that is the most important problem among the many that must be dealt with as part of the effort to find new paths for development. The suggestion of setting up a national fund for economic restructuring and social development, an economic and political mechanism in which many sectors of society would be represented, is precisely a step in this direction.

Of course it is not possible to recommend a sole strategy for every one or even the majority of Latin American countries. The claim to have found a universal solution has perhaps been one of the most serious sins, both of the main strategies followed in the past and of the more recent ones, particularly those of the neoliberal type. Neoliberalism has ignored *both* the common and the particular features of the several Latin American economies. The import substitution strategy was based on a diagnosis of some of the fundamental structural characteristics common to the majority of the Latin American economies (although it did not make sufficient distinction among them). This is perhaps one of the principal reasons why ISI, in spite of having brought about serious imbalances of various kinds, at least made it possible to spur economic growth and modernization, thus undeniably creating the conditions for further development. Neoliberalism, on the other hand, not only did not achieve growth but often led to deindustrialization and made the problems of inequality, unemployment, and external imbalances even more acute. The claim of universality has been pushed to new extremes in the adjustment programs sponsored by the IMF, except in a handful of countries that were clever enough, politically and technically, to adopt their own adjustment policies or negotiate some variations in the IMF's formulas. But, it should be stressed that these compromises were short-term stabilization programs, not development strategies and policies, and this is, perhaps, one of their greatest weaknesses.

The new development strategies should be founded on a new pragmatism, based on the critical assessment of the failures and successes of the two main strategies followed up to now, with a realistic appreciation of the international conditions that exist at present and will surely continue to exist for the next few years; and they should concern themselves especially with the situation and the problems of each country in particular. If new policies are to lead to new development, it is fundamentally important to take into account the structural factors of development, such as the role of technology, the endowment of high-quality human resources, the degree of industrialization and urbanization, the social and political structure, and the role of the state. The Central American and Caribbean economies obviously cannot follow strategies similar to those of the largest and most industrialized countries in the region; proximity to the United States is a most important factor for Mexico; a decade of experience with extreme neoliberal development strategies creates a historical set of circumstances very different from that arising from a more moderate experience of adjustment.

In view of the traumatic experiences of the recent past and the somber prospects for the near future, the central theme of concern for the Latin American countries at this critical point in their history is the need to overcome as quickly as possible—in the short term—the cost of recessive adjustment, through an expansionist adjustment. But, such an expansionist adjustment should also constitute the basis for a transition toward a form of development that would provide strong support for democracy and would be sustainable in the medium and long runs. To find a positive way of linking the short and long terms, structural factors and functional variables, and the sociocultural, political, and economic aspects, it is necessary to go beyond the partial and unidimensional approaches that prevail at present. One way to achieve this is to distinguish between the short-term flows and the substantial endowments in human and natural resources and productive assets that have been acquired and accumulated over the very long term.

If we take a wider view of the three classic production factors—that is to say, labor, land, and capital—we must admit that the productive, organizational, and administrative capacities of Latin American countries have, in many cases, reached fairly advanced levels and cannot remain, nor will they remain, idle for much longer. In the present crisis, serious external imbalances in the flows of income and spending in the short run have reduced imports but have led also to a pronounced underutilization of sociocultural, human, natural, and productive resources. Latin America has potential real resources that might be mobilized, provided that such mobilization is freed from dependence on imported inputs.

Selectivity and Specificity in Development Policy

There is a wealth of knowledge, experience, and macroeconomic and sociopolitical proposals, and more detailed knowledge of a sectoral nature or of specific programs, that might serve to support concrete proposals for an expansionist readjustment, with its whole range of corresponding selective measures and programs. Many of those measures, in fact, are already being put into practice to cope with the crisis. These include programs aimed at large, medium, and small businesses and informal activities, in order to relieve the burden of poverty, provide employment, satisfy basic needs, produce exports, and replace imports. Among these measures one might mention the programs entailing the large-scale use of labor for the construction and reconstruction of housing, schools, hospitals, infrastructure, and equipment for collective services in working-class areas; for the construction, reconstruction, and maintenance of the highway network, public works, and human settlements in general; for protection against floods and other natural disasters; for reforestation, construction of terraces in areas where there is erosion, cleaning and protecting rivers and canals; for drainage and irrigation works; and for repair and maintenance of public buildings, machinery, and equipment.

These activities adapt very well, and at low cost, to the use and organization of labor on a large scale, and it is this quality that makes it desirable to adopt them in the present circumstances. At the same time, these activities mean a break with the predominant style of development, since they try to restore the importance of a work process designed to satisfy basic needs and to use the labor force and the underutilized potential to the full, while at the same time using fewer scarce factors such as capital and foreign inputs. In addition, these activities give rise to a different style of development, and a more vigorous, open, local cultural identity. However, they are most often adopted as emergency measures, tied to specific geographical contexts, daily experience, knowledge, and culture in those localities, and to the relationships formed by the natural ecosystem. It is vitally necessary to use this period of crisis to identify and foster such activities not only as immediate responses but as patterns having a more permanent character.

In the majority of cases, such projects involve some collective consumption or the utilization and expansion of the production infrastructure, not typically produced by private enterprise. The necessary investments are profitable only in the long run, either because they benefit low-income sectors whose monetary demand is very low or because the object is to create external economies or avoid external diseconomies, benefits that cannot be reaped easily by the private investor. In other words, they are activities and ventures that are normally the responsibility of the public sector.

The problems of poverty, of unemployment, and of utilization, preservation, protection, and improvement of the natural and artificial environment are not abstract concepts, but rather acquire their true significance in relation to concrete places, especially in countries that have highly varied local environments. Consequently, this is a field of public interest that is particularly appropriate for decentralization and community participation, two points of special interest and priority in the search for democratic planning and decisionmaking systems. Although the circumstances surrounding the crisis may trigger off this type of movement, the fact that it affects essential and widespread needs that have been systematically ignored offers the opportunity to introduce such programs as permanent characteristics of development, with the corresponding institutional and financial support and with a medium- and long-term outlook.

In this respect, a priority area for readjusting development models must be that of consumption and investment patterns, and the choices applied in the fields of technology and the handling of resources. Except in very special circumstances, it will be indispensable to place severe and selective restrictions on all types of superfluous demand that include, either directly or indirectly, many imported elements, and on all technology or designs that involve anything of this kind, while at the same time making an effort to replace imports by goods and services, technologies and designs that both depend on the use of national and local human and material resources and are essentially oriented toward satisfying basic needs.

All the lines of action proposed above imply the need for management of the environment. Expansion, preservation, maintenance, and protection of the environmental patrimony constitute a fundamental contribution to the standard of living and productivity. This necessarily implies greater awareness of the environment's potential, of the factors conditioning the ecosystems that determine its exploitation, and of the most efficient ways of administering these systems. The object is to make maximum use of the opportunities the environment offers, without destroying and damaging the ecology, so as to assure its survival in the long run. All of this means that in any plan for future development, we must give priority to the subject of natural resources and science and technology, adopting a long-term ecological perspective. In brief, it is a question of being fully aware of the material basis for sustaining development.

Stressing the exploitation of domestic resources means drawing a greater distinction both between countries and among regions within those countries. Development strategies must abandon their exaggerated level of abstraction and begin the concrete examination of the available natural and technological resources, the size and situation of the country, the relationship between its population and its resources, its position with regard to energy, and the degree and characteristics of its urbanization. This means that development strategies will necessarily have to be different for countries that are markedly different in these areas. It also means that development strategies will have to give special attention to the regional and spatial aspects (including the urban versus rural aspect). Because we must deal with resources of varying capacity and use potentiality, we must include in our plans diverse technologies having different levels of skill and methods of application—all of which is in acute contrast to the homogenizing tendencies that traditionally have been imposed on virtually every aspect of development, from crops to architectural design.

The method of planning that has been followed in the recent past—and especially the ingrained habit of relegating the state to a secondary role, under the influence of neoliberal thinking—has paid little attention to these considerations, because to a large extent this method—like the development strategies themselves—was determined by an orientation based fundamentally on imitating the industrialized countries' models of consumption and development, and dependent to an extreme degree on the national and international market.

From Inward-Looking Development to Development from Within

There now seems to be agreement that the development strategy of the past was overly biased toward ISI. However, although this criticism seems to be basically correct, it centers attention on the accessory and overlooks the central point. Fundamentally, the strategy of industrialization and development followed in the past was centered on the expansion of the domestic market, on fostering the local production of consumer goods that previously had been imported. This preference for consumption and the existing domestic market—that is, on the demands of the middle and upper classes—biased the industrialization strategy and determined the foreign trade policy (excessive protectionism), policies for encouraging consumption (subsidies, prices, and consumer credits), and investment policies aimed mostly at expanding the market for modern consumer durables, thus damaging, for example, savings and agricultural or manufacturing production for popular consumption.

In fact, it is not a question merely of criticizing partial aspects of the economic policies, such as tariffs or the exchange rate or controlled prices. It is the whole syndrome derived from a national industrial and consumer-oriented (populist) strategy that the crisis of the 1930s and World War II and its aftermath forced upon Latin America, and that persisted because it brought good profits. It has been difficult to break with this strategy and reorient Latin American economies because, beyond simply liberalizing domestic markets, it is necessary to undertake a wide-ranging overhaul, nothing less than an overall development strategy based on the conquest of world markets, with all the profound and complex implications that this carries for a country's international relations, and, in the domestic sphere, for intersectorial relations, for standards and patterns of consumption, for the reallocation of investments, for the creation of innovation capacity, for technological adaptation, for the reorientation of credit from fostering consumption to fostering exports, as well as for the more obvious and elementary aspects that affect the exchange rate, tariffs, and other economic policy tools.

It is well known that in the literature of Latin American development it has been customary to distinguish between the stages of outward-looking development, before the 1930s, and inward-looking development through ISI from that decade on. However, in one of Raúl Prebisch's pioneer works (1950b), he distinguished between the two stages in terms of offsetting the dynamic stimulus from abroad, which had become insufficient, by means of development *from within*.[4] Prebisch was thinking of a domestic industrialization process capable of creating a mechanism for capital accumulation, technical progress, and improved productivity like that which had emerged from the Industrial Revolution in the central countries. Prebisch pointed out that Japan would be incorporated into the universal propagation of technical progress when it "decides to rapidly assimilate the Western modes of production." The choice of words is particularly revealing: It is a question of assimilating, not transferring, copying, or reproducing, technical progress, and the accent is unmistakably placed on modes of production, that is, on supply.

In contrast, "inward-looking development," instead of placing the accent on accumulation, technical progress, and productivity, stresses demand, the expansion of the domestic market, and the replacement of formerly imported goods by local production. This last formulation leads to a strategy resting on more domestic consumption and on locally reproducing the consumption patterns and industrial and technological production of the central countries, through an import substitution process oriented basically toward a narrow and biased domestic demand, shaped by the unequal distribution of income.

Industrial development from within has very different implications. In the final analysis, it, too, is expressed in terms of import substitution, but it starts from industries that were considered, at that time, to be the pillars of what we have come to call the *basic endogenous nucleus* for industrialization, accumulation, creation and dissemination of technical progress, and productivity gains. It was, then, a question of mobilizing the iron and steel industries, the electrical and engineering industries, the basic chemicals industry, the infrastructure of energy, transport, and communications, of tapping the natural resources that had not been made use of, and of articulating the national territory.

The strategy of development from within is not oriented toward the satisfaction of the final consumer demand of the middle and upper classes, nor does it prejudge in favor of import substitution, which would eventually lead to an impasse. It leaves the options open for orienting industrialization from within toward particular domestic, regional, and foreign markets. This dynamic linkage does not proceed from final demand to inputs to capital goods to technology, but the reverse, from these latter elements to the satisfaction of domestic and external demands that are considered to be priorities in a long-term strategy. In the crisis that now confronts Latin America, the transition should not be from inward- to outward-looking development but toward a future of development and industrialization *from within* that promises a dynamic process of accumulation, innovation, and productivity gains.

Sustainable Development

The distinction between short- and long-term policies is of great importance when trying to cope with both recession and a structural crisis. At first glance, long-term policies—such as those affecting the preservation of the environment and natural resources, the population, education, science and technology, international relations, and the forms of social organization—apparently have little relation to short-term problems. But, as I have tried to explain, such policies are rich in opportunities for helping to solve short-term problems: for example, job creation, the satisfaction of basic needs, the development of new export products, and the substitution of imports. Conjunctural policies can be created which are designed both to cope with recession and to preserve and improve social and production structures and services in the long run, instead of exacerbating their waste and decline. Consequently, close collaboration between those who are concerned about short-term imbalances and those whose job it is to take care of medium- and long-term development may be useful and fruitful, provided that both keep in mind the need to achieve a sustainable development.

One of the difficulties affecting coordination between short- and long-term development policies is the fact that short-term economic policy falls within the sphere of influence of economists and administrators from finance ministries and central banks, whereas development plans, programs, and projects are the responsibility of planning offices, semiautonomous state-owned enterprises responsible for energy and natural resources, and the ministries responsible for public works, regional and urban development, education, science and technology, and the productive and social sectors of the economy. It is necessary to provide an institutional solution to improve the coordination between short-term crisis intervention and the planning of long-term development.

Past experience, both recent and longer ago, offers examples of development strategies and policies that—looking back on them—turned out to be unsuitable and led to deep-seated crises. Latin American economic and social history is marked by cycles of boom and bust based on the exploitation of specially favorable natural resources.

The most recent cycle is the most remarkable and the most lamentable. It is remarkable insofar as it was based on the exporting of a myth, that is to say, confidence in the miraculous capacity of the free market (both national and foreign) to exploit resources; and lamentable insofar as it led to a severe overexploitation of some resources and areas, a big step backward socially and economically, and to a foreign debt of extremely grave proportions. These characteristics weigh heavily on the possibilities for future growth and development.

It is necessary to accept the basic premise that development in the future will not depend, as it did in the past, on any large-scale inflow of foreign resources. On the contrary, it is likely that net external funding will be very scarce over the next few years. In simple terms, Latin America will have to ration its use of funding, either through successive devaluations and/or exchange and import controls. Moreover, a time will come when it will be impossible to continue importing luxury cars, electrical and electronic appliances, wine and spirits, and other luxury goods while there is a shortage of food and other essential goods or raw materials, and social injustice becomes ever more blatant. The countries of Latin America will have to be more self-sufficient; they will have to grow basically by using their own means, their own natural resources, their own environmental conditions, and their own labor, inventiveness, technology, and organization, and must develop great skill at finding their particular niches in world markets. Any foreign contributions that may turn out to be necessary will be complementary and selective and no longer the predominant and leading elements. Latin America will have to adjust to this new reality; otherwise, it will be irremediably torn apart. Limited resources must be shared equitably over the whole population, or those who manage to maintain, perhaps for a few more years, a standard of living similar to that of the developed countries will become an increasingly isolated minority, surrounded by an ever larger majority of the unemployed, outcasts, and the poor.

There is an enormous task implicit in the renewed challenge to achieve a steady development. It requires, on the economic plane, an adequate level of accumulation, efficiency, and creativity; and in the social sphere, a reasonable margin of justice, opportunities for work, and a decent standard of living. In the international arena, Latin American countries should be accepted as respectable members of the community of nations and must have the capacity to maintain satisfactory international relations. In the sphere of human rights, the essential rights of the individual, the family, and the basic organizations of society should be respected; in the cultural sphere, the achievement of a certain level of identity, adhering to the best values and traditions that shape and distinguish these nations, and the necessary creativity and maintenance of an acceptable degree of legitimacy, renovation, representativeness, and responsibility on the part of the authorities, and the participation of the people in government; in the environmental sphere, the certitude that the cultural, environmental, and natural patrimonies inherited from the past will be handed down to future generations, enriched by the best of our knowledge of how to use, preserve, and replace resources in order to assure an improved material basis for the survival and welfare of the generations to come.

Notes

This chapter was translated by Pauline M. Marmasse, CIDE, Mexico.

1. See the series of studies published by ECLA under the general title *Analyses and Projections of Economic Development*, including separate volumes on case studies of Brazil (1956), Colombia (1957), Bolivia (1958), Argentina (1959), Peru (1959), Panama (1959), El Salvador (1959), Honduras (1960), and Nicaragua (1966). There also were a study on Costa Rica, published by the university of Costa Rica, and unpublished studies of Chile and Mexico.

2. This characterization must be modified in the case of Chile in the last few years, since it has managed to recover from the deep recession of 1982/83, maintaining its stability and exhibiting a strong expansion in exports. However, it must be remembered that this positive macroeconomic behavior occurred when there was an exceptional shift in the terms of trade, with prices that were unusually high for copper exports and low for oil imports.

3. The following reasoning is based to a great extent on three works: Sunkel (1984); Sunkel (1985); and Griffith-Jones and Sunkel (1986).

4. See Sunkel (1987b). The discussion is to be found in Prebisch (1950b: 5). The English translation reads "by means of internal development." The original Spanish text is "el desarrollo desde dentro," which should be rendered in English as "development *from within*," as is done here.

9

Science, Technology, and Development

Dilmus D. James

Available evidence indicates that even during the high-growth decades of the 1960s and 1970s, the contribution of technological advance to Latin American economies was far from robust (Chenery 1986). If the region is to enjoy long-term growth once again, on a more sustainable basis and accompanied by socioeconomic development, it is imperative that internal generation, importation, diffusion, adaptation, and mastery of technologies become more effective.

Selecting Research and Development Projects: How Much Freedom?

There is reason to believe that in many Latin American countries, university researchers are, by and large, free to select their own projects. Speaking of Brazilian universities, for example, Pastore (1978: 270) observes that "the state has generally supported a liberal and individualistic style of scientific work." Although individual researchers may be less able to select their own projects in research and development (R&D) institutes in parastatal enterprises, government laboratories, and other agencies outside of academia, the institutes themselves appear to have wide latitude in choosing and perpetuating lines of inquiry that suit them.

How free should research institutes and the individual researchers within them be to choose R&D projects in a developing country context? There is little doubt that under ideal conditions relatively unfettered scientific pursuit, including choosing the most promising projects and avenues of investigation, would maximize social returns to society's investment in R&D activities. However, science and technology (S&T) in developing countries operate in an environment that is far from ideal—indeed, so far that I have, very reluctantly, concluded that a considerable net gain in social

159

returns from indigenous S&T efforts can be obtained if a set of inducements and sanctions are employed that will shift the center of gravity of S&T activity at the project and institute level. S&T shortcomings are so severe that some external influence is warranted. The current system is simply not working well from several standpoints.

Intrainstitutional Inefficiencies

Perhaps the most striking set of conditions constraining effective R&D output in the Third World is found within research institutes. Mexico uncovered a constellation of intrainstitutional inefficiencies in the mid-1970s (Consejo Nacional de Ciencia y Tecnología [CONACYT] 1976; James 1980). Frequently, the institute director, rather than those who would actually use equipment, specified what research materials were to be ordered; 60 percent of equipment was unusable because of poor maintenance; only about 10 percent of institutes had collaborative research arrangements with other agencies; sharing of expensive pieces of equipment was rare among departments within the same institute; and top researchers spent a good deal of their time in routine recording and bookkeeping activity because of the shortage of technical assistants.

A more recent and comprehensive glimpse of these intrainstitutional "housekeeping" problems has been provided by Gaillard and Ouattar (1988). In 1985 they surveyed 489 researchers in sixty-seven developing countries that held research grants from the Stockholm-headquartered International Foundation for Science. They found that one-third have no access to catalogs of scientific instruments and only 17 percent have access to current catalogs. Very often, when catalogs are available, they include equipment from only one or two firms. Basic errors are often made in ordering equipment, such as ignoring what cycles and voltage are standard in the receiving country or the availability of three-pronged sockets. Attempts to adapt the equipment ex post often result in malfunctions.

"Big ticket" pieces of equipment are often acquired for prestige purposes—electron microscopes, X-ray and nuclear magnetic resonance units, or high-resolution spectographs sit unused much or all of the time. Donor agencies do not have clean hands here. In Ethiopia, a survey of six thousand pieces of laboratory equipment donated by aid agencies, worth about $50 million, revealed that only 10–15 percent of the thirty-eight Ethiopian institutions prepared their own equipment specifications. The remaining organizations had equipment donated with minimum participation in defining needs. When equipment is sent abroad for repairs, as it often is, well over half such repairs take five months or longer; between 5 and 10 percent take fifteen to eighty-four months. Red tape for getting repairs accomplished locally is so daunting that researchers limit the number of users or even find it easier to order a new piece of equipment. In developed countries, the ratio of researchers to technical assistants supporting them is about 1:1 (France and Germany) and 1:1.5 (Sweden), compared with 6:1 (Indonesia), 2.5:1 (Philippines), and 3:1 (Egypt).

These intrainstitutional inefficiencies are not directly related to R&D project selection, but the same set of incentives and sanctions devised to improve research undertakings should serve to foster a more rational use of research agencies' resources.

Critical Minimum Thresholds

Another set of difficulties for achieving an effective use of resources devoted to science and technology revolves around the choice of research projects. For openers, the literature is replete with claims that a lack of direction in focusing R&D undertakings—another way of referring to an overly liberal framework for individual or institutional selection of projects—leads to such a proliferation of projects and such thinly spread resources that the majority of research activities come to naught because of a failure to achieve some critical minimum threshold of effort. Emphasis is usually placed on the minimum number of researchers that are needed, although clearly a deficiency in equipment, access to information, or financial resources can be equally damaging.

Thus, as usually stated, a critical minimum threshold refers to the number of active and interacting researchers for a project, below which the probability of success is very low. Two things seem obvious: (1) the critical minimum will depend on the scope and nature of the research; and (2) there is no scientific way to pinpoint precisely a minimum threshold—it is a matter of judgment, preferably informed by past experience regarding similar research efforts.[1]

Patently, there are some projects that can be conducted effectively by one researcher, and the activity need not be full-time. Moravcsik, a keen observer of S&T activities within developing countries, believes that, after taking into account appropriate qualifications regarding the abilities of the researchers, the field under investigation, and "other factors," "the number is certainly not larger than five, well within the capabilities of a budding institution" (1975: 54). In these days of organized team research, this figure seems excessively optimistic. We are fishing in murky waters here but, as reference points, Brown (1973: 24) puts the minimum for basic research within a single university at about ten scientists, and Robinson (1973: 88) reports that "it was found [in the United Kingdom] that research units of less than ten people were almost purely channels of communications and not adding to knowledge." In complex R&D activities the estimates range far higher: "To produce fruitful results, most drug companies feel it necessary to have a critical mass in their research groups. Some firms indicate that at least 200 employees per research unit are required for this critical mass" (National Academy of Sciences 1973: 33). Wionczek (1979: 222) believed research establishments in most fields require a minimum of twenty professionals to do effective work. Segal (1987a) recommends that research units in Africa that have fewer than ten professionals be disbanded.

In the early 1970s Venezuela's Department of Sociology and Statistics recorded 3,744 research projects being pursued by 2,536 researchers, an average of about one and a half researchers per project (Peñalver 1973: 217). In addition, we can presume that in keeping with the norm in Latin America, many of the individuals involved were part-time employees. Mexico's CONACYT (1976: 15, 32) reported that in 1974, 64.4 percent of research institutions employed five researchers or fewer and only 3.5 percent had more than twenty. Per project, there was less than one full-time researcher. In the mid-1980s Schwartzman (1986) surveyed a sample of research units in the Brazilian states of Rio de Janeiro, São Paulo, Rio Grande do Sul, Minas Gerais, Pernambuco, Bahia, and the Federal District (Brasilia) in the fields of biological, medical, exact and earth sciences, technology and agricultural research. For 4,774 "research units" the average number of scientists was 5.6.

A priori, it would seem to me that, based on the fragmented information at hand (not to mention opinions by a variety of knowledgeable observers), a large chunk of R&D projects in Latin America (and one would surmise in the Third World generally) suffers from a failure to mount a critical minimum effort. Even if numbers per project were identical for both wealthy industrial countries and Third World nations, there is reason to believe that the latter would be at a disadvantage. First, as we have seen, the paucity of technical assistants means inevitably that Third World scientists spend an inordinate amount of their time in routine activities.

Second, the count of scientists is likely to overstate the number of productive researchers. The observations of Sarukhán (1989: 268–269), Rector of Universidad Nacional Autónoma de México (UNAM), on the Mexican count is enlightening. As opposed to counts ranging from fourteen thousand to sixteen thousand, he figures that in 1987 Mexico had about 3,526 scientists who worked full-time at their profession and had published within the last three to five years, an estimate obtained by using the membership rolls of the Sistema Nacional de Investigadores. In order to adjust for the bias that membership might entail, Sarukhán adjusted for nonmembership at UNAM and extrapolated the findings to Mexico, estimating that there are about 5,500 individuals in the natural sciences and engineering engaged in some level of research activity; nine thousand if social sciences are included. In similar investigations, Schoijet (1979: 381) has remarked on the number of part-time researchers in Mexico—in the late 1970s only 49 percent had full-time positions. Vessuri (1984: 227), speaking of Venezuela, says that "there are also many teachers who have survived by teaching or through their political connection; the latter are counted as scientists or research workers without having done any research." Vessuri also comments on the lure that administrative positions have for scientists. Citing Layrisse (1985), she points out that approximately 60 percent of Bolivian scientists are in occupations unconnected with research (1986: 28). In national surveys, these individuals are likely to be listed as scientists.

A third reason that a critical minimum of researchers for a given task is likely to be larger in a developing country vis-à-vis a mature industrial nation is the paucity of formal and informal linkages to other research agencies and supporting institutions.

Lack of Relevance

The claim is also made that much of the research conducted in developing countries, Latin America included, is not really relevant to the needs of the country concerned. Morales (1989: 244) believes that postgraduate education in Latin America is almost always divorced from important national problems, and, according to Vessuri: "Frequently those branches of science which are most developed in a Latin American country, and which are closer to the point where they could cease being imitative of work at the world centre of science, are the least related to practical economic problems" (1984: 7). Schoijet's assertion would also be typical of many observers: "Most of the scientific communities of the poor countries are inert and unproductive, but in their most productive areas they look outwards and not within the country" (1979: 384).

Although not conclusive, there is some evidence to support these allegations. Krauskopf and associates (1986) surveyed Latin American– and Caribbean-authored scientific and technical articles indexed by the Institute for Scientific Information in 1981. They found, as others had in earlier studies, that scientific activity is concentrated in the life sciences, with less emphasis on mathematics ("almost non-existent"), chemistry, and physics, fields that are needed to support industrial development. Agricultural research was also lower than expected, although the authors point out that several useful journals in this field are not indexed in their source.

In another review of Latin American scientific publications, sponsored by the IDB, de Arregui obtained similar results. Between 1973 and 1984 there was a lack of growth (relative to total publications) in chemistry and mathematics, although engineering showed a slight increase and physics was on the rise. Still, she concluded: "The heavy concentration on life sciences . . . has been a characteristic of the research efforts of the underdeveloped countries, as has the scanty emphasis on chemistry, physics and engineering" (1988: 295).

Proportion of Effort Along the Pure-Applied Spectrum

This brings up a closely related, but by no means identical consideration; namely, the balance of research activities along a spectrum ranging from pure or fundamental research to applied activities. The majority opinion seems to hold that Latin America and other developing regions have unduly skewed the composition of their research activities toward fundamental and experimental science.

But, before continuing, what is wrong with this? Several champions of science in developing countries are not overly alarmed about the situation. Sábato (1969: 183), for example, has recommended that the distinction between good science and bad science should be the primary concern, not whether research leans more toward basic or applied undertakings; the latter distinction, he believed, should only become a real issue once the scientific community and investigative activity has reached the necessary critical threshold. Moravcsik (1975: 111) claimed that the improvement of the quality of applied research and the fostering of stronger linkages along the entire pure-applied spectrum "should be the primary targets of attention, not the redressing of numerical ratios between the two."

No one can quarrel with the advisability of stamping out bad science, improving research quality wherever it appears along the spectrum, and forging stronger links within the entire research and development community. Yet, economists fancy that there is indeed a productive distinction to be made between the pure and applied terminals of the continuum. As we scroll through the spectrum toward pure science, economists are convinced that: success for any given project becomes more unpredictable; it is more difficult for the research entity to capture the full economic benefits from a successful outcome;[2] and, ordinarily, any social and/or commercial payoff is further down the road. For all of these reasons most economists advise developing nations to bias their research budgets in favor of applied projects compared to the configurations of S&T expenditures in the wealthier nations.

Be that as it may, this does not appear to be what is taking place in Latin America specifically, or the developing countries in general. For some earlier evidence, one might note Herrera's (1972: 22) estimate that over 50 percent of total S&T spending in Latin America goes for basic research. In 1972 Venezuela's combined spending on free basic research and oriented basic research amounted to 37.3 percent of its total. This compared with roughly 10 percent for England and France and 20 percent for other Western countries (Peñalver 1973: 215). More recently, Schwartzman (1986) found that 21 percent of leaders of research units in the Brazilian states preferred to do "mainly pure research" and 17 percent preferred "all types of work"—a category that would include some pure investigation.

Science Policy and Technology Policy:
How Much Integration?

Should science and technology fall under a single all-encompassing policy or should each enjoy its own separate constellation of support measures and policy prescriptions? Wionczek made it clear that he would not endorse either extreme, but he did seem to favor a great deal of autonomy, both for science planning and policy and the counterparts in technology. Although he did not advocate their divorce (1979b: 177), he felt that "[S&T planning] must make a distinction between science planning and technology planning" (171) and that "scientific planning offers a different sort of challenge, and calls for approaches and methodologies different from those involved in technological planning" (172). Hodara perhaps even more strongly advocates distinct policies for science and technology. In critiquing what he calls "a holistic approach," he points out dangers inherent in blurring "institutional boundaries among science, technology and economics," which, in turn, "overlooks the distinctive requirements of science as a fledgling product" (1979a: 182).

Both Wionczek and Hodara believed that a misguided acceptance of the "linear" concept of scientific and technological progress, usually expressed as the notion that scientists produce the necessary raw knowledge that is then turned into socially useful products and processes by technicians, helped inspire a holistic approach. Others have had harsh words about the linear concept in the context of S&T planning in Latin America. In their critique of Venezuela's First Science and Technology Plan, Antonorsi-Blanco and Avalos Gutiérrez (1980) asserted that one of the primary reasons that planning was faulty at the outset was that its formulators accepted the linear model. According to Vessuri—who agrees—part of the blame for the plan, which was elaborated by the Consejo Nacional de Investigaciones Científicas y Tecnológicas (CONICIT) to cover 1976–1980, can be placed on the definitional categories and planning-style recommendations of UNESCO, which leaned heavily on the linear concept (1984: 230–231). As she observed in the same article (231):

> [Venezuelan planners] were therefore unable to recognize that technological development has a certain immanent tendency, an autonomous potentiality of growth from within, just like the autonomy of scientific knowledge. The local planners failed to understand that technological development is not simply an epiphenomenal function of the development of basic science. They did not see that although technology, especially in the contemporary situation, is very much affected by scientific progress, and is indeed in many ways dependent on it, the promotion of basic science is not a guarantee of technological development.

Before going further, perhaps it should be said that, although the complex interrelations between science and technology are still being mapped out, I think it fair to say that the old idea that innovations march in lockstep from basic science through directed basic science and experimental design, finally to emerge at the applied research and pilot phases, is no longer acceptable. This progression is but one of many permutations, and historical examples of other sequences abound. The piano, steam engine, zipper, and ballpoint pen leaned lightly, if at all, on scientific knowledge (Clarke 1985: 5), and semiconductors and fractional distillation techniques were in use before they were subjects of scientific investigation (Rosenberg 1982). Experimentation by amateurs with shortwave radio stimulated scientific research that led to greater understanding of the ionosphere, and the behavior of metals in steel furnaces motivated metallurgical research into their properties (Rosenberg 1982). Sabet (1985: 206) believes that in agricultural research the impetus usually flows from the applied end of the spectrum in the direction of basic research. Although he does not address the interrelation of science and technology explicitly, Clark (1987) has made a convincing case that technological trajectories are similar (but not identical) to scientific counterparts, thus at least implying that technological progress has a great deal of elasticity with respect to scientific change.

While I fully share Wionczek's and Hodara's acceptance of nonlinearity, it seems to me this justifies *greater* integration between science and technology policies, not less. Pronounced separation will not only run the risk of prolonging scientific undertakings less than optimally suited to long-run development needs, it presents a barrier to beneficial feedback of stimuli to the scientific community from technological and commercial activities.

Virtually all observers of S&T activities in the Third World express concern over inadequate linkages among many of its components. If my analysis, which builds on Wionczek's observations about Mexico, is on the mark, there is serious disarticulation between S&T practices and prevailing political priorities, social preoccupations, and cultural modes. Hodara (1979a) reveals the gulf between science and technology when he highlights the hostility between scientists and engineers who have reached the policymaking level.[3] Perhaps the most publicized weak link is between the results of S&T efforts taken as a whole and the needs of the productive sector, which constitutes the largest potential user of locally generated knowledge. A collection of papers (Williams Silveira 1985) of the United Nations Center for Science and Technology for Development (UNCSTD) panel, that met in Lima, is replete with laments about the dearth of demand-pull signals from productive entities.

The interstices that could bolster this link are legion—one might mention industrial liaison among R&D institutes and users of technology, consulting engineering services, development promotion, technical assistance, demonstration projects, extension services, technical and market feasibility studies, and market-testing. And even this catalog omits the all-important hookup with some source for funding. Wionczek and Hodara were very much aware of these shortcomings. However, they tended to see this as warranting less integration between science policy and technology, whereas it seems to me that the reverse is true.

This in no way is meant to endorse an extremely holistic approach, but I do believe that science, technology, and production policies must be intimately interconnected. Allowing the three to proceed in a parallel fashion (and neither Wionczek or Hodara suggested that they should) is folly, and mere coordination, it seems to me, is inadequate. Once again, we might mention Hodara's (1979a) concerns, drawn from experience, about scientists and engineers cohabiting important policymaking agencies and constantly at each others' throats. My point is that if some mechanism, or process, or shared experience cannot engender a substantial degree of cooperation and appreciation of the potentially symbiotic nature of the two professions, then "the jig is up." I am not convinced that dual policies will rectify the problem. Two rival factions would still remain—the only difference would be that the hostility would be interagency rather than intra-agency. There is an express need for consciously designed instruments to foster healthy interfaces among the participating components.

Incomplete Socialization of Science and Technology

A dramatic illustration of the lack of appreciation of the contributions that science and technology can make to socioeconomic development is the demise of a carefully prepared plan in Mexico during the mid-1970s. The Plan Indicativo de Ciencia y Tecnología (CONACYT 1976) was devoted to bringing some order out of chaos through elaborating goals, priorities, and planning instruments for S&T policy. It provided a detailed examination of scientific and technological infrastructure and technology policy instruments, and priority research areas were specified by economic sector. The plan concentrated on the 1976–1982 period, but in an obvious attempt to overcome the *sexenio* barrier—a tendency to confine planning and actions to each six-year presidential term—some elements of the plan extended well into the 1990s. It was widely hailed as the state of the art in Third World S&T planning.[4]

The Plan Indicativo never really got off the ground, a fact that was bitterly disappointing to its creators. Two short-term events adversely affected the plan: It appeared just before a presidential succession, and thus the usual (in Mexico) shuffle in administrative personnel and shifts in priorities took place; in addition, the appearance of the plan coincided with the economic and financial discord associated with downward adjustments of the Mexican peso that occurred in 1976. While the framers of the plan recognized these proximate difficulties, they believed the problems were far more deep-seated. After all, in the boom years of 1978–1981 there was no serious move to resurrect the plan, implying that economic and financial matters were not the only impediments.

On reflection, many observers came to believe that the socialization of science and technology in Mexico was incomplete and inadequate to muster support for a systematic national approach from the political arena, business groups, and even from within the scientific community itself. As one of the architects of the plan, Wionczek (1979c: 230), put it, "The authors . . . overestimated the interest of the Mexican political system in science and technology, at the same time underestimating the dead weight of federal bureaucracy and parochial interests of the small national scientific and technological communities." "The absence of political modernization, the severely deficient social organization, the very poorly designed educational system, and scientific and technological backwardness" combined to retard Mexico's development (1979c: 220). Wionczek (1979b: 75) pointed out that, as of the early 1980s, "there is not even one fairly competent history of the development of science and technology in Mexico." Finally, in retrospect, he regarded the support for the plan as temporary and circumstantial (Wionczek 1981: 62).

Wionczek is not alone in his opinion. Hodara (1979b: 20) believes that the "scientific spirit" wherein "the intrinsic value of science and technology as an expression of human culture is taken for granted has only been precariously internalized in Mexico." Amadeo (1979: 158) faults the political receptivity accorded S&T policy when he alleges that "the political support given to CONACYT was more formal than real and was conditioned to the changes in the bureaucratic structure of the government."

It is also interesting that when Mexico initiated a scheme to keep researchers from leaving the country and achieved some geographic dispersion of research activities in 1985, the objectively administered standards for disbursing material incentives unmasked many incompetents who had "sailed for years under the flag of genius masquerading as saviors of science" (Roche 1985: 171). Furthermore, in a telling observation, Schoijet (1979: 411) reminds us that there was no organized protest by the S&T community when the plan was scrapped despite the fact that over two hundred people had actively worked on drafting it, indicating "both the fragile nature of the consensus achieved and the lack of coherence of the Mexican scientific community." Urquidi (1986: 187) underscores Mexico's political indifference when he states: "Although the director of CONACYT was supposedly the 'science advisor' to the President and a member of the Cabinet, decisions were in fact taken on industrial policy, public investment, education, and not least, financial and monetary policy, that did very little to enhance Mexico's own capacity in R&D."

Aside from political apathy, the educational system is often assigned a good deal of the blame. Schoijet (1979: 392) faults an educational bureaucracy, itself trained in a humanistic or legal tradition, that is "only perfunctorily interested in scientific and technological education." Evidently, these difficulties are not confined to Mexico. Because of the lack of a scientific tradition in Latin American universities, an overexpansion that diluted quality, and political interference both within and outside academe, there has been a serious debate about giving up on universities as the flagship institutions for conducting R&D in Latin America. As described by Vessuri (1986: 34–35), Ernesto Mayz Vallenilla, former rector and founder of the Simón Bolívar University in Venezuela, and Francisco Sagasti, an economist directing a think tank in Peru, argued that the lion's share of R&D should be located in agencies outside institutions of higher learning.

There are socialization problems within R&D entities as well. Lomnitz (1979), in a case study of a Mexican university's medical and biological studies institute, found that the only sure way for scientists to advance their careers was to go into administration. There was a feeling that it was impossible to compete with foreign science, a sense of poor communication within the institute, and a suspicion that a critical mass of resources had not been attained. She also found a rather rigorous hierarchy that, on balance, was probably not conducive to learning or producing science. We have already noted the estimate by Layrisse (1985) that 60 percent of Bolivian scientists have been syphoned off into other pursuits.

As additional evidence of the lack of socialization of science and technology in Latin America, I mention the targeting of the scientific community during periods of military suppression (Street 1981b). Furthermore, analyses of Latin American fictional literature indicate that technology tends to be seen in a negative light (Lyon 1987; Robinette 1987).

Selected Policy Suggestions

The recommendations made here are highly selective and do not pretend to "cover the waterfront." Indeed, there is a whole mountain of issues that have not been broached here, including technology policies of multinationals, the poor R&D showing of the Latin American private sector, the extent to which recommendations apply to extremely poor nations,[5] the role of alternative technologies—the catalog could be extended. My intent here is merely to make a meaningful if limited contribution to policy deliberation.

Two cautionary remarks are in order. The objectives of S&T policy should not be overstated. There is a need for fewer R&D projects with better funding and staffing for those that survive; project composition should shift more in the direction of applied R&D; and demand-pull from social and commercial needs should have more influence on what scientists and technicians are doing. The aims of planning and policy should include safeguards that make it highly unlikely that the most egregiously wasteful R&D projects can be perpetuated over any considerable length of time. A system is needed that can assure modest improvements in project efficiency, at both the internal margin of existing R&D and the external margin of new R&D agencies or projects. Fostering excessively high expectations, especially for science, is a mistake, and will cause Latin American societies to become even less appreciative of the potential contributions of S&T.

Thus, I am positing an approach that attempts to bring about improvements along the lines indicated above, followed by efforts to better the system through experimentation and learning from what seems to work well and what does not. This is another way of saying that any attempt to achieve an optimum S&T system based exclusively, or even heavily, on reductionist reasoning will fail and disappoint.[6]

Another caveat is warranted regarding the desirability of altering the mix of R&D projects more toward applied endeavors, because it is a recommendation easily misunderstood. No "basis bashing" is implied—no conscious dismantling of the fundamental end of the R&D spectrum is contemplated. Nonlinearity does not mean that *some* new products and processes, important ones at that, do not progress in linear fashion. Langer (1989: 96) makes a case that Brazil's development of physics in earlier years—uncharacteristic, as we have seen, of Latin America as a whole—helped set the stage for that country's contemporary computer industry. Wionczek (1979a: 172) offered another compelling reason for preserving basic science: "Science has other important functions besides supporting the expansion of technical know-how. The most important function, perhaps, is that of providing a base for a general scientific culture, badly needed for an increased degree of overall rationality in LDC societies." He goes on to say that science offers a source of national satisfaction and prestige, while providing important links to the outside world. Thus, we are considering a matter of proper proportions along the spectrum, not an either/or proposition.

Socialization

I am afraid that I am devoid of any bright ideas on how to accelerate and deepen the socialization of S&T in Latin America and other developing areas. Clearly, education and popularization are important,[7] and one might surmise success will beget success. Enhancing the quality and productivity of S&T output can lead to greater social acceptance and appreciation of what science and technology can (and cannot) accomplish for development. Fellow institutionalists, and those with similar bents, who are interested in pursuing the matter might find Hayden's (1982a, 1982b, 1986) social fabric matrix useful in this regard.[8]

Improving Linkages

We need to know much more about how constructive bonds can develop between R&D and productive sectors in developing countries. Efforts by UNCSTD have shed much light on the many facets of the problem and how they manifest themselves (Williams Silveira 1985), but little has been accomplished in identifying institutional changes that could remedy the situation. In particular, we need insights as to to how successes have come about. I am happy to report that this is exactly what UNCSTD is undertaking. Williams Silveira and her colleagues are putting together a collection of case studies involving linkages between the results of biotechnological research and the users of that technology.[9] This is a step in the right direction, but much more remains to be done.

In addition, there is a place for institutional experimentation. I cite as an illustration the case of the Centro para Inovación Tecnológica (CIT), a relatively small center associated with UNAM. CIT offers courses on various aspects of S&T policy, both for academic credit and certificate, and sponsors roundtables and public lectures on S&T affairs. More to the point of our concern here, CIT stands ready to take a laboratory result that seems promising and follow through with the necessary steps to get it accepted commercially. UNAM's rector originally wanted to require that all ideas coming from the university's considerable number of research laboratories be channeled through CIT, but, much to his credit, Mario Waissbluth, who eventually became CIT's director, would not accept that idea. He wanted CIT to be judged on the basis of its track record rather than by administrative fiat.[10] The last time I visited CIT's offices, during 1986, the center had a portfolio of approximately two dozen projects that were being pursued. Similar institutional experiments might pay dividends, but whatever institutional mechanisms are devised, they should be deliberately included as an integral part of S&T planning.

Small and Medium-Sized Enterprises

Efforts to expand the number of external sources for technology should be continued and reinforced. The expansion of technology transmission through joint ventures, or other contractual arrangements, with small and medium-sized enterprises (SMEs) appears especially promising. A series of surveys conducted by UNCTAD[11] in the early 1980s indicated that SMEs were at a disadvantage in operating in developing countries by reason of their inability to carry out large-scale projects. In addition, SMEs have traditionally had more difficulty in getting inside the "information loop" and finding out who is in the market for what.

Compared to large multinational firms, however, SMEs have the following attractions for Third World hosts: They are more flexible both in decisionmaking and in their production processes; they have a greater propensity to procure material inputs locally; they are more willing to sell specialized technical components or technologies rather than to insist on an investment package; they are more willing to engage in joint ventures; they are more willing to provide unpatented technology; they are more willing to offer the latest technology and know-how; and, because of more balanced bargaining power between buying and selling parties, with SMEs there tend to be fewer restrictive clauses in agreements and more favorable terms regarding training of local employees and future transfers of improvements in the technology that is involved.

What specific actions can encourage a more active competition of SMEs with larger foreign firms investing in Third World nations? First, the disadvantages of SMEs can be partially offset if, on large projects, they are considered for appropriate subcontracting roles, and if public support is forthcoming for developing international, commercial, on-line data bases. Subcontracts, especially, should be awarded in foreign aid projects, "an area which until now has been almost exclusively reserved for major national consultancy, engineering and manufacturing enterprises" (Herbolzheimer and Ouane 1985: 145). Perhaps it is not too naive to suppose that aid recipients can convince donors to experiment with including SMEs in assistance packages. Regarding the pooling of information: as of 1982 there were in excess of one thousand commercial data bases, mainly in developed countries; data bases are needed that are specifically geared to advertising technology on the "wish lists" of public and private enterprises in developing regions.

Second, red tape, bureaucratic delays, and excessive amounts of paperwork are inordinately burdensome to SMEs, in part because they cannot afford specialists to deal with these matters. A conscious effort by Third World governments to streamline the rules of the game would be beneficial.

Other, more imaginative, institutional changes might be tried, but the main motivation should come from the real possibility that SMEs can be a source of technology that can often be obtained on a more advantageous basis than from the multinationals.

In Situ R&D

Often it is suggested that developing countries should give high priority to R&D projects that make sense locationally or geographically. Such projects are much more likely to be relevant to local development needs, while being less likely to require technology obtained from abroad. Segal (1987a, 1987b), a strong advocate of in situ projects, suggests that R&D pertaining to natural resources, climatic and environmental conditions, tropical agriculture, marine biology, hydrology, geology, applied biotechnology, renewable energy systems, agriculture, and appropriate technology would be good bets for Latin America and the Caribbean. I regard this as sound advice and add that many such research areas were mentioned in the sectoral lists of priorities in Mexico's Plan Indicativo.

By way of illustrating R&D in this mold, let us consider mineral extraction through microbial leaching in the Andean countries. Bacterial leaching takes place under natural conditions but, with controlled intervention by scientists and technicians, the process can be accelerated enormously. The proper microbes are introduced into a mine, old mining dump, or a prepared mound of mineral ore, along with a feeding solution, and, after leaching has occurred, the solution is pumped out and various extraction methods are applied. Copper is the primary metal involved, but application to other metals is possible. Peru, in cooperation with Bolivia, is at the cutting edge of this technology, in part because the developed world has not advanced it sufficiently and in part because it is site-specific in terms of size, mineral content, heat, porosity, and other factors (Warhurst 1984). Mineral extraction is thus perfect for exploiting local R&D talent and building indigenous technological capacities. Another by-product of site-specificity is that laboratory scientists and mining engineers in the field are compelled to work together cooperatively, thus cementing a link that is often weak or missing in Latin America. Chile also is investigating microbial leaching under a tripartite agreement among the University of Chile, the Institute of Technological Research, and the National Copper Corporation (Blackledge 1985: 41). The development of a portfolio of such in situ R&D undertakings seems worth the effort.

Technological Partnership

It may well be an opportune time to press for some major form of collaboration on technological matters within the Americas. If such a technological partnership materializes, clearly the brunt of the financing would fall on the United States, thus running smack against conservative fiscal concerns. Yet, the U.S. stake in the solution of Latin America's problems is becoming patently obvious. The United States is concerned by political instability and for the survival of fragile democracies in the region; environmental worries range from pollution of California's beaches by sewage from Tijuana to the degradation of the rain forests in the Amazon Basin; Latin American external debt management has a direct influence on

U.S. exports and constitutes a threat to the U.S. domestic banking industry. Escalating U.S. attention to Latin America as a source of drugs makes it ever more clear that some of the United States' options are not pleasant, and there is trepidation about illegal migration from south of the border for economic, political, and health reasons. As it sinks in that these problems are extremely serious, are not getting any better, and, above all, are inextricably intertwined, there may be some chance that a more constructive role for the United States will gain support.

Surely, assisting Latin America to achieve some degree of technological mastery is one important ingredient in restoring sustained economic growth; furthermore, it may be achieved at bargain-basement prices compared to having to deal with a deteriorating situation further down the line. Several such proposals are surfacing. One, authored by two former science advisors to the U.S. Embassy in Mexico, is being polished in light of critiques by selected colleagues and could serve as a basis for discussion.[12] All I am suggesting here is that the Latin American nations and the United States should actively explore some substantial technological collaboration that would be in the best interests of all.

Boom and Bust

Latin American S&T budgets have by no means been isolated from the stop-go syndrome so commonly experienced by the region's national economies. As an example, national expenditures on science and technology in Mexico climbed by 26.1 percent in real terms in 1978 and plummeted by 18.7 percent in 1980 (Velasco 1981: 405). Ernesto Palacio Pru, speaking as the president of Venezuela's CONOCIT (cited in Vessuri 1984), tells of his budget that began at 6 million bolívares, rose to 93 million, and fell to 73 million in 1984. After adjusting to predevaluation purchasing power, he calculated that the 1984 budget was about equal to that of 1976. Palacio Pru characterized this situation as a "dromedary" policy because of its likeness to the hump of the Arabian camel. Schwartzman (1985: 111) describes how, "in Brazil, the number of research groups and institutions increased very rapidly when money was available, an expansion that was curtailed very rapidly by the general economic crisis that started to become more evident in the mid 1970s."

Sharp cyclical swings, harmful to an economy as a whole, are especially pernicious when experienced by the S&T community. Curtailment of funding can involve partial or total loss of sunk costs invested in long-term R&D projects, affect morale adversely (Vessuri 1984), and lead to factional fights where contests for survival depend more on political clout than on effective research (Schwartzman 1985). It is perhaps too much to ask that S&T activities be isolated from booms and busts in the economy or major shifts in political priorities, but some measures would ameliorate the intensity of the fluctuations: Exercise some restraint through avoiding a proliferation of new institutes when times are good; during the good times, allocate much of the surplus funds to improving equipment, maintenance, and incentives for existing R&D establishments; and encourage international donor agencies to be particularly generous when curtailment of S&T activities threatens, especially since downward swings are often linked to foreign exchange crises, making it difficult to import scientific supplies and equipment.

Conclusion

Institutional, or evolutionary, economists are often criticized, with some justification, for couching their arguments in such general terms that they do little to inform the beleaguered decisionmaker confronted with day-to-day problems. Some of my past work has been painted with broad strokes and therefore is not immune from accusations along these lines. In this chapter, I have attempted to make amends by providing concrete, specific policy recommendations:

1. Considerably more mileage can be garnered from Latin American S&T budgetary outlays if glaring inefficiencies within R&D institutes can be reduced, if project composition can be shifted to include fewer but more soundly funded and staffed investigations, and if a greater emphasis is placed on R&D geared to ameliorating local socioeconomic problems.

2. External reviews of R&D performance would provide incentives for improving research agencies' performance and represent a vehicle for "creative destruction" of institutes or major projects that become an unwarranted drain on scarce R&D resources.

3. Channeling R&D activity toward appropriate in situ projects would be a move toward relevant, applied undertakings, and deliberately promoting institutional arrangements for bridging the discontinuity between R&D results and the requirements of the productive sector would allow demand-pull incentives to exercise a healthier influence on the selection of R&D projects.

4. Vigorous pursuit of alternative sources, such as SMEs, for procuring technology from abroad is a worthy objective, as are measures insuring some fiscal stability to S&T budgets during fluctuations in the general economy.

5. Finally, in view of the manifest interest throughout the Americas in reinstating sustained economic growth and development in Latin America, the time is ripe for considering an important collaborative initiative to promote the transfer and, above all, the effective absorption and mastery of technology within the region.

Notes

1. C. Richard Bath and I (1979) have attempted to distinguish four critical minimum thresholds: (1) a microminimum for a single, narrowly defined research project; (2) a mesominimum for large, interdisciplinary projects; (3) a macrominimum, beyond which the scientific community could exercise some influence over the allocation of national resources; and (4) a megaminimum, beyond which science and technology affect society's cultural values and the way people view their physical environment.

2. For two seminal articles dealing with the economics of basic research, see Arrow (1962) and Nelson (1959).

3. The problem, evidently, is not confined to Latin America. Choudhuri (1985) recounts the profound disengagement of the majority of university science teachers from R&D activities in India, and universities are relegated to a secondary or tertiary role in China's overall R&D efforts (Jing Su 1990).

4. See, for example, Nadal Egea (1977: 25), who characterizes the plan as "the most important effort for the establishment of a general framework for the S&T policy, not only in Mexico, but among the LDCs, and can only be compared to the S&T plan by India."

5. Some of the ideas I express here were aired before science policy officials in Egypt and Ethiopia while I was on a lecture tour in June 1989. Judging by the reaction, some do apply to very low-income countries.

6. One of Hodara's (1979a) objections to a holistic approach to S&T planning was that it was founded on and helped perpetuate excessive reliance on reductionist thinking.

7. For ideas on popularization, see Anandakrishnan (1985, esp. pt. 2).

8. I want to thank my co-editor, Jim Dietz, for suggesting this point.

9. Personal communication with Williams Silveira.

10. Personal communication with Waissbluth.

11. For citations, see Herbolzheimer and Ouane (1985: 132).

12. Reynaldo Morales and Ronald Lohrding presented a proposal, "A Technological Partnership for the Americas," before the North American Economics and Finance Association, December 28–30, 1989, in Atlanta. James Dietz, Francisco Thoumi, and I each responded to their suggestions, which provide a useful point of departure for further discussion.

10

Technological Autonomy, Linkages, and Development

James L. Dietz

The political will required to build on the existing indigenous technological capability is a world away from the easy declarations about endogenous development at international meetings.

—Kenneth King (1984: 34)

My purpose is to suggest the foundations of a concrete, policy-oriented development strategy that promises both economic growth and greater equity. The approach proposed here has the merit of being connected to verifiable successes in its application elsewhere; it is a strategy borne not of theory but of practice. Ironically, perhaps, it seems to require continual restatement as the cornerstone of successful development despite volumes of implicit evidence in its favor. In a very important sense, then, I restate and recast old truths that have been ignored or forgotten by orthodox, particularly neoliberal, policymakers concerned with development in recent years.

Just how to accelerate progress in the underdeveloped world is a concern that has preoccupied development economics and development economists for a half-century. Still, relatively little consensus has emerged over the appropriate strategy of development, so there remains space for renewed theoretical and empirical intervention in the debate, even though the argument advanced here may be considered by some to be old wine in a new bottle. But, as any epicure will confirm, old wine is valued for a reason.

I will call the development path discussed, recommended, and defended here the technological strategy. At the heart of this approach is the national pursuit of technological autonomy, an aspiration with the blessing that it can be and has been embraced, if not fully understood or implemented, by governments with widely different political ideologies. Moreover, the technological strategy tends to create a dynamic process of social and economic reorganization that transforms the status quo in progressive and equity-enhancing directions, irrespective of the ideological orientation of the state—an especially important consideration in much of the contemporary Third World.

Technological autonomy as the key component for spurring economic development replaces—or, better, is more fundamental than—the more traditional strategies focused on spurring industrialization, such as balanced or unbalanced growth or the creation of an export-oriented trade regime, both of which have been suggested, to one degree or another, by the majority of development economists as the proper road to development, regardless of the weight put on either axis. Industrialization strategies per se, however, have been no panacea for backwardness; there are far too many instances of semiindustrialized but still obviously underdeveloped nations, particularly in Latin America but also in Asia, that suggest the incompleteness of such a policy (Ranis 1981; in Asia, India is an outstanding example of failed industrialization).

My fundamental argument is that where industrialization, whether of the import substitution or export-oriented variety, has been able to foster sustainable economic growth and development, it has done so only when technological autonomy has been integral to the overall strategy, which itself must, of necessity, extend beyond simple, early, or horizontal ISI with its intrinsic limitations (see Chapter 2).[1] Neither can export promotion—the now-fashionable, theoretical cure-all for development ills that emanates from such multilateral aid agencies as the World Bank and the IMF and from far too many in the academy—alone be the engine that drives the process of economic development, like some deus ex machina. A first principle for successful transformation in Latin America requires that *development be internally propelled by improvements in local control over production, founded on a base of unfolding, indigenous technological autonomy.*[2]

An export focus for the economy in the absence of increasing technological autonomy will tend only to sustain the backward productive structures that already are arresting the required transformations; it would perform just as woefully as any misdirected ISI policy in stimulating development. In fact, export-dominated strategies have been effective in ensuring sustained development only when there has been a prior ISI strategy coupled with the maturing, indigenous capacity for domesticated technological adoption and adaptation, and deepening control by domestic factors of production over the process of production (Ranis 1981). Puerto Rico is a striking case of an export-oriented model that failed as a consequence of a skipped-over ISI stage and the absence of an indigenous technological capacity (Dietz 1989: Epilog).

In other words, what most development economists have chosen to emphasize as strategic means to promote development—balanced or unbalanced industrialization, foreign investment, export expansion, or aid—cannot be shown to be sufficient. In fact, the traditional strategies are compatible with both economic development and the reproduction, even strengthening, of economic backwardness in new and sometimes stronger forms. What underlies the successful cases of flourishing economic development is an ever-maturing capacity for indigenous technological adaptation founded upon the widest dissemination of the principles of a technological culture among the population (Shinohara, Yanagihara, and Kim 1983; also see Chapter 9). The necessity for these two constituent elements—progress toward technological autonomy and the inculcation of a technological culture—transcends the nature of the mode of production of an economy or its particular, phenomenal forms of channeling technology into production. The real underpinning for robust economic development, then, is this threshold capacity for technological self-sufficiency supported by a culture increasingly immersed in the values of a technological society.

Elements of the Technological Strategy of Development

At the core of the technological understanding of the process of economic development, and the technological strategy, is the constant dualistic tension existing between technology and the prevailing ceremonial structure of a society (Ayres 1978). Technology—meaning not only the entire accumulated complex of scientific and machine-tool knowledge and the tools themselves, but also the human understanding, skills, education, and training essential for making use of such knowledge and tools—is the indispensable source of greater productivity, expanded output, and higher income, as any economist will admit. The more rapidly technology is able to advance the more rapid will be the pace of economic growth. Slower technological progress means, pari passu, slower economic growth and reduced possibilities for augmenting or creating the social mechanisms that promote greater equity.

What is less well understood by many development economists is how some of society's existing social and economic institutions—including class structure, land tenure, finance and banking, ideology, religion and superstition—as well as the commitment of society to education and free inquiry, and the nature of the ties between industry and the scientific and educational infrastructure, are paramount forces in determining the extent to which technology is able to perform its dynamic and transformative functions. Many of these institutions are Ayresian ceremonial institutions that exist always and in all societies; they are tradition-bound and operate on other than scientific principles by nature. Although it is inconceivable to have a socioeconomic system wherein there are not some such ceremonial institutions—structures that are past-binding and nonprogressive by definition—in those societies whose ceremonial structure is, on balance, relatively weak, facilitating, and complementary to change (or—and this is most important—made so by appropriate state policies), technology will be better able to combine with the production process and contribute to greater productivity and output. On the other hand, in societies whose ceremonial institutional structure is retrograde, especially powerful, and not facilitating of change, and wherein the state does not act to debilitate these structures and ways of thinking and acting, technology is less apt to be adapted, created, or applied to production, and hence the likelihood of greater income and social justice will be adversely affected (see Chapter 7).

Technology, and particularly the enrichment of the human-resources component of technology—often inaptly termed "human capital" accumulation—has been widely identified as a contributor to economic growth beginning at least with the path-breaking work of Denison (1967: 299, 315), who found it responsible for over 40 percent of growth in the United States and the United Kingdom. Kuznets's work also has amply identified the significance of technological change, broadly interpreted, to productivity and economic growth (see Solow [1988] for a succinct overview of the evidence for the empirical significance of technological change); Solow (1988: 314) notes that over 90 percent of increases in output can be accounted for by technology and education.

It is something of an orthodox doctrinal curiosity, then, that—despite the extreme empirical importance that mainstream economists accord to technology in the historical record of economic growth—so little attention is paid to the fundamentals of the technological process in theorizing about economic growth, other than, typically, the disembodied 'A' in Cobb-Douglas or CES production functions. Just as oddly, in the economic history of economic development little has been made of the significance of markets per se as contributors to growth. It is markets and prices, nevertheless, that neoclassical general and partial equilibrium models and their derived development strategies so often stress, leaving out the historically determined and verified role of technology as the primary determinant of growth. As a consequence, the stylized orthodox models from which development strategies originate have focused on factor proportions and substitutability in competitive (or at least contestable) markets where it is relative prices, and not policies, and the invisible hand, not the visible, that dominate, and where technology is afforded, at best, a passive role when it is mentioned at all.

ECLAC's empirical studies have ignored neither technology nor markets, but it must be said that neither has ECLAC's theorizing about development put either markets or technology near the center of its strategies for promoting development in Latin America. ECLAC investigators, like most observers, have understood technology far too narrowly as machines, tools, and processes rather than as a way of thinking, doing, and valuing. And considerably too much of ECLAC's attention has been directed at external factors thwarting the development process, with too little recognition, or at least explicit discussion, of how and why internal constraints have exerted ˉequal or greater opposition to dynamic change in the region.

North American institutionalist theory, which is the basis for the technological view adopted here, offers important insights that may help to enrich ECLAC's theorizing in its search for a new paradigm for development (see *CEPAL Review* [April] 1988; Chapter 3). Institutionalism cannot be faulted for inattention to the central significance of technology to economic growth and to social progress in general. Technological and scientific development, understood in their broadest meanings to include the vital and parallel development of human resources, lies at the heart of institutionalist thinking about development in the Third World as much as in the First and, by extension, although it is only latent in institutionalist analysis, in the socialist world. What has been conspicuously absent from the institutionalist paradigm, however, is any explicit analysis of just how existing backward and technologically retarding ceremonial institutions in Third World nations, which so far have proved so resistant to change, might now be superseded in the face of powerful interests impervious to the need for such a transformation and indifferent to the wider social welfare (Ayres left the door open for social revolution in such circumstances [1978: xxix]).

Recent theoretical extensions, based upon a micro-understanding of individual national development projects that have succeeded, however, make it possible to identify a concrete path—leading from underdevelopment over the threshold of development—that is consistent with, and complementary to, the institutionalist and ECLAC analyses; a path centered on technological change and a maturing, indigenous, and domesticated autonomous technological capacity. Technological autonomy is an aspiration that structural economists of the ECLAC school have come very close to expounding, although perhaps without fully appreciating. Thus, the convergence of North American institutionalist and Latin American structuralist thinking on the problems of underdevelopment and the necessary conditions for overcoming it is even closer than it was when Street (1967) first compared the two schools of thought more than two decades ago. ECLAC economists such as Sunkel increasingly recognize the need to afford greater attention to technology as institutionalists define it. One of the hopes behind this chapter and this book is that a greater measure of communication among structuralists, institutionalists, and other like-minded development economists and policymakers can be the basis for a renewed and dynamic theoretical intervention in development that can, as in the 1950s and 1960s, form the basis for progressive development policies in Latin America into the twenty-first century.

Significantly, the technological autonomy strategy discussed here can be, in fact should be, as important for the Cubas, Chinas, and Nicaraguas of the world where social revolutions have occurred as for the Chiles, Puerto Ricos,

South Africas, and Irans where they have not but where poverty and backwardness continue to dominate amid retarding ceremonial structures. Arguably, technological autonomy is an ideologically neutral strategy necessary for economic development in all societies. Although the precise nature of the political culture of any country will certainly shape specific aspects of the particular strategy selected for achieving technological autonomy and the nature of the technology itself, the strategy is absolutely necessary if successful economic growth is to be achieved, regardless of the nature of the political regime or the prevailing mode of production. It is progress on the path toward an indigenous technological capacity that provides the essential and irreplaceable foundation for economic development; industrialization, export expansion, and the promotion of industrial linkages are only means to realize and to channel the outputs following from the successful creation of an indigenous technological capacity, be it within a capitalist or socialist context.[3]

The Necessity of Technological Autonomy and a Technological Culture

Ayres wrote, in a famous and oft-quoted passage, that "the most important factor in the economic life of any people is the educational level . . . of the community. A technically sophisticated community can and will equip itself with the instrumentalities of an industrial economy. There is no instance of any such community having failed to do so" (1978: xxix). Economic development is thus indistinguishable from technological progress, and, without continuing technological change, economic development falters. Technological change is the result of scientific discovery, experiment, and innovation. In any country, the successful introduction of technology into the domestic production process—what can be called domestic innovation—requires a scientific establishment capable, first, of adopting and adapting foreign-produced technological knowledge (including machines and tools) to local conditions, and, later, of conducting its own research, designing its own experiments, and recognizing the potential of, and sometimes the dangers of, its own discoveries when applied to the domestic economy. Dore (1984: 65–68) refers to these two capacities as ITLC and ITCC—an "independent technology *learning* capacity" and an "independent technology *creating* capacity." ITLC is the initial but fundamental stage on the path to what is here called technological autonomy. Creating an ITLC is the first step toward greater technological self-sufficiency and toward reducing international dependence. It is ITLC that has undergirded the Japanese, Korean, and Taiwanese development "miracles." ITCC comes later, with the further maturation and deepening of the ITLC process that logically precedes it. An

ITLC is essential to achieve development; an ITCC may be necessary to continue development over the longer term, after the initial gains from technological autonomy become more difficult to sustain, as Japan would appear now to be learning (Lynn 1988).[4]

Ayres undeniably introduced an element of determinism in his analysis of the relation between education (and the improvement of human skills in general) and the process of development: "There is no instance of any . . . community" failing to develop once "equipped" with a level of "technically sophisticated" education and training. But, it is a determinism widely if only implicitly shared by most development economists (Rosenberg 1982: 275). Still, this insistence on the absolute primacy of a mass, technologically based education to social and economic development marks an important distinction between institutionalist/technological thinking about the development process and that of most other economists, including those of the ECLAC school. While education and all types of "human capital accumulation" do contribute to furthering economic development in the orthodox theory, they are treated as adjuncts to a supposedly wider and more fundamental process of physical capital accumulation. There is in the neoclassical view an a priori methodological importance assigned to additions of physical capital, which can be "disembodied" from technology, to the production process, as is clear from the nearly exclusive attention devoted to the level of savings and gross domestic investment as the determinants of growth in most macroeconomic and growth models and in the concomitant development policy recommendations of most strategies as applied to the Third World. Human resources are accorded but secondary and derived attention.

Not so in institutionalist/technological analysis: Education and human-resource skills are so integral to the development process as to be wholly inseparable from the process and progress of capital/technological accumulation.[5] In institutionalist analysis, capital disembodied from technology can have no meaning, since physical capital is created from and of the extant fund of technological knowledge and human skills. At times, technology does manifest itself as physical capital and specific machines, but it cannot be disembodied and made to stand alone as a thing. Technology exists as an intangible and accumulating body of knowledge at the world level, capable of being utilized by any given country only to the degree that it has developed a "technologically sophisticated community" (that is, an ITLC) that can use the existing pool of knowledge to employ implements of production to further its own economic progress. As one study properly put it, people, not tools, "are the real agents of technology transfer and diffusion" (Radhakrishna 1980: 170). The institutionalist argument thus stands the entire neoclassical edifice on its head: Rather than capital embodying technology, it is technology, or some of it at any rate, that embodies capital.

Technology, then, is not a "thing," but a way of thinking that molds culture and behavior and that may manifest itself phenomenally as machines and tools.

The technologically sophisticated community in institutionalist thinking is composed not only of knowledge workers, such as scientists, engineers, and researchers, but just as importantly of an indigenous entrepreneurial center of aggressive agents able to appreciate the potential of new ways of producing and able and willing—really, driven—to make use of them through constant innovation in the domestic production process. Also essential is a sufficiently large body of production workers endowed with the requisite skills and attitudes that make them capable of operating and adapting to the constantly and rapidly changing productive methods introduced by the entrepreneurial center. The activities of the entrepreneurial center will be concentrated predominately in the private sector, but in the underdeveloped world the state, directly or indirectly, may need to play a role, and it is here that state macropolicies can either inhibit or contribute to rapid development.

However, absent effective institutions such as universities and independent research centers, including corporate R&D operations, that allow the emerging ITLC to participate at a world-class level in technological adaptation, training, development, and implementation, progress toward technological autonomy will surely stumble. Primary and secondary education must also be structured so as continuously to inculcate students into the culture and values of a technological society in support of the goal of ITLC (Japan's education ministry, for example, is officially the Ministry of Education, Science, and Culture [Lynn 1988: 166 n. 7]).

This indigenous technological capacity, supported by a technologically supportive cultural milieu, is necessary since the preconditions for development absolutely cannot be borrowed (Street 1987a: 1878, 1881; also see the interesting analysis in Reséndiz Nuñez 1987–1988). Technology, properly conceptualized, cannot be imported off the shelf as a bundle of things because "technological progress can be understood only by recognizing that human skills and the tools by and on which they are exercised are logically inseparable" (Ayres 1978: xv). It is thus not possible to effectively borrow the manifestations of technology—physical capital, tools, and implements, which are the usual focus of technology transfer—and expect to become developed, if the human skills and the culture required to make effective use of this fragment of technology are absent or but poorly formed within the borrowing country (see Reich [1989] for a consideration of what the United States needs to do to compete with Japan in this regard; his analysis is complementary to mine).

It is the human-resource and social dimension of technology that makes an indigenous technological capacity so important to any successful process of development. Technology is more than tools, blueprints, and machines; it is a complex, value-laden social process imbedded in key institutions of society, from the family to the schools to the state, that inculcates an unconscious but deeply formed technological culture as an integral aspect of society's ideology and canon. This culture must exist, or be in substantial formation, if there is to be any hope for meaningful technological borrowing and adaptation, let alone for technological progress that is at least partially internally generated and then applied to domestic production processes.

An insistence on technological autonomy as a requisite for economic and social development, as opposed to simply expanded use of the implements of technology diffused from technology-producing countries, although not a recent emphasis, still is not widely appreciated or understood (James, Street, and Jedlicka 1980: 588; James 1988; Chapter 9).[6] From the 1960s at least, the necessity of creating an indigenous technological capacity has been recognized by some analysts and governments, although all too often studies on what was needed to create autonomous technology made it seem as if there was some automatic connection between the creation of universities and polytechnics and an ITLC (see Latapi 1980: 24 for a critique). In the 1970s and 1980s, a sharp turn was made with the increasing recognition given to enriching the meaning of endogenous technological development, expressed programatically in, for example, the Organization of African Unity's Lagos Plan of Action for the Economic Development of Africa (King 1984: 32–34).

One official study went so far as to state that "the desire of all developing countries is to become technologically independent" (Radhakrishna 1980: 169). As true as that may be, what has been lacking in all such plans is a sophisticated sensitivity as to what technological independence or self-sufficiency really means beyond the strongly felt sentiment to reduce dependence on the North. Too often, policy efforts have been directed primarily at gaining preferred access to the manifestations of technology rather than to acquiring domestically the capacity "to do" technology, that is, an ITLC strategy.

Until quite recently, this could perhaps be explained by the belief, held even by many institutionalists, that technological diffusion or horizontal technology transfers (McIntyre 1986: 10) from the First to the Third World could help poor countries skip over stages of domestic technological development. In this way, they would be permitted to enter directly into the intensive stage of technology utilization. It was believed that such diffusion of machines could materially contribute to a more rapid narrowing of the income gap between the center and periphery. Many countries have attempted to follow this diffusion path by attracting multinational investment, the major source for cutting-edge technology, and yet they still have failed to become developed. And they have failed to become developed not because of any generalized conspiratorial plot by MNCs to keep the Third World backward, as some commentators have argued, but because countries of the Third World to which MNCs have brought, sold, or licensed technology have yet to create a technological culture and a capacity for technological autonomy that would permit the benefits of tool and machine diffusion to be realized through learning at the point of production (see Gordon [1965: 174–177] for an early argument making this point).

Hirschman long ago warned of the inherent dangers of technological borrowing, particularly when it is mediated by MNCs' direct investment, as so much of it is in Latin America. He (1971: 227–229) cautioned that attempting to attain technology through direct foreign investment may act more to "harm the quality of local factors of production" than be a spur to the expansion of the "missing" local inputs, including innovating entrepreneurs. Rather than serve as a complement to local technological development and as a boost to locally controlled and directed production, foreign inputs can become substitutes for the local factors in environments where the necessary ITLC strategy has not been implemented, further stunting the possibility of developing the institutions and individuals capable of, and necessary for, learning from the tool and machine implements of technology developed and used by MNCs. But, this factor substitution or, better, factor displacement and factor atrophy effect, is not caused by the MNCs so much as it is permitted and even desired by the local ruling elites, which too often are actually uninterested in seeing technological autonomy achieved (Radhakrishna 1980: 168).

Institutionalists should never have fallen prey to such mechanical technological diffusion optimism. Technology must be understood, used, and applied; it cannot, by itself and coming from outside, spin straw into gold, turn an underdeveloped nation into a developed one. Technological progress—and hence economic development—flourishes only in an appropriate and facilitating environment. If that climate, composed of the entire ceremonial-institutional, ideological, and class structure of society, is not already conducive to, and supportive of, indigenous scientific adaptation and discovery and technological creation and application—and, thus, if that society is not already on the path to technological autonomy and an ITLC—it is a highly dubious proposition to presume that those same sociostasis ceremonial structures will be open to exogenous sources of technological change that equally threaten the reproduction of the prevailing, power-augmenting ceremonial structures already holding back change (Gordon [1965: 179] and Urquidi [1964: 107–109] long ago seem to have made the same case, although less unconditionally than I make it here). Profit-oriented private MNCs, which naturally strive to contain the positive externalities generated by their valuable and expensively created proprietary technological knowledge, are very often ideal agents for recalcitrant elites who wish to minimize the technological contamination of the economic and social processes they wish to continue to control. "The dominant classes know that technological development cannot be introduced merely as an isolated input to production; but is part of a global process, which once started is very difficult to stop, and which endangers the stability of the social structure on which their privileges are based" (Herrera 1973: 35).

The Role of Education in Development

To understand why Latin America remains relatively underdeveloped it is necessary to probe more deeply into why the human-resource base has not been expanded and why the pursuit of an indigenous technological capacity has been disregarded to such a significant degree. And, to understand these factors it is necessary to come to grips with the role of state power in Latin America.

Education and State Power

The provision of education is a basic responsibility assumed by the state in all countries. Government expenditures and government policies directed toward education and research give shape to a country's educational and scientific infrastructure and the resulting skills and values of the population passing through all levels of the educational structure. Even where private educational facilities significantly contribute to schooling, the state still plays a significant role through, for example, tax policies affecting private schools and by the setting of minimum standards of acceptable performance. This makes an examination of the role of the state and state power essential for understanding a country's level of educational attainment, for appreciating the "technological sophistication" of the community, and for evaluating that nation's possibilities for sustained and autonomous development.

Conventional neoclassical wisdom, at least that particularly self-conscious segment associated with Milton Friedman and the Chicago School, has tended to presume that liberal capitalism can best contribute to fulfilling the promises of democracy, and that the full development of society will follow if it is not burdened with unnecessary state intervention into the market, including into the sphere of education. Two axioms underpin this perspective: first, that capitalism is productive of democracy; and second, that liberal capitalism is productive of technological development and economic progress without state interference into the "natural laws" of a market capitalist economy.

The experience of the 1970s, when Friedman and his ideological disciples had virtual carte blanche to test the validity of their hypotheses in the Southern Cone (Foxley 1983; Street 1984), casts considerable doubt on the general validity of this theoretical perspective. Capitalist development and politics in the Southern Cone, filtered through military regimes closely advised by "los Chicago Boys," came loaded with heavy and expensive doses of ideology, repression, violence, dictatorship, the suspension of individual rights and freedoms, and severe economic crisis (Foxley 1983). To argue that democratic regimes have now emerged from this disarray (though not yet in Chile at this writing, despite Patricio Aylwin's election) is substantially to miss an important lesson: Democracy is not inextricably linked to capitalism, and capitalist organization does not automatically guarantee economic progress—meaning technological development—particularly in peripheral nations lacking a democratic tradition.

What should now be obvious is that there can be democratic capitalism or authoritarian capitalism, just as there can be democratic socialism or authoritarian socialism. What is critical for the discussion of the links among education, technology, and development is not the prevailing mode of production in a country but rather the nature of historical political life; that is, whether civil society has been democratically or dictatorially dominated in ways that contribute to, or detract from, greater ITLC. This returns us to a consideration of state power and, for our present purposes, the relation of state power to the educational system and technological progress.

Street (1983a) focused our attention on the importance of state power to the development process as this is reflected through the institutionalized educational process. In Chile, Argentina, and Uruguay in the 1970s, Chicago School–motivated liberal capitalist models imposed by military regimes failed to contribute to either democracy or development or even to reducing the growth of monetary aggregates and inflation, something that monetarism has at the core of its belief system. The economic policies of the military governments were devised to create ideal-type economies open to international market pressures in both commodity and financial sectors, by imposing a monetaristic, austerity policy package, reinforced by a climate of repression, that pushed wages and real incomes down.

Underlying the seemingly technocratic vision of these neoconservative experiments, however, was a scarcely hidden concern for the changing balance of class and state power, a concern that provides a clue to the continuing technological backwardness of Latin American society. In Brazil, Chile, and Argentina, the 1960s and early 1970s had witnessed shifting power bases and the introduction of institutionalized structures and forms that helped to empower and strengthen such historically dispossessed classes as workers and the landless (Foxley 1983). Greater, if still limited, democracy had been attained, and new, multiple centers of power began to press their interests. The reaction to this shift in power relations from the traditionally dominant classes and their constitutional defenders—the repressive ceremonial institutions of the military and police—was to unleash vicious military coups that overthrew elected, egalitarian-prone governments throughout the region (in Brazil, official repression was milder, although not entirely absent).

These undemocratic coups were accompanied not only by prolonged political repression but by severe economic compression; in the productive sphere, the austerity measures of open economy monetarism, learned by way of Chicago, fit the bill precisely for dominant elites interested in detaining and then reversing the popular gains of the previous period. For public and international consumption, the military dictators (and Friedman) justified the economic shock treatments that dramatically depressed incomes as unfortunate but necessary corrections to the ill-advised and failed statist policies of their predecessors; ECLAC policymakers often received the brunt of the criticism for past policy errors. Street (1984: 638) convincingly argues, however, that the real purpose of the neoconservative agenda was quite different, being "nothing less than a fundamental restructuring of society to establish centralized forms of control and to redistribute income according to a hierarchical scheme that had strong appeal to the most conservative elements in society" who wished to turn the tide in their direction once again. These "conservative elements," of course, were those traditional urban and rural elite classes—occupants of powerful but backward-looking hierarchal-class ceremonial institutions—with the most to lose from any significant redistribution of power and wealth within their societies. They acted as their elite-class interests dictated by setting the repressive ceremonial military and police institutions against the newer, more progressive, and potentially technological institutions that posed a threat to their privileged positions.

As Street (1983a) argued in a moving and poignant essay, the damage to civil society and the economy following the 1970s military coups in the Southern Cone of Latin America—and also that already inflicted under military rule and dictatorship in many other countries in the region—went deeper than most observers imagined. One ingredient of the civil repression was the interventions into universities, research centers, and other institutions of critical (that is, science- and technology-oriented) thinking, on the grounds that these were hotbeds of subversion and insurrection.[7] The educational system, particularly at its higher reaches, was short-circuited as administrators, academics, and researchers were dismissed, exiled, "disappeared," and assassinated. For Street, as for a few other perceptive observers (e.g., Herrera 1973: 33; Latapi 1980: 25–26), the consequences of the interventions in universities and other research centers went beyond the appalling human and personal sacrifices of so many individuals and their families.

Intervention interrupted, unfortunately not for the first time,[8] the activities of the key institutions endowed with the potential for creating knowledge, advancing human resource skills, and developing new technology; in short, intervention severely intruded upon those institutions most capable of making basic contributions to an indigenous technological capacity and to economic progress through the understanding, adaptation, use, and creation of technology. Intervention converted universities from potentially nonceremonial and technological institutions to decidedly ceremonial, past-binding, backward, and status quo–oriented structures, and this has severely curbed "the inveterate restlessness of human hands and brains" that drives all technological advance (Ayres 1978: xvi). As biologists, doctors, economists, engineers, agronomists, physicists, philosophers, sociologists, botanists, geologists, and political scientists were persecuted, and the educational process was disrupted through school closures and the expulsion of students and faculty, the human-resource raw material necessary for domesticating, adapting, creating, evaluating, and implementing new technology was depleted with long-term and wholly negative effects.[9]

Education and Technological Autonomy

Absent such effective institutions as universities and independent research centers capable of participating in technological adaptation, development, and implementation, progress toward technological autonomy is impeded. Hence, concern over academic freedom, the educational process, and the nature of the paths toward training, research, and scientific investigation embraces concern about the ability of technological autonomy to contribute to development. After all, if technology really could be fully borrowed and diffused from outside sources, along with any other critically needed factors of production, then the impact of "disruptions" in education and science in any country would not extend beyond the social and humanistic concerns that repression always raises. If borrowing were truly possible, the domestic environment would be significantly less important, and the question of development would dissolve to the technical considerations of capital accumulation characteristic of the Keynesian approach to foreign aid.

As I argued above, however, technology is not just an inanimate object, a technical relation, or a datum; it is a social force transformative and potentially disruptive of the whole array of existing ceremonial institutional, social, and class structures and forces in tradition-bound, underdeveloped nations (Kransberg 1986: 38). In deeply divided undemocratic societies—a description quite fitting for Latin America—the great ceremonial inequities of wealth and income, particularly those originally based on land and now increasingly reproduced in the industrial and financial sectors, have bred a bias against technological change and unmediated scientific inquiry borne of the fear of losing great wealth. Latin America's dependence on an exogenous scientific and technological base, one that can be selectively and somewhat sanitarily applied without the need to build autonomous, domestic, technology–adapting and creating institutions, has contributed to the preservation of these dominating and backward ceremonial structures, while at the same time successfully maintaining the distance of the local scientific and technological establishment from the local production structures that might give them strength (Cooper 1973: 5).

The resulting technological dependency does not conflict with the needs of at least a segment of the dominant and ruling elites, however; it is rather an integral part of their worldview and closely meshed with their particular class interests.[10] From the perspective of national development, continued technological dependency—and the elite classes it supports—may be judged perversely ceremonial. To precisely those same elite classes, however, technological dependency is instrumental to their continued economic and political domination, and thus it serves them as a functional ceremonial institution for maintaining existing class relations and for thwarting change that might undo ingrained patterns of inequality. Technological autonomy, as a policy, clashes with the interests of this segment of the elite; for this reason, when those interests exercise palpable power, institutions such as universities, normally charged with generating technological progress, *always* will be interfered with to greater or lesser degree to block the spread of expanded autonomy (Radhakrishna 1980: 168).

As Herrera (1973: 33) has persuasively argued, then, it is not actually an absence of policies toward science and technology that characterizes most countries in Latin America; it is the existence of an "implicit science policy" hostile to all broader, uncontrolled applications of science and technology, originating from indigenous or exogenous sources. Such an implicit policy can be seen to operate regardless of the explicit policy statements in favor of technological autonomy that appear in the programs of most governments. It is this implicit, hostile attitude toward science and technology that inclines at least a segment of the dominant classes toward technological dependency. The lack of technological development in Latin America, then, is the price of entrenched internal class barriers to technological change, with their strong bias in favor of technological dependency, precisely because more rapid change would threaten the existing class structure that thrives not on progress but on maintaining the prevailing configuration of inequality. External interests (for example, the MNCs) certainly have a stake in preserving control over their own technology, but it is not correct to argue that technological dependency can be blamed exclusively or even primarily upon the MNCs or any other outside force, such as imperialism. *Technological dependency is something that the policies of a country create and perpetuate in the interests of a narrow, albeit powerful, elite against the interests of the majority who lack access to power.*

What gives us hope for change is that technological dependency is not in the interests of all members of the dominant elite. Many emerging industrialists are favorably predisposed toward a policy of technological autonomy and ITLC, as they increasingly require the tools of technology and the knowledge to use them in order to be competitive on the world market and in the less-protected internal markets. Where the influence of the modernizing fragment of the elite has been strong and growing, as in Brazil (Adler 1987), the changeover in state policies toward technology-creating institutions has been remarkable, at least in certain sectors (Solingen 1989). Vigorous state promotion of technological progress—from education to science policy and research, to support for R&D, to favorable treatment accorded the production process for local S&T efforts—is essential to the success of the pursuit of technological autonomy, certainly in the late twentieth century, since technological progress can be demonstrated to exhibit substantial public goods characteristics, accompanied by significant positive externalities over the longer term (Adler 1988).

In countries arriving late to the continuing S&T "revolution"—and Latin American countries are certainly in this category regardless of the reasons—building a capacity to develop any comparative advantage in science and technology requires the critical microminimum infrastructure to overcome the "lumpiness" and discontinuous character of the S&T creation process (Bhalla and James 1986: 457; James, Street, and Jedlicka 1980: 593).[11] Absent a preexisting S&T infrastructure, the state—as the sole entity with the capacity both to finance the major costs of an autonomous technology policy and to realize and internalize the spill-over benefits of greater autonomy, if only through the tax system—must act in the role of collective planner and entrepreneur. Just how to get the state to behave in a way that promotes technological autonomy when the dominant elites have not already seen it as in their interest to do so is the essential barrier to be overcome, but the existence of fragmented interests within the dominant elite certainly opens the possibility of progressive change taking place.

So, too, interestingly and perhaps inadvertently, do IMF policies, which function as "pressure mechanisms" (Hirschman 1984: 94) in forcing greater integration of the Latin American economies with the international economy as a solution to the debt crisis. The pressure of integration tends to compel policy initiatives that will help to improve the international productivity of domestic enterprises. There is an exceptional opportunity, and necessity, for an ITLC strategy to be introduced in response to these external pressures for internal renovation, or the chance for change may be lost for some time. Still, as Cooper (1973: 15) reminds us, "the self-perpetuating powers of a system of technological dependence, inappropriate technology and alienated science are, to say the least, considerable," and they should not be underestimated.

Autonomy and Linkages

If technological autonomy/ITLC is understood as an "industrial activity" in the broadest sense, then Hirschman's (1958, 1977) extremely rich theory of linkages can be exploited to demonstrate, empirically, to decisionmakers the significance of the technological strategy to any development process. A technological development process has the general effect of fostering a matrix of technological linkages. Rather than a particular industry or group of industries providing the center or growth pole for a chain of backward and forward linkages throughout the economy—the exceedingly creative focus of Hirschman's original linkage analysis (1958)—it is the ITLC strategy itself that permits a whole series of productive linkages to proliferate, following a Hirschmanian unbalanced growth process, as the benefits of technological learning are unleashed.

In fact, without the beginnings of an ITLC strategy in place, without the genesis of a technological culture inculcated in at least a significant portion of the work force, Hirschmanian backward and forward linkages are significantly less likely to form and to flourish, and that perhaps explains why Hirschman's linkage analysis has been less successful as the basis for effective development planning than it had promised to be. It is not that particular industries are not important in providing the breeding grounds for productive linkages (Evans [1986] has shown just how important they can be for pharmaceuticals in Brazil); it is just that the spread and effectiveness of particular industrial linkages are positively and fundamentally a function of a successful ITLC strategy, and of the specific industrialization strategy but secondarily. While backward and forward linkages are important categories for analyzing the potential spill-over benefits likely to accompany the growth of particular industries, even more basic are the technological linkages resulting from the ITLC strategy that provides the domestic raw material—and especially trained human resources—from which such specific industrial linkages might be formed. Without this foundation, the input of domestic technological knowledge may be too low to permit backward and forward production linkages to emerge to any substantial degree.

The technological strategy also is essential for augmenting outside linkages that can expand the benefits of national development.[12] The strategy of technological autonomy and the effort to broaden the base of the technological culture can promote the diffusion of domestic entrepreneurial activity to new groups of potential producers, a growing number of whom will have the requisite skills to compete with existing producers. The expansion of such outside linkages will augment the base of the industrial sector, and participation in it of domestic inputs, by utilizing more fully the increasingly sophisticated and technologically driven domestic factors of production (from labor to finance to management) being formed by the effort toward technological autonomy. In other words, the technological strategy tends to stimulate the growth of outside linkages (control of domestic industrial expansion by new, enhanced, domestic human-resource inputs) by progressively reducing the rationale for monopolized inside linkages. In the Latin American context, this means a reduction in the rationale for dependence on foreign inputs, particularly those mediated by MNCs, and on the entrenched domestic elite that dominates the production process without generating significant spread (that is, outside linkage) effects.

The technological strategy, which must be focused on product and process innovation and not just on basic science,[13] also enhances what Evans (1986: 15–16) has called managerial linkages. As the strategy affects ever-expanding segments of the economy and an ever-larger proportion of the population, it "provides an outlet for the skills and organizational capabilities generated" by the success of the strategy itself. It is not just the expansion of industry, as important as it is, that facilitates managerial linkages through a process of learning by doing, which is Evans's focus; at least as significant is the level of success of the ITLC strategy in providing the basic training ground prior to, and concurrent with, the industrial experience, which speeds up the acquisition of learning and accelerates the spread of managerial and technological linkages into new phases of production. Thus, the spread of technological linkages speeds the possible managerial linkages likely to be formed as new industries become feasible.

The linkage effects of the technological strategy on expanding and supporting a process of industrialization and on accelerating economic growth are compelling. What is still missing are the means by which powerful and ceremonial ruling elites, or their representatives, might be convinced that the strategy is not only essential, but that it meshes with their interests. After all, I have argued that there has been a conscious choice by many ruling elites in the Third World not to pursue technological autonomy because it threatens their ruling and, not incidentally, their pecuniary interests. As Adler (1987) contends, the implementation of such a policy redirection must first be won in the realm of ideology and in the fierce interplay of ideas.

The Role of "Subversive Elites"

In a finely argued theoretical and comparative empirical study of technological policies in Brazil and Argentina, Adler (1987: 90–95, 329, passim) has drawn attention to the role of "subversive elites"[14] in creating the conditions for technological and social progress through a strategy of technological autonomy. The subversive elites are made up of engineers, economists, scientists, and civil servants of all stripes who are imbued with a particular ideological perspective on the need for more independent development vis-à-vis the center countries. This ideology coalesces around the need for technological autonomy as the means to enhance peripheral independence. Through their influence on policymakers—deriving from their level of education, skills, and writings, and often from their key decisionmaking and consultative positions in government—the subversive elites can, under the proper circumstances, create a broader-based ideological consensus around technological autonomy and a path of development decreasingly dependent on foreign capital, foreign ideas, and foreign tools (although, as Solingen [1989] makes clear, there are sectoral explanations having to do with organizational structures that are compelling forces in permitting such ideas to become reality).

Strategies for Implementing Technological Autonomy

The technological autonomy/ITLC strategy has the possibility of being made attractive to governments with widely differing ideological projects, and not just in Latin America. For Third World nations with continuing balance of payments deficits and/or debt problems, moving in the direction of technological autonomy is a concrete means to save, over the medium and long term, valuable foreign exchange and to improve both the balance of trade and the other components of the current account balance. The extent to which import-substituting domestic technological progress saves on scarce foreign exchange reserves can, by itself, be a strong bargaining chip in convincing higher-level government officials—ministers, senators, representatives, perhaps even presidents—in positions to make laws, to approve spending, to suggest projects, and to create appropriate institutions, to pursue a technological autonomy strategy.

The balance of payments linkage effects resulting from import-substituting domestic technological progress (to further extend the Hirschmanian terminology) may provide the most convincing evidence of the benefits of the technological strategy for recalcitrant ruling elites in the Third World, the great majority of whose governments face binding foreign exchange constraints. Balance of payments linkages can be measured on an even more encompassing scale to demonstrate the longer-term, cumulative effects on export growth, import savings, and factor service income outflows (reduced payments for direct-foreign-investment profits, management service contracts, licensing, etc.) accruing to the strategy. Technological autonomy encourages the evolution of new domestic import-substituting industries, particularly in the more-advanced fields such as computers, machine goods, and chemicals where world markets also are important. To the extent that exports of the new products are stimulated—and there is every reason for designing government policies that do precisely that through subsidies or tax incentives that are part and parcel of the ITLC strategy (Shinohara,

Yanagihara, and Kim 1983)—the balance of payments linkage effects can indeed be strongly positive.

Significantly, the export angle of the technological strategy meshes with the dominant strain of orthodox policy advice now being offered Latin America and much of the Third World and, hence, is more likely to be ideologically digestible than a nationalistic, antidependency argument in favor of technological autonomy, which ruling elites may be more prone to reject on class grounds. What is so satisfying about this approach, and of course what makes it "subversive," is that this strategy combined with an export orientation (though not an export strategy alone; the domestic technology link is critical) will contribute to further progressive change that can help to transform the existing ceremonial structures as a consequence of the pursuit of technological autonomy itself. And all without having to wage a high-level, potentially divisive battle over dependency, imperialism, and pernicious elite control that would solely serve to make the strategy anathema to ruling elites. Instead, it is only necessary to establish that an export orientation will be significantly more successful in improving any external imbalance when it is founded upon technological autonomy that also saves foreign exchange. That has been the basis of the Japanese, Taiwanese, and South Korean "miracles"; as that is better understood, and given the need to accumulate foreign exchange reserves, the chances for the technological strategy improve (Amsden 1985, 1989).

In the domestic framework, it also is possible to demonstrate the income and tax linkage effects resulting from the technological autonomy strategy: More-rapid technological progress creates more productive workers whose incomes rise; increased income expands domestic expenditures that then stimulate other industries through the normal income multiplier effects. The spread of technological linkages will permit and then force new backward and forward production links among domestic entrepreneurs that further broaden the tax base. The increased revenues generated from greater production and income can then be used by the state to recover at least a part of the expenditures required by the technological autonomy strategy itself. Here, a supply-side argument can help to strengthen the case in favor of the technological strategy as an increasingly self-financing policy that, combined with the balance of payments linkage effects, only makes it look more necessary in the face of the continuing internal and external disequilibriums plaguing so many nations.

Conclusion

I have posited that technological autonomy provides the base for all successful development efforts. The dilemma of underdevelopment, then, is understanding that this strategy is often in opposition to the interests of ruling elites that, although they may pay lip service to such a strategy, work to frustrate its realization. Given the crisis of growth brought on by the debt overhang facing the majority of Latin American countries, the possibility that a drive for technological autonomy can improve their balance of payments positions through import-substituting technological savings and the expansion of export linkages enhances the feasibility of the adoption of such schemes on a wider scale. And this would open the door to more rapid and progressive change in the region.

Notes

1. Gustav Ranis's (1981) fine comparison of the Latin American and East Asian economies, although not focused on technological autonomy, supports this conclusion.

2. The goal, it is worth stressing, is technological autonomy, not technological autarky, an obviously impossible and foolish objective.

3. This argument is based upon an underlying assumption that is perhaps better made explicit: that even socialist economies for the foreseeable future will be subject to the rhythms of the international economy (and events in Eastern Europe give no cause to doubt this). In other words, no economy, and certainly no small one, can reasonably expect to thrive without a substantial degree of commercial and financial intersection with the international economy, which is undeniably organized on a capitalist basis. This intersection does not necessarily mean a socialist economy will be "determined by" international capitalist relations; it does suggest that the socialist economy will be "subject to" such relations, meaning that the broad rules of the game defined by the international market are binding to at least some degree.

4. ITLC involves both know-*how* and increasing progress on the path of "know-*why*," or deep technological learning, to use Lall's (1984: 116–117) distinction. A schematic representation of the relations might look thus:

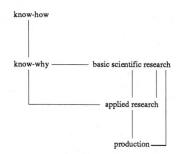

5. Of interest is the view of Kuznets, who is perhaps midway between institutionalism and the mainstream: "Far more important [than physical capital to economic growth] in retrospect are the economic and social

characteristics that reside in the capacities and skills of an economy's population, determine the efficiency of the institutions that direct the use of accumulated physical capital, and guide the current production into proper channels of consumption and capital investment" (1968: 272). Kuznets's view on education, at least as expressed in this quotation, fits nicely with the broad institutionalist/technological interpretation, a similarity that Street (1988) has noted more generally throughout Kuznets's work.

6. UNCTAD, which was headed for a time by Raúl Prebisch, has called for something like technological self-determination for the Third World. However, the concept of technology adopted by UNCTAD has focused on the machine aspect of the technology spectrum with little attention to the knowledge aspect that is being stressed here as fundamental to successful development (Adler 1987: 30). However, see the comment in Landes (1969: 7), an early observer who comes closer to the mark: "The one ingredient of modernization that is just about indispensable is technological maturity and the industrialization that goes with it; otherwise one has the trappings without the substance, the pretence without the reality."

7. Given the unequal income, wealth, and power structures characteristic of most Latin American countries, at least some research and teaching was likely to target for critical investigation existing social and economic structures; any resulting recommendations as to needed changes could be interpreted as threatening specific elite interests. From the wider viewpoint of the welfare of society, there was no overt or immediate subversive threat from such research, but social workers, doctors, economists, sociologists, psychologists, lawyers, and many other professionals who seriously, objectively, and critically investigated their own societies were nonetheless suspect in the eyes of the ruling elites.

8. Street (1983a) dates the institutionalization of intervention into universities to the 1940s Peronist regime in Argentina, which purged, among others, Raúl Prebisch. There is, perhaps, some argument to be made, too, that the backwardness of inherited structures from Latin America's colonial past continue to haunt the educational systems of the late twentieth century.

9. An alteration in the nature of political life from authoritarianism to greater democracy and back to authoritarianism can also endanger a strategy that is moving toward an ITLC. Thoroughly authoritarian societies, such as South Korea, are perfectly capable of making progress on the path to ITLC as long as it can be restrained within acceptable boundaries that benefit new elites in their struggle to consolidate economic and political power against old elites, and this would seem to be true as well of the Brazilian case (Solingen 1989). When technology cannot be so contained, then conflict sets in that can threaten to interrupt the entire development process.

10. My analysis is quite different from other explanations that have been advanced, some by institutionalists, to explain technological dependency. For example, Bath and James (1979: 16–17) suggest that inability to reap the advantages of economies of scale and the argument that infant industries should be protected are barriers to indigenous research in Latin America. The point being made here, and one clearly in the Veblenian-Ayresian tradition, is that the major factor explaining technological dependency is the existing distribution of class power and wealth. Other barriers are, at best, of second-order significance.

11. It will be remembered that Ricardian comparative advantage analysis assumes that trading partners are able to produce both (all) goods under

analysis. Given that science and technology can also be "exchanged," the comparative advantage analysis requires the ability to produce science and technology by both (all) parties. The absence of a productive capacity is not, a fortiori, evidence of the absence of comparative advantage except in the simple case of constant costs, an unlikely hypothesis for the S&T industry. Hence, the absence of scientific and technological production in Latin America is not an ipso facto case for its irrationality.

12. "Outside" is used in the sense of outside the existing network of involved individuals. An outside linkage, then, is one that kindles the activity of new participants within the production process, while an inside linkage only enlarges the sphere of activities of those already operating within the existing network of production. In this usage, an outside linkage is one that augments the participation of domestic factors of production in decisionmaking positions at the expense of (certain) inside linkages; of particular importance in Latin America would be substitution of domestically controlled factors in those activities controlled by foreign factors of production.

13. This is a distinction that Adler (1987: 8, passim) found to be important. He determined that Argentina's S&T policies were associated with an emphasis on basic science, while in Brazil there was an emphasis on linking science with industry. The more successful Brazilian strategy emphasized innovative technology, i.e., the application of new knowledge to the production process.

14. Adler also called these subversive elites "pragmatic antidependency guerrillas" (1987: 5).

11

A Latin American Development Model for the Future

James L. Dietz
Dilmus D. James

The 1980s proved to be a paradoxical decade for Latin America. In most countries, as nonelected military dictatorships disappeared, there emerged greater political participation and promising, if still tentative, steps toward democratization (Central America, torn by civil war and external pressures, remained marginalized from this process to a substantial degree). But the trend, despite despair over recalcitrant repressive regimes, can be counted as a positive one, certainly by comparison with the retreat from democracy so depressingly characteristic of the 1970s.

Progress on the political front, however, was not accompanied by any parallel economic advance. Indeed, the 1980s are destined to be remembered as the "second Great Depression" in the region. Real income per person, measured by gross domestic product (GDP) in constant 1988 dollars, declined from $2,512 in 1980 to $2,336 in 1988, a decrease of slightly more than 7 percent. Some nations escaped this trend, but among IDB member countries, twenty of twenty-five had lower real per capita incomes in 1988 than in 1980, and seven had real 1988 incomes below their 1970 levels (IDB 1989: 463, table B-1). If reliable GNP figures were available, and taking into account income distribution effects, the visible loss in real income would be even more dramatic than the GDP-based averages suggest. Chapter 1 identified some indicators that begin to put the depth of the crisis in perspective.

How is one to understand the causes of this economic downturn? Just as the 1980s have been a period of political readjustment away from military dictatorship, the 1970s and 1980s proved to be a remarkable time for rethinking economic theories and for experimenting with alternative development models, particularly the neoliberal, extreme orthodoxy that has impacted on policies in most countries. It is likely that the exhaustion of the ISI model and the failure of Latin America to enter a more dynamic post-ISI path, as discussed by Alexander in Chapter 2, account for a considerable part of the success of the economic counterrevolution and its assault on existing policies in the region. A contributing factor that must be faced, too, is the relatively limited reach of alternative economic strategies and their inability to successfully supplant the ideological power of the orthodox, neoliberal strategy that began to gain hegemony at the highest levels of decisionmaking, particularly after the onslaught of the debt crisis (see Chapters 1 and 4).

Throughout this book, perhaps most strongly in Chapter 1 by James and Dietz, Chapter 4 by Cypher, and Chapter 8 by Sunkel, the rising influence of neoliberal, free market economics has been assailed for its inappropriateness to Latin America's development needs. The classic model of development that had been followed in the region, based on ISI, was undoubtedly passé to some degree, at least in its stagnated form; it no longer performed as robustly as it had in the past, despite the fact that the successes of the ISI strategy and its absolute necessity at an early stage of transformation in all developing countries were always much greater than its critics allowed.[1] A fresh approach to Latin America's development problems was urgently required by the 1970s, and the neoliberal strategy increasingly gained the advantage in the debate over appropriate policies and the proper roles for the market and government as structuralism turned its back on many pressing problems.

But, the neoliberal critics of structuralism and ISI strategy—which is closely associated with the ECLAC—focused on the surface manifestations of economic crisis in the region rather than on the root causes. It is necessary to ask *why* Latin America has not progressed significantly beyond the ISI strategy, why a post-ISI development model has not been pursued, why Latin America's stylized development path has diverged so widely from that of the East Asian success cases held up as prototypes, and why alternative development models, other than neoliberalism, have gained so little ground. The various contributors to this book submit that the failure of economic policy in the region is not due to any simple failure of policy implementation or of theory (although some of our authors, especially Cypher, certainly do find such failure) but is the consequence of, broadly speaking, entrenched institutional barriers that support particular financial and social interests. These entrenched interests will and do impede the process of economic transformation when it threatens their well-being.

In other words, the failure of Latin American economic progress and policy in the 1970s and early 1980s, of a "stalled" strategy of development, and of ECLAC's role in promoting such "failed" policy, was not inherent in the policies themselves but rather in the limited capacity of an important segment of Latin America's ruling elites to overcome their own special interests, since any post-ISI model, especially of the East Asian variety (Ranis 1981), would have conflicted with their claims. The so-called economic failures of ISI, in this view, were no such thing; rather, the economic crisis of excessive and inefficient state intervention and prolonged ISI within a protectionist "hothouse" were brought on by the nature of political and economic power in the region, which made the self-executing evolution of Latin America's economic model a virtual impossibility in the absence of some deep crisis that could force change upon conservative elites.[2] Given the institutionalized structure of political and economic power, Latin American policy simply could not get beyond the first stages of industrialization, an industrialization forced upon the region in the first place by earlier crises. Latin America's poor performance was not caused by failing to "get policies or prices right," but rather by not "getting *politics* right."

Unable to pass beyond the former development strategy without threatening substantial changes in the existing internal balance of economic and political power, and faced with a growth and then a debt crisis after 1982, Latin America's ruling elites, supported by the international lending agencies and financial institutions, chose to retreat from ISI. Instead of moving forward by implementing a strategy more along the lines of a Ranisian East Asian model in which there remained a leading role for intelligent government intervention that respected international market forces (without being subservient to them), in which ISI was integral to creating an indispensable manufactured goods export capacity, and in which the economic power of some of the elite was sacrificed to obtain the benefits of a more fully modernized productive structure, Latin America's elites took the low road of simple neoliberalism, which promised economic progress through unleashing international market forces. More importantly, it promised this without threatening entrenched interests; if anything, neoliberal policies were geared to reconstituting elite interests that had been eroded by the relative economic and political progress of the 1960s and 1970s (Foxley 1983).

When and if the economic corrections promised by neoliberal policies failed to materialize, Latin America's elites could and did shift the blame to intervention by the international lending agencies, especially the IMF (see Chapter 5 by Phillips), which have trumpeted the necessity for such an orthodox reorientation of policy. In the process, Latin America's ruling elites were let off the hook for a crisis, rooted in their own unequal economic and political power, that made neoliberalism not only politically and economically acceptable to them, but positively desirable.

There is consensus, then, among the contributors to this book that the neoliberal, open economy, market-dominated strategy will fail to provide for Latin America's development needs over the future. What emerges is a proposed neostructuralism, a loosely defined path of development and its conditioning policies that builds upon the base of a complex understanding of ECLAC structuralism (see Chapters 2–4), rather than the bastard structuralism (to borrow the adjective Joan Robinson applied to what came to be taught as Keynesian economics) applied in practice by most governments.

This neostructuralism, it is argued, can be strengthened by the intervention of the technological insights of institutionalism, and Chapters 3 (Sunkel), 4 (Cypher), 7 (Cole), 9 (James), and 10 (Dietz) put forward specific suggestions about how to improve policy and the prospects for future development consistent and/or complementary with the thrust of ECLAC structuralism. Schwartz's interesting analysis of Argentina's policies toward manufactured exports (Chapter 6), while not expressed in the same institutionalist/structuralist terminology, provides important and corroborating insight into the entrenched barriers to industrialization and exports. His insight meshes well with the analyses of other chapters and strengthens the effort to promote a neostructuralism that can extricate the region from ten years of acute and open crisis and decades of repressed but no less harsh suffering for the great majority of Latin Americans.

Imperfect as they are, especially in an immature industrial setting, the market and its attendant pricing system must play a much larger role in Latin America than was the case during the ISI period.[3] We agree with González (1988: 15) when he says: "The international market's price structure is useful as a basic point of reference for the behavior of the various economic sectors and as a tool for economic decision-making and for the management of the development process." We would go further and say that, by and large, domestic prices should be a rough gauge of static efficiency—or at least such prices should be a useful point of departure before adjusting for externalities, monopolistic elements, imperfect knowledge or perception (see Schwartz, Chapter 6), or the potential for dynamic gains not reflected in the current price structure. Multitudinous interventions, often made on ad hoc bases in an extremely politicized atmosphere and frequently having contradictory impacts, muddy the water so severely that only in unusually transparent cases can one say with confidence that an economic activity is either efficient or inefficient; but this only stresses the need for a more comprehensive market orientation that respects and understands what information the market is capable of providing, as well as that which it cannot. This point of view does not imply that the market should dominate all decisions or that it is always a perfect substitute for well-crafted policy.

There is general agreement that neostructuralism must place considerably more emphasis on short-term policy measures that exercise greater control over monetary, fiscal, and balance of payments variables.[4] Structuralist policies, at least in practice, and sometimes in theory, underestimated the damaging effects of hyperinflation, fiscal deficits, and large and growing trade deficits. What were sometimes considered to be necessary evils at an earlier stage of development turned out to be far worse when allowed to persist, particularly when the underlying causes that led structuralists to be somewhat permissive in their attitude toward such disequilibriums were not being eliminated.

Neoclassical economics has plenty to offer regarding both markets and monetary and fiscal instruments, and it is a mistake to reject all orthodox findings out of hand simply because of their origin. A case in point is the careful and well-designed research on labor markets in Mexico by Gregory (1986), which implied that labor markets were more efficient than previously thought; cast doubt on the existence of surplus labor à la Arthur Lewis; critiqued the way surplus labor had been measured; and shot a few holes in some of the elements of the Todaro explanation of rural-to-urban migration. Our purpose is not to defend Gregory's findings, which are quite consistent with orthodox precepts, but to say that neostructuralists or any other heterodox economists in Latin America ignore these studies at their own peril. Nor does it advance the cause when such research is not ignored but attacked on rather flimsy grounds. It matters little, in this context, that orthodox economists often ignore or treat inadequately heterodox schools of thought; to use Ffrench-Davis's expression (1988: 38), we need to seek "co-optable inputs from the orthodox approach" if more-serviceable knowledge is to be available for more-informed decisionmaking. The Latin American economies function within an international market environment in which quite a few "economic laws," about which neoclassical economics has something to say, cannot just be wished away. It is necessary to respect market pressures and the useful signals they provide, and to utilize them for speeding development, which is possible, if Japan and other East Asian economies are any indication, without becoming enslaved by, or to, the market.

We should note, along with Bitar (1988: 47), that the use of market forces does not preclude planning, particularly if planning is indicative, decentralized, and focused on limited problem areas. These generalities having been established, we must say emphatically that there are a variety of areas and circumstances that do call for a departure from market forces, at times to supplement the price system, at times to reduce the exposure of an economic activity from the dictates of the market for reasons of equity or growth. Again, it is the East Asian cases that provide a reasonable guide to the possibilities (Amsden 1989). Most of the remainder of our suggestions revolve around this simple but significant proposition.

In spite of the current vogue of privatization in several Latin American countries, largely inspired by IMF directives and U.S. influence, we believe that parastatal enterprises, which are not fully subject to market pressures, will continue to play a significant role in key sectors of most Latin American economies. This does not mean that the elimination or privatization of some state enterprises should not be part of the package; Brannon and Baklanoff (1987) on Mexico's state-run henequen industry provide us with a good candidate for selling, killing, or drastically restructuring. Cole's case (Chapter 7) for the privatization of the backward and unproductive communal ejido agricultural system in Mexico, while no doubt controversial and emotional within the context of Mexican agrarian reform, is also worthy of serious discussion in a neostructuralist paradigm.

In some instances, disaggregation of existing enterprises should be considered, especially when the benefits from economies of scale are overpowered by the social diseconomies of excessive political clout. Sheer size often can endow those involved in such enterprises with substantial power, prestige, and wealth. Whatever the method, "considerable importance should be attached to increasing the efficiency of public enterprises" (Bitar 1988: 59). A good deal of the problem of inefficiency in state enterprises can be explained by the differential in attention economists have devoted to private vis-à-vis public entities. The effort spent on theoretical analysis of state enterprises pales beside the enormous emphasis on the behavior of private firms. Serious study of parastatals is under way, yet much more needs to be known about motivations and decisionmaking within different classifications of these enterprises. Both structuralism and institutionalism, having embraced a multidisciplinary framework, are perhaps better equipped for undertaking the requisite investigations that will form the neostructuralist understanding of parastatals.

Another fundamental policy consideration in any neostructuralist analysis carries over from the older ECLAC tradition; namely, that there are compelling supply-side bottlenecks that cannot be solved, indeed may be perpetuated, by suppressing aggregate demand when inflationary pressures arise. An illustration of this is the Mexican transportation system in the late 1970s and early 1980s. The economy was overheated and large amounts of grain were being imported from the United States; freight ships waited off Mexican ports, sometimes for weeks, at a cost of thousands of dollars per day, because the rail system could not handle the rising volume of traffic. Storage areas were inadequate, which led sometimes to using scarce rail cars for storage, thus further extending delays (also, some rail cars were being used for dwellings and hence were not available for transport purposes). Most of Mexico's system was single-track, with very few turnoffs. The shipping and rail bottlenecks threw a heavy burden on the trucking industry, where another nightmare emerged. Frequently, because of an imprudent and inefficient state licensing system, one truck was forced to off-load its cargo at a state line only to load it onto another truck on the other side. Compressing demand—the neoliberal panacea when inflation emerges—can certainly obscure problems of this nature, but it cannot cure them. As structuralists have long insisted, these bottlenecks require time and proper policy to vanquish, and reducing demand would release a pressure point for change that growth, even when accompanied by supply-side inflation, can help to overcome.

We are particularly convinced that S&T policy should be front and center in the neostructuralist scheme (see Chapters 9 and 10). As mentioned in

Chapter 1, we are unaware of any neoliberal delineation of how technological dynamism can come about in Latin America. In an excellent article reviewing neoliberalism and neostructuralism, Ffrench-Davis (1988) compares seventeen elements in both paradigms. Technology is simply not there! Perhaps this is because no counterpart exists in the neoliberal theory with which to compare it. Perhaps, too, structuralists are still not fully attentive to the centrality of S&T and related policies within the development process. We are also mystified, but less surprised, by how a leading neoliberal work, titled *Toward Renewed Economic Growth in Latin America*, can fail to discuss the role of technological innovation, but it does (Balassa et al. 1986).

As Sunkel points out in Chapter 3, structuralists have always afforded S&T an important position in their development thinking, but it would seem that often either a general statement was made, or the rate of industrialization, or direct foreign investment, was used as a proxy for technological change and technological development. It would be preferable to see the issue of technology internalized within the neostructuralist paradigm and to witness a contingent of neostructuralists "getting their hands dirty" in the many pressing problems in the area (see Chapter 9) in the tradition of Daniel Chudnovsky, Jorge Katz, Francisco Sagasti, Francisco Sercovich, and Miguel Wionczek, to mention but a few. Above all, attention must focus on how the importation and the domestic generation of technology can contribute to the accumulation and domestication of technological capacities within the Latin American region (see Chapter 10). To use Leslie Sklair's term, "technology relocation" will not get the job done. It is this richer understanding of technology that neostructuralism must incorporate.

Ex post, it is an academic point as to whether the cost of pushing the industrial sector during ISI, with special emphasis on heavy industry over time, was too costly. Future economic growth will or should exhibit much more sectoral balance than in the previous decades with agriculture (including smallholder producers); light and medium manufacturing units; the traditional raw commodity–exporting sector; the service sector (including small enterprises and informal urban activities); and education and health delivery systems will or should share in national resource allocations and efficiency-enhancing investments and innovations.

If the old-style ISI "umbrella" approach is agreed to be outmoded, this does not preclude encouraging specific manufactures through protecting infant industries.[5] One possibility is carefully to select a limited number of narrowly defined industries, believed to be reasonably close to international competitiveness, for state support. Thus, a more limited range of economic activities could be stimulated with a set of measures spanning the spectrum from modest protection to direct assistance, such as technical support, access to new technology, and manpower policies. The portfolio of prioritized industries could be revolving: That is, when an industry becomes competitive, it is gradually weaned from the leading policies and another industry is picked up. If we read the situation correctly, this is precisely the model employed by South Korea on its path to a higher stage of development (Pack and Westphal 1986) and seems, too, to have been the Japanese strategy.

We are acutely aware of the many differences between South Korea and Latin America in general, yet we think some properly adjusted variant of the approach is worth a try. Criteria for the selection of industries could include: a reasonable expectation that success can be attained within five years, or in no case more than ten (Bell, Ross-Larson, and Westphal 1984); a strong base of human capital; a recent good record in cost-cutting and/or quality-upgrading innovations; and a high ranking regarding positive stimuli to other industries through consumption, supply-connected (i.e., backward), and learning linkages. Regarding technical learning, capital goods producers are likely to be good candidates for support, but we stress the importance of narrowly defining "an industry"—one of the prevailing problems with capital goods production in Latin America is the attempt to make too many types and variations of producer goods in individual countries.

Overpowering as international concerns appear to be, certainly in the current period, a larger proportion of neostructuralist thought, energy, and actions needs to be channeled toward domestic policies—in short, we agree with Cypher's sharp observations (Chapter 4). The tasks of shaping short-term fiscal, monetary, and exchange rate policies, of coping with the maldistribution of income and surplus labor, and of forging approaches and instruments for sectoral applications are challenging indeed, but, despite the risk of spreading resources too thinly, these issues must be met head-on while simultaneously wrestling with more global concerns.

Finally, neostructuralists and institutionalists still have much to learn from one another. We trust that this book, especially Sunkel's eloquent statement (Chapter 3), will encourage a reciprocal trade agreement between the two paradigms for the future and that the suggestions for a new paradigm that can lead to "development from within" (Sunkel, Chapter 8) found in all the chapters will help to mark a new stage of renovation in Latin America.

Notes

1. See Alexander, Chapter 2, for a spirited defense of ISI as an appropriate and necessary strategy when it was introduced; also see Ranis (1981) for a broader perspective on the instrumentality of ISI.

2. A reference to the opening to the West in Eastern Europe in late 1989 can, perhaps, provide a parallel example. Prior to that year, the entrenched leaders of the Communist regimes had found it impossible, even in the face of economic crises, to reform the old style of development. But it was not the old

policies that were causing the crises; it was the power structure and ruling elites of the East European countries that blocked the necessary evolution toward new policies that could have moved those societies forward. It took a severe political and economic crisis to push the ruling elites in new directions, although the ultimate outlines of those policies remain unclear, and the outcome may be one those elites find themselves unable fully to control.

3. The ideas contained in this discussion already had been sketched out before we read, with great profit, four articles in the *CEPAL Review* that share, and anticipated, our suggestions; see Bitar (1988), Ffrench-Davis (1988), González (1988), and Rosales (1988).

4. Structuralism's "emphasis on the structural characteristics of socioeconomic phenomena led to a kind of unconcern for short-term instruments of economic policy"; further, "there is also such a thing as an error of omission, and in this case it should be recognized that the structuralist paradigm underestimated the potential of monetary, fiscal and exchange rate policy to combat inflation" (Rosales 1988: 27). One shortcoming of structuralism "was its limited concern with the management of short-term macroeconomic variables, in that the analysis and definition of areas in which action might be taken with respect to fiscal deficits and monetary liquidity occupied a secondary place in structuralist thinking" (Ffrench-Davis 1988: 38). See Bitar (1988: 47, 49) for similar statements.

5. González (1988: 16) recommends essentially the same approach except he maintains the term *import substitution*: "When all is said and done, the term 'import substitution' signifies the development of new sectors which are essential to the incorporation and dissemination of technology. From this standpoint, the possibilities of import substitution have not been exhausted, nor will they be, at least not for a long time."

References

Adams, John. 1987. "Trade and Payments as Instituted Process." *Journal of Economic Issues* 21 (December): 1839–1860.

Adler, Emanuel. 1987. *The Power of Ideology: The Quest for Technological Autonomy in Argentina and Brazil.* Berkeley: University of California Press.

———. 1988. "State Institutions, Ideology, and Autonomous Technological Development." *Latin American Research Review* 23, no. 2: 59–90.

Aguirre Beltrán, Gonzalo. 1967. *Regiones de refugio.* Mexico City: Instituto Indigenista Interamericano.

Alam, Shahid. 1989. *Governments and Markets in Economic Development Strategies.* New York: Praeger.

Alexander, Robert J. 1978. *The Tragedy of Chile.* Westport, CT: Greenwood Press.

Allais, Maurice. 1948. *Économie et intérêt: Exposition nouvelle des problèmes fondamentaux, relatifs au rôle économique du taux de l'intérêt et de leurs solutions.* 2 vols. Paris: Librairie des Publications Officielles.

Amadeo, Eduardo. 1979. "National Science and Technology Councils in Latin America: Achievement and Failure of the First Ten Years." In Babatunde Thomas and Wionczek, *Integration of Science and Technology with Development.*

Amsden, Alice H. 1985. "The State in Taiwan's Economic Development." In *Bringing the State Back In,* ed. P. Evans, D. Rueschemeyer, and T. Skocpol. Cambridge: Cambridge University Press.

———. 1989. *Asia's Next Giant: South Korea and Late Industrialization.* New York: Oxford University Press.

Anandakrishnan, M., ed. 1985. *Planning and Popularizing Science and Technology in Developing Countries.* Oxford: Tycooly Publishing.

Antonorsi-Blanco, Marcel, and Ignacio Avalos Gutiérrez. 1980. *La planificación ilusoria: ensayo sobre la experiencia venezolana en política científica y tecnología.* Caracas: Editorial Ateno.

Argentina, Central Bank. 1980–1988. *Estimaciones sobre oferta y demanda global.* Buenos Aires: Central Bank.

Arrow, Kenneth. 1962. "Economic Welfare and the Allocation of Resources for Invention." In *The Rate and Direction of Inventive Activity,* ed. Richard R. Nelson. Princeton, NJ: Princeton University Press.

210

Ayres, C. E. 1962. *The Theory of Economic Progress*. New York: Schocken Books.
————. 1978. *The Theory of Economic Progress*, 3d ed. Kalamazoo, MI: New Issues Press.
Babatunde Thomas, D., and Miguel S. Wionczek, eds. 1979. *Integration of Science and Technology with Development: Caribbean and Latin American Problems in the Context of the United Nations Conference on Science and Technology for Development*. New York: Pergamon Press.
Balassa, Bela. 1978. "Exports and Economic Growth: Further Evidence." *Journal of Development Economics* 5 (June): 181–189.
Balassa, Bela, and Associates. 1982. *Development Strategies in Semi-Industrial Economies*. Baltimore, MD: Johns Hopkins University Press.
Balassa, Bela, et al. 1986. *Toward Renewed Economic Growth in Latin America*. Washington, DC: Institute for International Economics.
Balassa, Bela, and Constantine Michalopoulos. 1985. *Liberalizing World Trade*. Development Policy Issues Serial Report, VPERS 4. Washington, DC: Office of the Vice-President, Economics and Research, World Bank.
Ballestero, Florencio, and Francisco Thoumi. 1988. "The Instability of Intra-Latin American and Caribbean Exports and Exchange Rates." In *Foreign Investment, Debt and Economic Growth in Latin America*, ed. Antonio Jorge and Jorge Salazar-Carrillo. London: Macmillan.
Banco Central de Venezuela. 1988. *Informe económico, 1987*. Caracas: Banco Central.
Baran, Paul. 1957. *The Political Economy of Growth*. New York: Monthly Review Press.
Barkin, David. 1980. "Intervención del estado en la agricultura mexicana." In *Conflicto entre ciudad y campo en América Latina*, ed. Iván Restrepo. Mexico: Editorial Nueva Imagen.
Bath, C. Richard, and Dilmus D. James. 1979. "The Extent of Technological Dependence in Latin America." In *Technological Progress in Latin America: The Prospects for Overcoming Dependency*, ed. James H. Street and Dilmus D. James. Boulder, CO: Westview Press.
Bell, Martin, Bruce Ross-Larson, and Larry E. Westphal. 1984. "Assessing the Performance of Infant Industries." *Journal of Development Economics* 16 (September–October): 101–128.
Bell, Martin, and Don Scott-Kemmis. 1985. "Technology Import Policy: Have the Problems Changed?" *Economic and Political Weekly* 20 (November): 1975–1990.
Bernal Sahagun, Víctor. 1980. *Pensamiento latinoamericano: Cepal, R. Prebisch y A. Pinto*. Mexico City: UNAM.
Bhalla, Ajit S., and Dilmus D. James. 1986. "Technological Blending: Frontier Technology in Traditional Economic Sectors." *Journal of Economic Issues* 20 (June): 453–462.
Bitar, Sergio. 1988. "Neo-Conservatism versus Neo-Structuralism in Latin America." *CEPAL Review* 34 (April): 45–62.
Blackledge, James P. 1985. "The Potential for Contribution of R&D to the Production System." In Williams Silveira, *Research and Development*.
Blejer, Mario I., and Adrienne Cheasty. 1988. "Some Lessons from 'Heterodox' Stabilization Programs." *Finance and Development* 20 (September): 16–19.

Blomström, Magnus, and Bjorn Hettne. 1984. *Development Theory in Transition. The Dependency Debate and Beyond: Third World Responses.* London: Zed Press.

Bonilla, Arturo. 1980. "Las ideas principales de la CEPAL: Comentarios." In Bernal Sahagun, *Pensamiento latinoamericano.*

Brannon, Jeffery, and Eric N. Baklanoff. 1987. *Agrarian Reform and Public Enterprise in Mexico: The Political Economy of Yucatán's Henequen Industry.* Tuscaloosa: University of Alabama Press.

Brett, E. A. 1983. *International Money and Capitalist Crisis.* Boulder, CO: Westview Press.

Brinton, Crane. 1965. *The Anatomy of Revolution*, rev. and expanded ed. New York: Vintage Books.

Brown, Harrison. 1973. "The Role of Science and Technology in Development." In *Symposium on the Scientific and Technological Gap in Latin America*, ed. Roberto Esquinazi-Mayo et al. Lincoln: Institute for International Studies, University of Nebraska.

Bush, Paul D. 1983. "The Structural Characteristics of a Veblen-Ayres-Foster Defined Institutional Domain." *Journal of Economic Issues* 17 (March): 35–66.

Canterbery, E. Ray, and R. J. Burkhard. 1983. "What Do We Mean by Asking Whether Economics Is a Science?" In *Why Economics Is Not Yet a Science*, ed. A. S. Eichner. New York: M. E. Sharpe.

Carballo de Cilley, Marita. 1987. *¿Qué pensamos los argentinos?* Buenos Aires: Ediciones El Cronista.

Cardoso, Fernando Henrique. 1977a. "The Consumption of Dependency Theory in the United States." *Latin American Research Review* 12: 7–24.

———. 1977b. "The Originality of a Copy: CEPAL and the Idea of Development." *CEPAL Review* 4 (2d Semester): 7–40.

———. 1979. "The Originality of the Copy: The Economic Commission of Latin America and the Idea of Development." In *Toward a New Development Strategy.* Rothko Chapel Colloquium. New York: Pergamon Press.

Cardoso, Fernando Henrique, Aníbal Pinto, and Osvaldo Sunkel. 1969. *El pensamiento de la CEPAL.* Santiago: Editorial Universitaria.

Chapin, Mac. 1988. "The Seduction of Models: Chinampa Agriculture in Mexico." *Grass Roots Development* 12: 8–17.

Chenery, Hollis. 1986. "Growth and Transformation." *In Industrialization and Growth : A Comparative Study*, ed. Hollis Chenery et al. New York: Oxford University Press.

Chevalier, François. 1963. *Land and Society in Colonial Mexico.* Berkeley: University of California Press.

Choudhuri, A. R. 1985. "Practicing Western Science Outside the West." *Social Studies of Science* 5 (September): 475–505.

Chudnovsky, Daniel. 1985. "El comercio de bienes de capital en América Latina y la creación de Latinequip." *Comercio Exterior* 35 (September): 848–855.

Clark, Norman. 1980. "The Economic Behavior of Research Institutions in Developing Countries—Some Methodological Points." *Social Studies of Science* 10 (March): 75–93.

———. 1987. "Similarities and Differences Between Scientific and Technological Paradigms." *Futures: The Journal of Forecasting and Planning* 19, no. 1: 26–42.

Clarke, Robin. 1985. *Science and Technology in World Development*. Oxford: Oxford University Press/UNESCO.

Cohen, Stephen D. 1985. *Uneasy Partnership: Competition and Conflict in U.S.-Japanese Trade Relations*. Cambridge, MA: Ballinger.

Cole, William E., and Richard D. Sanders. 1970. *Growth and Change in Mexican Agriculture*. Knoxville: Center for Business and Economic Research, University of Tennessee.

———. 1974. "The Impact of Agriculture's Domestic Terms of Trade." *Growth and Change* 5 (July): 36–40.

Colombian Information Service. 1986. *Colombia Today* (New York) 21, no. 2.

Conaghan, Catherine. 1988. *Restructuring Domination: Industrialists and the State in Ecuador*. Pittsburgh, PA: University of Pittsburgh Press.

Consejo Nacional de Ciencia y Tecnología (CONACYT). 1976. *Plan nacional indicativo de ciencia y tecnología*. Mexico City: CONACYT.

Cooper, Charles, ed. 1973. *Science, Technology and Development*. London: Frank Cass.

Cortazar, Rene. 1989. "Austerity Under Authoritarianism." In *Paying the Cost of Austerity in Latin America*, ed. Howard Handleman and Warner Baer. Boulder, CO: Westview Press.

Cypher, James. 1988. "The Crisis and Restructuring of Capitalism in the Periphery." In *Research in Political Economy*, vol. 11, ed. Paul Zarembka. Greenwich, CT: JAI Press.

———. 1989. "The Debt Crisis as Opportunity." *Latin American Perspectives* 16 (Winter): 52–78.

———. 1990. *The Unmaking of the Mexican State*. Boulder, CO: Westview Press.

Darity, William, Jr., and Bobbie L. Horn. 1988. *The Loan Pushers: The Role of Commercial Banks in the International Debt Crisis*. Cambridge, MA: Ballinger.

De Arregui, Patricia M. 1988. "Comparative Indicators of the Results of Scientific and Technological Research in Latin America." In Inter-American Development Bank, *Economic and Social Progress in Latin America, 1988 Report*. Washington, DC: IDB.

Denevan, William M. 1982. "Hydraulic Agriculture in the American Tropics: Forms, Measures, and Recent Research." In *Maya Subsistence*, ed. Kent V. Flannery. New York: Academic Press.

Denison, Edward. 1967. *Why Growth Rates Differ: Postwar Experience in Nine Western Countries*. Washington, DC: Brookings Institution.

Dietz, James L. 1980. "Dependency Theory: A Review Article." *Journal of Economic Issues* 14 (September): 751–758.

———. 1986. "Debt and Development: The Future of Latin America." *Journal of Economic Issues* 20 (December): 1029–1051.

———. 1988. "Democracy, Education, and Technology in Latin America." Paper presented at the Southwestern Economics Association meetings, Houston, Texas, March.

———. 1989. *Historia económica de Puerto Rico*. Río Piedras, PR: Ediciones Huracán.

Dietz, James L., and Dilmus D. James. 1988. "Introduction of Award Recipient: James H. Street." *Journal of Economic Issues* 22 (June): 323–326.

Dietz, James L., and James H. Street, eds. 1987. *Latin America's Economic Development: Institutionalist and Structuralist Perspectives*. Boulder, CO: Lynne Rienner.

Di Tella, Guido, and Rudiger Dornbusch. 1989. *The Political Economy of Argentina, 1946–83.* Pittsburgh, PA: University of Pittsburgh Press.

Dixon, William J. 1987. "Progress in the Provision of Basic Human Needs: Latin America, 1960–1980." *Journal of Developing Areas* 21 (January): 129–139.

Dore, Ronald. 1984. "Technological Self-reliance: Sturdy Ideal or Self-serving Rhetoric." In Fransman and King, *Technological Capability in the Third World.*

Earl, Peter E. 1983. "A Behavioral Theory of Economists' Behavior." In *Why Economics Is Not Yet a Science*, ed. A. S. Eichner. New York: M. E. Sharpe.

Economic Commission for Latin America and the Caribbean (ECLAC). 1986. *Exportación de manufacturas y desarrollo industrial: Two Studies on the Argentine Case (1973–1984).* Working Paper 22. Buenos Aires: ECLAC.

———. 1987. *Statistical Yearbook for Latin America and the Caribbean, 1986.* Santiago: ECLAC.

El cultivo del maíz en México. 1980. Mexico City: Centro de Investigaciones Agrarias.

Esteva, Gustavo. 1983. *The Struggle for Rural Mexico.* South Hadley, MA: Bergin & Garvey.

Evans, Peter. 1982. "Reinventing the Bourgeoisie." In *Studies of Labor, Class and State*, ed. Michael Buroway and Theda Skocpol. Chicago: University of Chicago Press.

———. 1986. "General Linkages in Industrial Development: A Reexamination of Basic Petrochemicals in Brazil." In *Development, Democracy, and the Art of Trespassing: Essays in Honor of Albert O. Hirschman*, ed. A. Foxley et al. Notre Dame, IN: Notre Dame University Press.

———. 1989. "Declining Hegemony and Assertive Industrialization." *International Organization* 43 (Spring): 207–238.

Fajnzylber, Fernando. 1989. *Industrialización en América Latina.* Santiago: Naciones Unidas.

Fernández, Roque B. 1984. "Implicaciones dinámicas de la propuesta de Simons para reforma del sistema financiero." *Ensayos Económicos*, Banco Central de la República de Argentina, Buenos Aires (March): 1–30.

———. 1985. "The Expectations Management Approach to Stabilization in Argentina during 1976–1982." *World Development* 13 (August): 871–892.

———. 1987. *Negociación y capitalización de la deuda externa.* Working Paper 57. Centro de Estudios Macroeconómicos de Argentina, Buenos Aires.

Fernández y Fernández, Ramón. 1959. "La clientela del crédito ejidal." *El Trimestre Económico* 26 (January): 31–48.

Ffrench-Davis, Ricardo. 1988. "An Outline of a Neo-Structuralist Approach." *CEPAL Review* 34 (April): 37–44.

Filgueira, Carlos. 1981. "Consumption in the New Latin America Models." *CEPAL Review* 15 (December): 71–110.

Fisher, Irving. 1945. *100% Money*, 3d ed. New Haven, CT: City Printing.

Fisher, Joseph L. 1967. "Natural Resource Problems and the TVA." In *The Economic Impact of TVA*, ed. John R. Moore. Knoxville: University of Tennessee Press.

Fortune. 1977. "The IMF Lays Down the Law" (July): 102.

Foster, Elizabeth Andros. 1950. *Motolinia's History of the Indians of New Spain.* Westport, CT: Greenwood Press.

Foster, Fagg. 1981. "The Effect of Technology on Institutions." *Journal of Economic Issues* 15 (December 1981): 907–913.

Foxley, Alejandro. 1983. *Latin American Experiments in Neo-Conservative Economics*. Berkeley: University of California Press.

Frank, Andre Gunder. 1979. *Mexican Agriculture 1521–1630: Transformation of the Mode of Production*. London: Cambridge University Press.

Frank, Andre Gunder, Rodolfo Fuiggros, and Ernesto Laclau. 1972. *América Latina: ¿feudalismo o capitalismo?* Medellín: Ediciones La Oveja Negra.

Fransman, Martin, and Kenneth King, eds. 1984. *Technological Capability in the Third World*. Hampshire, England: Macmillan.

Friedman, Milton. 1960. *A Program for Monetary Stability*. New York: Fordham University Press.

Gaillard, Jacques F., and Said Ouattar. 1988. "Purchase, Use and Maintenance of Scientific Equipment in Developing Countries." *Interciencia* 13 (March–April): 65–70.

Gatica Barros, Jaime. 1989. *Deindustrialization in Chile*. Boulder, CO: Westview Press.

Gershenkron, Alexander. 1962. *Economic Backwardness in Historical Perspective*. Cambridge, MA: Harvard University Press.

Gibson, Charles. 1964. *The Aztecs Under Spanish Rule*. Stanford, CA: Stanford University Press.

Girton, Lance. 1974. "SDR Creation and the Real-Bills Doctrine." *Southern Economic Journal* 36 (July): 57–61.

Glade, William P. 1987. "Multinationals and the Third World." *Journal of Economic Issues* 21 (December): 1889–1920.

Gómez Contreras, Hugo. 1988. "Chile con Pinochet." *Uno más Uno* (Mexico) (October 15): 12.

Gómez-Pompa, Arturo et al. 1982. "Experiences in Traditional Hydraulic Agriculture." In *Maya Subsistence*, ed. Kent V. Flannery. New York: Academic Press.

González, Norberto. 1988. "An Economic Policy for Development." *CEPAL Review* 34 (April): 7–17.

Gordon, Wendell. 1965. *The Political Economy of Latin America*. New York: Columbia University Press.

Greenberg, Martin H. 1970. *Bureaucracy and Development: A Mexican Case Study*. Lexington, MA: D. C. Heath.

Gregory, Peter. 1986. *The Myth of Market Failure: Employment and the Labor Market in Mexico*. Baltimore, MD: Johns Hopkins University Press.

———. 1987. "The Mexican Labor Market in the Economic Crisis and Lessons of the Past." In *Mexico's Economic Policy: Past, Present and Future*, ed. William E. Cole. Knoxville: Center for Business and Economic Research, University of Tennessee.

Griffith-Jones, Stephany, and Osvaldo Sunkel. 1986. *Debt and Development Crises in Latin America: The End of an Illusion*. Oxford: Clarendon Press.

Gurrieri, Adolfo. 1982. *La obra de Prebisch en la CEPAL*. 2 vols. Mexico City: Fondo de Cultura Económica.

Hamilton, David. 1984. "Economics: Science or Legend?" *Journal of Economic Issues* 18 (June): 565–572.

Handleman, Howard, and Werner Baer. 1989. "Introduction." In *Paying the Costs of Austerity in Latin America*, ed. H. Handleman and W. Baer. Boulder, CO: Westview Press.

Harberger, Arnold. 1966. "Comment." *Economic Development and Cultural Change* 15 (October): 87–90.

Hayden, F. Gregory. 1982a. "Organizing Policy Research Through the Social Fabric Matrix: A Boolean Digraph Approach." *Journal of Economic Issues* 16 (December): 1013–1026.

———. 1982b. "Social Fabric Matrix: From Perspective to Analytical Tool." *Journal of Economic Issues* 16 (September): 637–662.

———. 1986. "Defining and Articulating Social Change Through the Social Fabric Matrix and System Digraph." *Journal of Economic Issues* 20 (June): 383–392.

Herbolzheimer, Emil, and Habib Ouane. 1985. "The Transfer of Technology to Developing Countries by Small and Medium-Sized Enterprises of Developed Countries." *Trade and Development* 6: 131–148.

Herrera, Amilcar. 1972. "Explicit Science and Implicit Science Policy." *Journal of Development Studies* 9, no. 1: 19–37.

———. 1973. "Social Determinants of Science Policy in Latin America: Explicit Science Policy and Implicit Science Policy." In Cooper, *Science, Technology and Development*.

Hewitt de Alcántara, Cynthia. 1978. *La modernización de la agricultura mexicana.* Mexico City: Siglo Veintiuno.

Hirschman, Albert O. 1958. *The Strategy of Economic Development.* New Haven, CT: Yale University Press.

———. 1971. "How to Divest in Latin America and Why." In A. O. Hirschman, *A Bias for Hope.* New Haven, CT: Yale University Press.

———. 1973. *Journeys Toward Progress: Studies of Economic Policy-Making in Latin America.* New York: Norton.

———. 1977. "A Generalized Linkage Approach to Development, with Special Reference to Staples." *Economic Development and Cultural Change* 25 (Supplement): 67–97.

———. 1981. *Essays in Trespassing: Economics and Politics and Beyond.* Cambridge: Cambridge University Press.

———. 1984. "A Dissenter's Confession: The 'Strategy of Economic Development' Revisited." In Meier and Seers, *Pioneers in Development*.

Hodara, Joseph B. 1979a. "Science and Technology Policies in Latin America—Against a Holistic Approach." In Babatunde Thomas and Wionczek, *Integration of Science and Technology with Development*.

———. 1979b. "El intelectual científico mexicano: un tipología." *Interciencia* 3 (January–February): 20–22.

Husain, S. Shahid. 1989. "Reviving Growth in Latin America." *Finance and Development* 26 (June): 2–5.

IMF Survey. 1974. (May 6): 134.

INEGI (Instituto Nacional de Estadística, Geografía e Informática). 1985. *Estadísticas históricas de México.* 2 vols. Mexico: Secretaría de Progamación y Presupuesto.

Inter-American Development Bank (IDB). 1984–1989. *Economic and Social Progress in Latin America.* Washington, DC: IDB.

James, Dilmus D. 1980. "Mexico's Recent Science and Technology Planning: An Outsider Economist's Critique." *Journal of Interamerican Studies and World Affairs* 22 (May): 163–193.

———. 1988. "Accumulation and Utilization of Internal Technological Capabilities in the Third World." *Journal of Economic Issues* 22 (June): 339–353.

————. 1989. "In Memoriam: James H. Street, 1915–1988." *Journal of Economic Issues* 23 (March): 1–6.

James, Dilmus D., James H. Street, and Allen D. Jedlicka. 1980. "Issues in Indigenous Research and Development in Third World Countries." *Social Science Quarterly* 60 (March): 588–603.

Jing Su. 1990. "The Role of Technology Transfer in Fostering Internal Technological Capacity: A Case Study Of China's Computer Policy." M.A. Thesis, Department of Economics, University of Texas, El Paso.

Johnston, Bruce F. 1972. "Criteria for the Design of Agricultural Development Strategies." *Food Research Institute Studies in Agricultural Economics, Trade, and Development* 11: 35–37, 42–54.

Kahn, Mohsin. 1986. *Islamic Interest-Free Banking.* IMF Staff Papers 33 (March): 1–27.

Kahneman, Daniel, Paul Slovic, and Amos Tversky, eds. 1982. *Judgment Under Uncertainty: Heuristics and Biases.* Cambridge: Cambridge University Press.

Katz, Jorge. 1984a. "Domestic Technological Innovations and Dynamic Comparative Advantage: Further Reflections on a Comparative Case Study Program." *Journal of Development Economics* 16 (September–October): 13–37.

————. 1984b. "Technological Innovation, Industrial Organization and Comparative Advantages of Latin American Metalworking Industries." In Fransman and King, *Technological Capability in the Third World.*

————, ed. 1987. *Technology Generation in Latin American Manufacturing Industries.* New York: St. Martin's Press.

Kay, Cristóbal. 1989. *Latin American Theories of Development and Underdevelopment.* London: Routledge.

Kets de Vries, Manfred F. R., and Danny Miller. 1988. "Personality, Culture and Organization." In *Psychological Foundations of Economic Behavior,* ed. Paul J. Albanese. New York: Praeger.

King, Kenneth. 1984. "Science, Technology and Education in the Development of Indigenous Technological Capacity." In Fransman and King, *Technological Capability in the Third World.*

Kolbeck, Gustavo Romero. 1967. "Economic Development of Mexico." *Economic Development Issues: Latin America.* New York: Committee for Economic Development.

Kransberg, Melvin. 1986. "The Technological Elements in International Technology Transfer: Historical Perspectives." In *The Political Economy of International Technology Transfer,* ed. John R. McIntyre and Daniel S. Papp. Westport, CT: Quorum Books.

Krauskopf, M., R. Pessot, and R. Vicuna. 1986. "Science in Latin America: How Much and Along What Lines?" *Scientometrics* 10, no. 3/4: 199–206.

Krueger, Anne. 1978a. *Liberalization: Attempts and Consequences.* Cambridge, MA: Ballinger.

————. 1978b. *Foreign Trade Regimes and Economic Growth: Anatomy of Exchange Control.* Cambridge, MA: Ballinger.

————. 1980. "Trade Policy as an Input to Development." *American Economic Review* 70 (May): 288–292.

Kuznets, Simon. 1968. "Trends in Capital Formation." In UNESCO, *Readings in the Economics of Education.* Paris: UNESCO.

Laidler, D. 1984. "Misconceptions about the Real Bills Doctrine and the

Quantity Theory: A Comment on Sargent and Wallace." *Journal of Political Economy* 92 (February): 149–155.

Lall, Sanjaya, ed. 1984. Special Issue on "Exports of Technology by Newly-Industralizing Countries." *World Development* 12 (May–June).

Lamartine Yates, Paul. 1981. *Mexico's Agricultural Dilemma.* Tucson: University of Arizona Press.

Landes, David S. 1969. *The Unbound Prometheus: Technological Change and Industrial Development in Western Europe from 1750 to the Present.* Cambridge: Cambridge University Press.

Langer, Erick D. 1989. "Generations of Scientists and Engineers: Origins of the Computer Industry in Brazil." *Latin American Research Review* 24, no. 2: 95–111.

Lanus, Archibaldo. 1988. *La causa argentina.* Buenos Aires: Editores EMECE.

Latapi, Pablo. 1980. "Trends in Latin American Universities: Selected Problems and Perspectives." In UNESCO, *New Trends and Responsibilities for Universities in Latin America.* Paris: UNESCO.

Layrisse, Miguel. 1985. "Recursos humanos para ciencia y tecnología." *El Nacional* (Caracas) (March 26).

Lewis, W. Arthur. 1954. "Economic Development with Unlimited Supplies of Labour." *Manchester School of Economic and Social Studies* 22 (May): 139–191.

———. 1955. *The Theory of Economic Growth.* London: Allen & Unwin.

Little, Ian. 1982. *Economic Development: Theory, Policy and International Relations.* New York: Basic Books.

Little, Ian, et al. 1970. *Industry and Trade in Some Developing Countries: A Comparative Study.* New York: Oxford University Press.

Lomnitz, Larissa. 1979. "Hierarchy and Peripherality: The Organization of a Mexican Research Institute." *Minerva* 17 (Winter): 527–548.

Lynn, Leonard H. 1988. "Research and Development in Japan." *Current History* 87 (April): 165–168, 180.

Lyon, Ted. 1987. "Science and Technology in Contemporary Latin American Literature." *Bulletin of Science, Technology and Society* 7, nos. 5/6: 628–637.

Macario, Santiago. 1952a. "El institucionalismo como crítica de la teoría económica clásica." *El Trimestre Económico* 19 (January–March): 73–112.

———. 1952b. "Teoría positiva del institucionalismo." *El Trimestre Económico* 19 (April–June): 250–300 and (July–September): 481–509.

McCallum, Bennett T. 1986. "Some Issues Concerning Interest Rate Pegging, Price Level Indeterminacy, and the Real Bills Doctrine." *Journal of Monetary Economics* 17 (January): 135–160.

McIntyre, John R. 1986. "Introduction: Critical Perspectives on International Technology Transfer." In *The Political Economy of International Technology Transfer,* ed. John R. McIntyre and Daniel S. Papp. Westport, CT: Quorum Books.

Mallon, Richard D., in collaboration with Juan V. Sourrouille. 1975. *Economic Policymaking in a Conflict Society: The Argentine Case.* Cambridge, MA: Harvard University Press.

Mandelbaum, Karl. 1945. *The Industrialization of Backward Areas.* Oxford: Basil Blackwell.

Mayhew, Anne. 1987. "The Beginnings of Institutionalism." *Journal of Economic Issues* 21 (September): 971–998.

Meier, Gerald M., ed. 1987. *Pioneers in Development: Second Series*. New York: Oxford University Press.

Meier, Gerald, and Dudley Seers, eds. 1984. *Pioneers in Development*. New York: Oxford University Press.

Mints, Lloyd. 1945. *A History of Banking Theory*. Chicago: University of Chicago Press.

Mogab, John W. 1984. "The Mexican Experience in Peasant Agricultural Credit." *Development and Change* 15 (April): 201–221.

Morales, Reynaldo, and Ronald K. Lohrding. 1989. "A Technology Partnership for the Americas." Paper presented at the North American Economics and Finance Association, December 28–30, Atlanta, GA.

Morales, Víctor. 1989. "Los estudios de postgrado: ¿Para qué?" *Interciencia* 14 (September–October): 242–246.

Moravcsik, Michael J. 1975. *Science Development: The Building of Science in Less Developed Countries*. Bloomington: International Development Research Center, Indiana University.

Nadal Egea, Alejandro. 1977. *Instrumentos de política científica y tecnológica en México*. Mexico City: El Colegio de México.

Nash, Manning. 1967. *Handbook of Middle American Indians: Social Anthropology*. Austin: University of Texas Press.

National Academy of Sciences. 1973. *U.S. International Firms and R, D and E in Developing Countries*. Washington, DC: NAS.

Neale, Walter C. 1987. "Institutions." *Journal of Economic Issues* 21 (September): 1177–1206.

Nelson, Richard R. 1959. "The Simple Economics of Basic Scientific Research." *Journal of Political Economy* (June): 297–306.

Nogués, Julio J. 1986. *The Nature of Argentina's Policy Reforms During 1976–81*. World Bank Staff Working Paper 765. Washington, DC: World Bank.

————. 1988a. "La economía política del proteccionismo y la liberalización en la Argentina." *Desarrollo Económico* 28 (July–September): 159–182.

————. 1988b. *The Experience with Export Subsidies in Latin America*. Washington, DC: World Bank (unpublished typescript).

Nurkse, Ragnar. 1953a. *Patterns of Trade and Development*. Oxford: Basil Blackwell.

————. 1953b. *Problems of Capital Formation in Underdeveloped Countries*. New York: Oxford University Press.

O'Donnell, Guillermo A. 1973. *Modernization and Bureaucratic-Authoritarianism: Studies in South American Politics*. Berkeley: Institute of International Studies, University of California.

Orive Alba, Adolfo. 1970. *La irrigación en México*. Mexico City: Editorial Grijalbo.

Pack, Howard, and Larry E. Westphal. 1986. "Industrial Strategy and Technological Change: Theory versus Reality." *Journal of Development Studies* 22 (June): 87–128.

Palerm, Ángel. 1973. *Obras hidráulicas prehispánicas en el sistema lacustre del valle de México*. Mexico City: Instituto Nacional de Antropología e Historia.

Palma, Gabriel, and Mario Marcel. 1989. "Kaldor and the 'Discreet Charm' of the Chilean Bourgeoisie." *Cambridge Journal of Economics* 13 (March): 245–272.

Park, Yung-Chul. 1988. "Korea." In *The Open Economy: Tools for*

Policymakers in Developing Countries, ed. Rudiger Dornbusch and F. Leslie C. H. Helmers. New York: Oxford University Press.

Parsons, Kenneth H. 1985. "John R. Commons: His Relevance to Contemporary Economics." *Journal of Economic Issues* 19 (September): 755–778.

Pastor, Manuel. 1987. *The International Monetary Fund and Latin America: Economic Stabilization and Class Conflict*. Boulder, CO: Westview Press.

Pastore, José. 1978. "Science and Technology in Brazilian Development." In *Science, Technology and Economic Development: A Historical and Comparative Study*, ed. William Beranek, Jr. and Gustav Ranis. New York: Praeger.

Payer, Cheryl. 1982. *The World Bank*. New York: Monthly Review Press.

Pazos, Felipe. 1987. "Import Substitution Policies, Tariffs and Competition." In Dietz and Street, *Latin America's Economic Development*.

Peñalver, Luís Manuel. 1973. "The Situation of Science and Technology in Venezuela." In *Symposium on the Scientific and Technological Gap in Latin America*, ed. Roberto Esquinazi-Mayo et al. Lincoln: Institute for International Studies, University of Nebraska.

Phillips, Ronnie J. 1988a. "The Debate over 100% Reserves in the 1930s." Paper presented at the Atlantic Economic Society Meetings, New York, December.

———. 1988b. "Veblen and Simons on Credit and Monetary Reform." *Southern Economic Journal* 55 (July): 171–181.

Pinto, Aníbal, and Osvaldo Sunkel. 1966. "Latin American Economists in the United States." *Economic Development and Cultural Change* 15 (October): 79–86.

Prebisch, Raúl. 1950a. *The Economic Development of Latin America and its Principal Problems*. New York: United Nations.

———. 1950b. *Economic Survey of Latin America, 1949*. New York: United Nations.

———. 1981a. *Capitalismo periférico*. Mexico City: Fondo de Cultura.

———. 1981b. "Dialogue on Friedman and Hayek." *CEPAL Review* 15 (December): 153–174.

———. 1984. "Five Stages in My Thinking on Development." In Meier and Seers, *Pioneers in Development*.

———. 1985. "Power and Market Laws." In *Debt and Development in Latin America*, ed. Kwan Kim and David Ruccio. Notre Dame, IN: University of Notre Dame Press.

Radhakrishna, K., ed. 1980. *Science, Technology and Global Problems: Views from the Developing World*. Oxford: Pergamon Press.

Ramírez, Miguel D. 1989. "The Social and Economic Consequences of the National Austerity Program in Mexico." In *Paying the Costs of Austerity in Latin America*, ed. Howard Handleman and Werner Baer. Boulder, CO: Westview Press.

Ranis, Gustav. 1981. "Challenges and Opportunities Posed by Asia's Superexporters: Implications for Manufactured Exports from Latin America." *Quarterly Review of Economics and Business* 21 (Summer); reprinted as Ch. 9 in Dietz and Street, *Latin America's Economic Development*.

Redclift, Michael R. 1981. *Development Policy Making in Mexico: The Sistema Alimentario Mexicano (SAM)*. Working Paper. La Jolla: Program in U.S.-Mexican Studies, University of California.

Reich, Robert J. 1989. "The Quiet Path to Technological Preeminence." *Scientific American* 261 (October): 41–47.

Reséndiz Nuñez, Daniel. 1987–1988. "Science and Technology in Mexico: Looking Forward." *Voices of Mexico* 6 (December–February): 38–45.

Rincón Serrano, Romeo. 1980. *El ejido mexicano*. Mexico City: Centro Nacional de Investigaciones Agrarias.

Robinette, Jane. 1987. "Other Realities—Technology and Recent Latin American Fiction." *Bulletin of Science, Technology and Society* 7, no. 4: 507–511.

Robinson, E.A.G. 1973. "Discussion of the Paper by Professor Griliches." In *Science and Technology in Economic Growth*, ed. B. R. Williams. New York: Halstead Press.

Roca, Sergio. 1974. *Economic Structure and Ideology in Socialist Cuba*. Ph.D. diss., Rutgers University, New Brunswick, NJ.

Roche, Marcel. 1985. "Mexico's Example." *Interciencia* 10 (June–August): 170–172.

Rodríguez, Octavio. 1980. *La teoría del subdesarrollo de la Cepal*. Mexico City: Siglo Veintiuno.

Rosales, Osvaldo. 1989. "El neoestructuralismo en América Latina." *Pensamiento Iberoamericano: Revista de Economía Política* 14 (July–December): 394–406.

———. 1988. "An Assessment of the Structuralist Paradigm for Latin American Development and the Prospects for Its Renovation." *CEPAL Review* 34 (April): 19–36.

Rosenberg, Nathan. 1982. *Inside the Black Box: Technology and Economics*. New York: Cambridge University Press.

Rosenstein-Rodan, Paul. 1944. "The International Development of Economically Backward Areas." *International Affairs* (April).

———. 1943. "Problems of Industrialization of Eastern and South-Eastern Europe." *Economic Journal* 53 (June–September): 202ff.

———. 1957. "Notes on the Theory of the 'Big Push.'" Cambridge: Center of International Studies, Massachusetts Institute of Technology.

Rossi, Nicola. 1988. "Government Spending, the Real Interest Rate, and the Behavior of Liquidity-Constrained Consumers in Developing Countries." *IMF Staff Papers* 35 (March): 104–140.

Ruttan, Vernon. 1988. "Cultural Endowments and Economic Development: What Can We Learn From Anthropology?" *Economic Development and Cultural Change* 36 (April Supplement): S247–S271.

Sábato, Jorge A. 1969. "The Influence of Indigenous Research and Development Efforts on the Industrialization of Developing Countries." In *Industrialization and Development*, ed. H. E. Hoelscher and M. C. Hawk. San Francisco: San Francisco Press.

Sabet, Adel A. 1985. "Mechanisms for Achieving Self-Reliance in R&D Activities Useful to the Productive System." In Williams Silveira, *Research and Development*.

Sanders, William T., Jeffry Parsons, and Robert S. Santley. 1979. *Basin of Mexico: Ecological Processes in the Evolution of a Civilization*. Orlando, FL: Academic Press.

Sargent, T. J., and Neil Wallace. 1982. "The Real-Bills Doctrine versus the Quantity Theory: A Reconsideration." *Journal of Political Economy* 90 (December): 1212–1236.

Sarkar, Prabijit. 1986. "The Singer-Prebisch Hypothesis." *Cambridge Journal of Economics* 10 (December): 355–372.

Sarukhán, José. 1989. "The Status of Mexican Science and Technology Research: Potential Avenues for Collaboration Programmes with the United States." *Mexican Studies/Estudios Mexicanos* 5 (Summer): 265–280.

Schell, William, Jr. 1986. *Medieval Iberian Tradition and the Development of the Mexican Hacienda.* Syracuse, NY: Syracuse University Press.

Schoijet, Mauricio. 1979. "The Condition of Mexican Science." *Minerva* 17 (Autumn): 381–412.

Schwartz, Hugh. 1987. "Perception, Judgment and Motivation in Manufacturing Enterprises: Findings and Preliminary Hypotheses from In-Depth Interviews." *Journal of Economic Behavior and Organization* 8 (December): 543–566.

Schwartzman, Simon. 1985. "The Quest for University Research: Policies and Research Organization in Latin America." In *The University Research System: The Public Policies of the Home of Scientists*, ed. Bjorn Wittrock and Aant Elzinga. Stockholm: Almqvist & Wiksell International.

———. 1986. "Coming Full Circle: A Reappraisal of University Research in Latin America." *Minerva* 24 (Winter): 456–475.

Secretaría de Industria y Comercio. 1964. *VIII censo general de población.* 1960. Mexico City: Secretaría de Industria y Comercio.

Segal, Aaron. 1987a. "Africa: Frustration and Failure." In *Learning by Doing: Science and Technology in the Developing World*, ed. Aaron Segal et al. Boulder, CO: Westview Press.

———. 1987b. "Latin America: Development with Siesta." In *Learning by Doing: Science and Technology in the Developing World*, ed. Aaron Segal et al. Boulder, CO: Westview Press.

Shinohara, Miyohei, Toru Yanagihara, and Kwang Suk Kim. 1983. *The Japanese and Korean Experiences in Managing Development.* World Bank Staff Working Paper 574. Washington, DC: World Bank.

Silva Herzog, Jesús. 1952. "La concentración agraria en Mexico." *Cuadernos Americanos* 62 (March–April): 175–190.

———. 1959. *El agrarismo mexicano y la reforma agraria.* Mexico City: El Fondo de Cultura Económica.

Simons, Henry. 1948. *Economic Policy for a Free Society.* Chicago: University of Chicago Press.

Simpson, Lesley Byrd. 1962. *Many Mexicos.* Berkeley: University of California Press.

Singer, H. W. 1949. "Economic Progress in Under-developed Countries." *Social Research* 16 (March): 1–11.

———. 1950a. "The Distribution of Gains Between Investing and Borrowing Countries." *American Economic Review (Papers and Proceedings)* 40 (May): 473–485.

———. 1950b. *Economic Development of Underdeveloped Countries.* Published in Portuguese by the Fundación Getúlio Vargas, Rio de Janeiro.

———. 1953. "Obstacles to Economic Development." *Social Research* 20 (April): 19–31.

Solingen, Etel. 1989. "State Autonomy, Lateral Autonomy, and Sectoral Adjustments." Paper presented at the International Studies Association Meetings, London, January (mimeo).

Solow, Robert. 1988. "Growth Theory and After." *American Economic Review* 78 (June): 307–317.

Soustelle, Jacques. 1955. *Daily Life of the Aztecs on the Eve of the Spanish Conquest*. Palo Alto, CA: Stanford University Press.

Stakman, E. C., Richard Bradfield, and Paul C. Mangelsdorf. 1967. *Campaigns Against Hunger*. Cambridge, MA: Belknap Press of Harvard University Press.

Street, James H. 1967. "The Latin American Structuralists and the Institutionalists: Convergence in Development Theory." *Journal of Economic Issues* 1 (June): 44–62; reprinted as Ch. 7 in Dietz and Street, *Latin America's Economic Development*.

———. 1977. "The Internal Frontier and Technological Progress in Latin America." *Latin American Research Review* 12: 25–56.

———. 1980. "A Holistic Approach to Underdevelopment." In *Institutional Economics: Contributions to the Development of Holistic Economics: Essays in Honor of Allan G. Gruchy*, ed. John Adams. Boston: Martinus Nijhof.

———. 1981a. "Mexico's Development Plan." *Current History* 80 (November): 374–378, 388–391.

———. 1981b. "Political Intervention and Science in Latin America." *Bulletin of the Atomic Scientists* (February): 14–23.

———. 1983a. "The Reality of Power and the Poverty of Economic Doctrine." *Journal of Economic Issues* 17 (June): 295–313.

———. 1983b. "Mexico's Development Dilemma." *Current History* 82 (December): 410–414, 434.

———. 1984. "Values in Conflict: Developing Countries as Social Laboratories." *Journal of Economic Issues* 18 (June): 633–641.

———. 1985a. "Development Planning and the International Debt Crisis in Latin America." *Journal of Economic Issues* 19 (June): 397–408.

———. 1985b. "Monetarism and Beyond: The Dilemma of the Southern Cone Countries: A Review Article." *Journal of Economic Issues* 19 (December): 923–937.

———. 1987a. "The Institutionalist Theory of Economic Development." *Journal of Economic Issues* 21 (December): 1861–1887.

———. 1987b. "Mexico's Development Crisis." *Current History* 86 (March): 101–104, 127–129.

———. 1987c. "Raúl Prebisch, 1901–1986: An Appreciation." *Journal of Economic Issues* 21 (June): 649–659.

———. 1988. "The Making of an Applied Institutionalist." *Journal of Economic Issues* 22 (June): 327–337.

Street, James H., and Dilmus D. James. 1982. "Institutionalism, Structuralism, and Dependency in Latin America." *Journal of Economic Issues* 16 (September): 673–698.

Sunkel, Osvaldo. 1980. "The Interaction between Styles of Development and the Environment in Latin America." *CEPAL Review* 12 (December): 15–49.

———. 1984. "Past, Present and Future of the International Economic Crises." *CEPAL Review* 11 (April): 81–105.

———. 1985. *América Latina y la crisis económica internacional: ocho tesis y una propuesta*. Buenos Aires: Cuadernos del RIAL, Grupo Editor Latinoamericano.

———. 1987a. "Beyond the World Conservation Strategy: Integrating

Conservation and Development in Latin America and the Caribbean." In *Conservation with Equity: Strategies for Sustainable Development*, ed. P. Jacobs and D. Munro. Cambridge: IUCN.

————. 1987b. "Las relaciones centro-periferia y la transnacionalización." *Pensamiento Iberoamericano* 11 (January–June).

Sunkel, Osvaldo, and Edmundo Fuenzalida. 1979. "Transnationalization and its National Consequences." In *Transnational Capitalism and National Development: New Perspectives on Dependence*, ed. José J. Villamil. London: Harvester Press and Institute of Development Studies, University of Sussex.

Sunkel, Osvaldo, with Pedro Paz. 1970. *El subdesarrollo latinoamericano y la teoría del desarrollo*. Mexico City: Siglo Veintiuno.

Tamagna, Frank. 1965. *Central Banking in Latin America*. Mexico City: Centro de Estudios Monetarios Latinoamericanos.

Taylor, William B. 1972. *Landlord and Peasant in Colonial Oaxaca*. Palo Alto, CA: Stanford University Press.

Teitel, Simón, and Francisco E. Thoumi. 1986. "From Import Substitution to Export: The Manufacturing Exports Experience of Argentina and Brazil." *Economic Development and Cultural Change* 34 (April): 455–490.

Tobin, James. 1985. "Financial Innovation and Deregulation in Perspective." *Bank of Japan Monetary and Economic Studies* 3.

————. 1987. "The Case for Preserving Regulatory Distinctions." In *Restructuring the Financial System*. Kansas City: Federal Reserve Bank of Kansas City.

Tokman, Víctor E. 1982. "Growth, Underemployment and Income Distribution." In *Trade, Stability, Technology and Equity in Latin America*, ed. Moshe Syrquin and Simón Teitel. New York: Academic Press.

Tool, Marc. 1985. *The Discretionary Economy: A Normative Theory of Political Economy*. Boulder, CO: Westview Press.

Ungeheuer, Frederick. 1989. "A Chasm of Misery." *Time* (March): 64–66.

United Nations (UN). 1985. *Industrial Statistics Yearbook*, vol. 2. New York: UN.

Urquidi, Víctor L. 1964. *The Challenge of Development in Latin America*. New York: Praeger.

————. 1986. "Technology Transfer Between Mexico and the United States." *Mexican Studies/Estudios Mexicanos* 2 (Summer): 179–193.

Vaitsos, Constantine V. 1974. *Intercountry Income Distribution and Transnational Enterprises*. Oxford: Clarendon Press.

Valenzuela, Samuel, and Arturo Valenzuela. 1979. "Modernization and Dependence: Alternative Perspectives in the Study of Latin American Underdevelopment." In *Transnational Capitalism and National Development: New Perspectives on Dependence*, ed. José J. Villamil. London: Harvester Press and Institute of Development Studies, University of Sussex.

Veblen, Thorstein. 1904. *The Theory of Business Enterprise*. New York: Scribner's.

————. 1934. "The Opportunity of Japan." In *Essays in Our Changing Order*, ed. Leon Ardzrooni. New York: Viking.

————. 1954. *Imperial Germany*. New York: Viking.

————. 1966. *Imperial Germany and the Industrial Revolution*. Ann Arbor: University of Michigan Press.

Velasco, Ibeles. 1981. "Algunos hechos y muchos impresiones sobre la ciencia y tecnología en México: primera parte." *Interciencia* 6 (November–December): 402–407.

Venezian, Eduardo L., and William K. Gamble. 1969. *The Agricultural Development of Mexico: Its Structure and Growth Since 1950*. New York: Praeger.

Vessuri, Hebe M. C. 1984. "The Search for a Scientific Community in Venezuela: From Isolation to Applied Research." *Minerva* 22 (Summer): 196–235.

———. 1986. "The Universities, Scientific Research and the National Interest in Latin America." *Minerva* 24: 1–38.

Villarreal, Rene. 1984. *La contrarrevolución monetarista*. Mexico City: Fondo de Cultura.

Vuskovic, Pedro. 1986. "La crisis económica de América Latina." Paper presented at the seminar, Teoría del Desarrollo, IIEc, UNAM, Mexico City.

Warhurst, Alyson. 1984. "The Application of Biotechnology to Metal Extraction: The Case of the Andean Countries." In *Blending of New and Traditional Technologies: Case Studies*, ed. Ajit S. Bhalla et al. Dublin: Tycooly International Publishers.

Warman, Arturo. 1972. *Los campesinos: hijos predilectos del régimen*. Mexico City: Editorial Nuestro Tiempo.

Weeks, John. 1985a. *The Economics of Central America*. New York: Holmes & Meier.

———. 1985b. *Limits to Capitalist Development*. Boulder, CO: Westview Press.

West, Robert C., and John P. Augelli. 1966. *Middle America: Its Lands and Peoples*. Englewood Cliffs, NJ: Prentice-Hall.

Williams Silveira, Mary Pat, ed. 1985. *Research and Development: Linkages to Production in Developing Countries*. Boulder, CO: Westview Press.

Williamson, Oliver E. 1985. *The Economic Institutions of Capitalism*. New York: Free Press.

Wionczek, Miguel S. 1979a. *Measures Strengthening the Negotiation Capacity of Governments in Their Relations with Transnational Corporations: Technology Transfer through Transnational Corporations*. New York: United Nations Center on Transnational Corporations.

———. 1979b. "Science and Technology Planning in LDCs." In Babatunde Thomas and Wionczek, *Integration of Science and Technology with Development*.

———. 1979c. "Science and Technology Planning Problems in a Large Circum-Caribbean Country (Mexico)." In Babatunde Thomas and Wionczek, *Integration of Science and Technology with Development*.

———. 1981. "On the Viability of a Policy for Science and Technology in Mexico." *Latin American Research Review* 16, no. 3: 57–78.

Wolf, Eric. 1959. *Sons of the Shaking Earth*. Chicago: University of Chicago Press.

World Bank. 1987. "The Latin American Depression: It Hit the Poor Hardest." *The World Bank Research News* 7 (Spring): 1–2, 11.

Yearley, Steven. 1988. *Science, Technology and Social Change*. London: Unwin Hyman.

Yotopoulos, Pan A., and Jeffrey B. Nugent. 1976. *Economics of Development: Empirical Investigations*. New York: Harper & Row.

Zaleznik, Abraham. 1988. "Decisions, Coalitions, and the Economy of the Self." In *Psychological Foundations of Economic Behavior*, ed. Paul J. Albanese. New York: Praeger.

About the Contributors

Robert J. Alexander is professor of economics, Rutgers University, New Brunswick. He is a prolific author, with more than twenty books on Latin American development and politics, including *Agrarian Reform in Latin America; Juan Domingo Perón; Labor Relations in Argentina, Brazil and Chile; Latin American Politics and Government;* and *The Struggle for Democracy in Latin America.*

William E. Cole is professor of economics, University of Tennessee, Knoxville. His research has focused on Mexico, particularly Mexican agriculture and technology transfer issues. His articles have appeared in the *Journal of Economic Issues* and *Growth and Change,* and in books and monographs.

James M. Cypher is professor of economics, California State University, Fresno. He is the author of *The Unmaking of the Mexican State,* an analysis of the Mexican development experience, and many articles on Latin American development, Mexico, debt, and issues of political economy.

James L. Dietz is professor of economics and Latin American studies, California State University, Fullerton. He is the author of *Economic History of Puerto Rico* and co-editor of *Latin America's Economic Development.* His articles have appeared in the *Journal of Economic Issues* and *Latin American Perspectives,* among others.

Dilmus D. James is professor of economics, University of Texas, El Paso. He is the co-editor of *New Technologies and Development* and *Technological Progress in Latin America,* among other books, and of articles in journals such as *Latin American Research Review* and the *Journal of Economic Issues.* He has worked for the International Labour Office in Geneva as a staff member of the Technology and Employment Branch.

Ronnie J. Phillips is associate professor of economics, Colorado State University, Fort Collins, and has been a visiting professor at Texas A&M University. His work has appeared in the *Southern Economic Journal* and the *Journal of Economic Issues*, among others.

Hugh Schwartz is an Argentine economist who for many years was senior economist with the Economic and Social Development Department of the Inter-American Development Bank in Washington, DC. He is currently engaged in a study of the behavioral approach to economic analysis.

Osvaldo Sunkel works for the United Nations Economic Commission for Latin America and the Caribbean in Santiago, Chile, and directs the Development and Environment Program. He has been associated with the Institute of Development Studies, Sussex, England, and is the author of classic works on Latin American development such as *El subdesarrollo latinoamericano y la teoría del desarrollo*.

Index